Dictionary of
SOCIAL
WELFARE

Noel and Rita Timms

Routledge & Kegan Paul
London, Boston, Melbourne and Henley

First published in 1982
by Routledge & Kegan Paul Ltd
39 Store Street, London WC1E 7DD,
9 Park Street, Boston, Mass. 02108, USA,
296 Beaconsfield Parade, Middle Park,
Melbourne, 3206, Australia, and
Broadway House, Newtown Road,
Henley-on-Thames, Oxon RG9 1EN
Set in 10pt Times by Saildean Ltd, Surrey
and printed in Great Britain by
Redwood Burn Ltd
Trowbridge, Wiltshire

Library of Congress Cataloging in Publication Data

Timms, Noel.

Dictionary of social welfare.
Bibliography: p.
1. Social service - Dictionaries.
2. Social policy - Dictionaries.   I. Timms,
Rita.   II. Title.
HV12.T54   361'.03' 21   82-5385

ISBN 0-7100-9084-6   AACR2

Introduction

Anyone attempting to compile a dictionary of social welfare develops a ready sympathy with the character in *Felix Holt* by George Eliot who remarks: 'Before I bring words to market, I should like to see 'em a bit scarcer.' The growing abundance of words is particularly evident if the dictionary aims, as does ours, to introduce users to the study of social work and of social policy. Attending to people's well-being through direct service, management, or the study and appraisal of social policies involves the use of a great many words; not only words, of course, and not mere words either. Even if it is decided to exclude the fascinating area of the working jargon of the professional ('on-going situation', for example), there is no commonly accepted theory of welfare to assist in the establishment of boundaries within which the words might be helpfully located. 'Welfare' itself, as Hobson (1929) observed, 'may mean anything from the most elevated conception of human character and destiny to the baths, refectories, and recreation grounds that figure so prominently in what is known as "welfare work".' The language of welfare reflects this description in so far as it is a mixture of the esoteric, the technical and the down-to-earth.

Students of social work and of social policy frequently refer to deprivation, to rights of various kinds, to the consequences of certain kinds of social stratification, and so on. Such reference obviously depends on psychological, sociological, and other usage, but the full significance of the terms cannot for welfare purposes be obtained simply by reference to dictionaries of psychology, sociology, and so on. Other terms used in welfare are not in any elaborate sense technical (e.g. abortion, advice, reform). Yet these too figure in social welfare discourse. They do not require much unravelling as terms, but they need to be placed in welfare talk by reference to recent developments in the practice of welfare or recent discussion in the literature. Such placing has been a major objective of this dictionary, since we believe that the simple stipulation of a necessarily brief synonym would give a false indication of the texture of the language of social welfare and would be of small benefit to the student.

In the entries that follow we indicate the meaning or range of meanings of a word and then outline its application in welfare, in legislation, policy, controversy, and use by welfare practitioners. Sometimes the exposition requires cross-reference to other terms in the dictionary and sometimes the cross-reference is to a connected term that might helpfully be considered alongside. (In each case the cross-reference is simply indicated in italics.) In addition, most entries are concluded by references which help the reader to a more extended treatment of the term or an elaboration of its application in the language of social welfare. (These criteria may result in reference to sources other than the most recent.) The aim in presenting such elements is to offer a practical aid to students of social work and of social policy in their conversation about social welfare. We hope that this dictionary will help them to enter and to participate in such conversation and also to 'go on' when they have been temporarily halted by doubt or perplexity about a term. The entries are not designed to present encyclopedic information but to offer sufficient for the user to 'continue'. To judge that the entries are thereby insufficient is, to use a metaphor of Wittgenstein, to suggest that because the light given by my bedside reading lamp has no sharp boundary it provides no real illumination at all.

We have said that the dictionary is intended to encompass the mutual interests of students of social policy and of social work. It may be considered that some of the entries are biased in the direction of social work; for instance the references to various psychological terms and theories. However, a psychology of some kind is necessary both for the practice of welfare and for understanding that practice, and we have referred to the psychological terms in use. Moreover, a psychology or a social psychology of social policy awaits development. A sociology of social policy is now clearly discernible (e.g. Room, 1979), but in the absence of any psychological development the psychology of the practitioner has to stand on its own.

The terms selected are the result of extensive discussions with teachers, practitioners, and students, but we may not have been able entirely to eliminate some elements of the arbitrary or the idiosyncratic. What we have attempted is to concentrate on terms that play an important role in our understanding of contemporary social provision or practice or have a place in significant controversy or simply because our own experience and that of others suggests they are initially puzzling or significantly contestable.

Hobson, J. (1929) *Wealth and Life: a Study in Values*, Macmillan, p. 10.
Room, G. (1979) *The Sociology of Welfare*, Blackwell and Martin Robertson.

Acknowledgments

We have had help and advice (including 'Don't attempt it') from a large number of friends and professional colleagues. We would acknowledge particularly help from the following, who, of course, bear no responsibility for the use we have chosen to make of their comments and suggestions:

Geoff Fimister, Senior Welfare Rights Officer, City of Newcastle-upon-Tyne.

Terence Finlay, General Secretary, Newcastle Council for Voluntary Service.

Colin Harris, Director, Centre for Research on User Studies, Sheffield University.

Kieron Hosty, Manager, Action Resource Centre (Tyne and Wear).

Phyllida Parsloe, Professor of Social Work, Bristol University.

Peter Selman, Department of Social Policy, Newcastle University.

Ian Sinclair, Director of Research, National Institute for Social Work.

Pamela Stewart, Social Science Liaison Librarian, University of Newcastle.

Janet Walker, Department of Social Policy, Newcastle University.

David Watson, Department of Social Administration, Bristol University.

We wish also to thank Mrs Vera Dunn for patient and accurate help in the form of typing.

Abortion Potts *et al.* define abortion as 'the loss of a pregnancy before the fetus or fetuses are potentially capable of life independent of the mother'. This general definition covers spontaneous abortion or miscarriage and induced abortion, but distinguishes both from premature birth, live or still. The subject of abortion is significant for current social policy and for social work for a number of different reasons. Legislation to legalise the medical termination of pregnancy has been promoted and criticised by the continuing action of different pressure groups (e.g. the Abortion Law Reform Society, founded in 1936, and the Society for the Protection of Unborn Children, 1967); the deep convictions in favour of abortion (and its extension to an on-demand service) or profoundly against the use made of present services have resulted in attempts to change the law in a less restricted or a more restricted direction; in addition, these convictions have led to the establishment of new voluntary services often of an 'advisory' or *'counselling'* nature. The conditions the 1967 Act was intended to rectify (e.g. back-street abortion, *illegitimate* and unwanted births) and the Act itself raise questions of a more moral and political nature: the justification of different grounds for termination; the conscientious objection of doctors and nurses; the rights of *women* to 'their own bodies'; abortion as part of explicit state policy in relation to family planning; the role of the state in preventing 'greater evil', and so on.

DHSS, (Lane) Committee on the Working of the Abortion Act (1974)
  Report, Cmnd 5579, HMSO.
Feinberg, J. (ed.) (1973) *The Problem of Abortion*, Belmont.
Potts, M., Digory, P. and Peel, J. (1977) *Abortion*, Cambridge
  University Press.

1

ACCEPTANCE

Acceptance Acceptance is usually taken in a social welfare context to refer to one of the *principles* of *social work* or to a desirable attitude towards the recipients of any social service on the part of those who administer it. It is best approached in terms of the implicit or explicit purposiveness of human behaviour: acceptance in the case of a social work client refers to active search for the point any behaviour has for the client and recognition of this as legitimate for him. 'Acceptance' illustrates the ambiguity of 'principle' in social work: it is justified as part of *respect for persons* or as a statement of what is in fact required for any effective social work. Unlike the *'non-judgmental attitude'* with which it also overlaps, 'acceptance' does not seem to suggest one refrains from anything. Moreover, 'acceptance' can be given a weak, dispassionate meaning, as in social work records when 'the social worker accepted this' means only that he made no comment, or a stronger meaning in which the social worker actively recognises elements in a situation as real. This more positive sense is sometimes exaggerated into descriptions of acceptance as a kind of love, but such rarefied 'hugging at a distance' is best left unpursued. Biestek notes that 'acceptance' is one of the vaguest in social work language, but argues for a clear distinction between acceptance and approval.

Biestek, F.P. (1961) *The Casework Relationship*, Allen & Unwin, pp. 67-88.

Accreditation Accreditation is the public attestation that a particular person or those who have successfully followed certain courses of study are worthy to be trusted in the pursuit of a certain range of activities. Accreditation is frequently statutorily enforced. For example, the Nurses, Midwives and Health Visitors Act 1979 provides for one statutory council to be responsible for the accreditation or approval of training, the registration of practitioners, and any necessary disciplinary procedures. In social work the idea and the practice of the registration of practitioners has been the subject of long debate. The Hospital Almoners' Association established a register in 1907, and the Association of Psychiatric Social Workers in 1961. Some system of accreditation (possibly through a General Social

Work Council modelled on the lines of the General Medical Council) is seen as providing protection for social worker and for client, as contributing to the enhancement of the status of social work as a profession, and as a stimulus to training.

Malherbe, M. (1980) *Accreditation in Social Work; Principles and Issues in Context*, Central Council for Education and Training in Social Work.

Acting-out A term from *Freudian theory* originally referring to the re-living of past experience recalled as a result of the work of the psychoanalyst. The term has come to be used more widely to refer to people who deal with their emotional tensions through behaviour directed towards others; they enact their intra-psychic problems rather than express them through the symptoms of a *neurosis*. Acting-out behaviour is characteristic of people with very low thresholds of tolerance who tend to react to others in terms of the past rather than the reality of the present. For such acting-out is a habitual but not very efficient mode of problem-solving. Acting-out behaviour is frequently associated with *character disorder*, but the term is also used very generally as a shorthand for behaviour creating difficulties for others, including social workers.

Action research A loosely defined type of research, contrasted with that undertaken on a strictly controlled experimental basis. The investigator interacts systematically with a service project, frequently on a small scale, in order to assess its operation and its outputs; the results of the research are fed back into the project. Halsey identified five possible types of action research, whilst Lees discusses a range of models. Action research has been a feature of social policy research at least since the *Educational Priority Areas*, and it has been used in social work (*case review system*). Some critics argue that the twin objectives of action and research are in contradiction (e.g. Marris and Rein) but Lees's more modest conclusion probably predominates: 'It is not clear that action research in social policy has to fail' (p. 69).

Halsey, A.H. (1972) *Educational Priority* (Reports sponsored by DES and SSRC): vol. 1, *EPA Problems and Policies*, HMSO.

ADDICTION

Lees, R. (1975) *Research Strategies for Social Welfare*, Routledge & Kegan Paul, pp. 66-72.
Marris, P. and Rein, M. (1967) *Dilemmas of Social Reform: Poverty and Community*, Routledge & Kegan Paul.

Addiction   Drugs have been used in most cultures, and for a long time in Britain were part of the accepted behaviour of the professional and upper classes. Only in the twentieth century has the law been increasingly invoked to control drug use, thus 'changing' the drug-addict from a respectable member of society to a common criminal. The laws are highly restrictive and selective, however, within a society which values the medicalisation of drugs. The precise definition of addiction is a matter of argument, but one key notion is that of a craving or overpowering desire for the consumption in one way or another of a particular substance, usually tobacco, alcohol, and drugs (e.g. non-opiates such as cannabis or barbiturates); recently solvents of various kinds have been misused. Other components of addiction are often described as psychological and/or physical dependence, tolerance of increased doses, and severe withdrawal symptoms. Socially preferred definitions of 'the addict' have changed over time from that of moral degradation through that of sickness to the present persuasive definition of drug-misuser, problem drinker, or alcohol abuser. Alcohol abuse has been defined variably, but one more acceptable definition refers to the intermittent or continual ingestion of alcohol, leading to dependence or harm. In social work it is usual to distinguish three categories of alcohol abuse – alcohol dependence, excessive drinking and alcohol-related disabilities; thus constituting a wide range of behaviours and associated problems. Addiction still persists as a term in fairly common use. In welfare discussion 'addiction' raises moral, social, including fiscal, and legal problems of *control*; social response to the problem includes a complex range of voluntary and statutory services, some of which are innovatory (such as detoxification units for habitual drinking offenders and street agencies for drug-misusers). Addiction leads to complex individual and family problems. Programmes of treatment and of health education are high in cost and of uncertain result.

Bean, P. (1974) *The Social Control of Drugs*, Martin Robertson.
DHSS and Welsh Office, Advisory Committee on Alcoholism (1978) *The Pattern and Range of Services for Problem Drinkers*, HMSO.
Grant, M. and Gwynner, P. (1979) *Alcoholism in Perspective*, Croom Helm.
Royal College of Psychiatrists, Special Committee (1979) *Alcohol and Alcoholism*, Tavistock.

Adjustment Adjustment is a change in outlook, belief or behaviour brought about to secure an improved orientation to another, to a situation, or to social norms. The term is used in discussion of individual cases and, more generally, as part of the criticism, negative and positive, of welfare activity and legislation. Thus, Marshall refers to 'the adjustment of the individual to his particular circumstances' and possibly 'a necessary condition for reaping the benefit of the welfare services that society offers him ... adjustment to blindness, to physical disablement, to old age, to desertion by a husband, to loss of parents and so forth.' Others suggest that social workers aim to adjust their clients to the intolerable, almost as directly as one would adjust one's dress. Social workers would now place less emphasis on a one-way change, preferring the idea of a double adaptation between 'society' and *client*. Charges that social work and social policy are primarily concerned with exacting adjustment to dominant social norms usually ignore differences between the kinds of conformity that can be enforced – of behaviour, of *attitude*, and of belief.

Marshall, T.H. (1981) *The Right to Welfare*, Heinemann, pp. 67-82.
Wilson, R. (1960) 'Unconformity in the Affluent Society', *Sociological Review*, 8, 119-28.

Admission Admission usually refers to formal entry into a residential provision or, more generally, to the *care* of an authority. Admission may be the result of agreement or of compulsion. Thus, a patient under S.5 of the Mental Health Act 1959 enters hospital voluntarily as an informal patient, but orders are made for compulsory admission under SS.25, 26, 29, and 135 of the same Act. Under the Child Care Act 1980, children may be received into the care of the local authority (sometimes this is referred to as admission to care rather than being committed to care, under the same Act), though this may not necessarily also mean admission to a children's home. Admission refers to the process and procedures whereby a person changes both status and location and becomes a resident of a local authority or voluntary home, hospital, etc. More recently, it has come to be used for formal entry into *day care*. A particular admission is often an immediate response to a *crisis* and constitutes a significant change for the persons concerned. Jones indicates that the admission procedures to any residential facility can be analysed in terms of mortification of self, an initiation rite, a life crisis, a socialisation process, and a necessary administrative process. For social workers and policy-makers the decision to admit, the participation of the person 'in need', and the criteria against which admission is tested are all matters of considerable importance.

Brearley, P. *et al.* (1980) *Admission to Residential Care*, Tavistock.
Jones, K. (1972) 'The Twenty-four Steps: an Analysis of Institutional Admission Procedures', *Sociology*, 6, 405-14.

Adolescence The terms 'adolescent' and 'young person' or '*youth*' are used interchangeably, but there is possible advantage in using the former as a psychological and 'youth' as a social category. Adolescence can be seen as a period of imbalance, not always severe, due to physical, emotional, and social changes marked by the appearance of secondary gender characteristics. It is difficult to suggest a chronology for the onset and the finalisation of puberty, especially if a cross-cultural comparison is intended. Thus, a World Health Organisation Report of 1977 (Technical Report Series 609, Geneva) used the age period of 10–20 years. There is also considerable individual variation in the onset and pace of puberty. Attempts have been made to divide adolescence into distinct periods, but it is perhaps more common to regard the whole developmental phase (including what has been termed prolonged adolescence) as centrally concerned with the establishment of *identity*. There is a tendency in planning programmes or in intervention in individual cases to regard 'adolescence' as essentially divorced from earlier phases of development (psychoanalytic ideas of adolescence as a period in which earlier phases of development are recapitulated have not been widely taken up) and from the psychological and social needs of whoever is in the parenting role at the particular time. Judging the degree to which particular 'disturbed' behaviour in an adolescent may be abnormal, calling for specialist help, is particularly difficult.

Jones, R. and Pritchard, C. (eds) (1980) *Social Work with Adolescents*, Routledge & Kegan Paul.
Laufer, M. (1975) *Adolescent Disturbance and Breakdown*, Penguin.
Meyerson, S. (ed.) (1975) *Adolescence: the Crises of Adjustment*, Allen & Unwin.

Adoption   Adoption is a legal and also a psycho-social process. The legal process is completed by a court order which confers a new legal status on adopters and the adoptee: the latter stands to the former as if born to them in lawful wedlock. The first adoption law was passed in 1926 and the most recent in 1976, though this has yet to be implemented. A high proportion of adoption orders involve a natural parent and a step-parent (some 60 per cent in 1980), though the Houghton Committee discouraged this in favour of custodianship. The pattern of adoptions has changed considerably as a result of the decline in numbers of white infants available, and serious efforts are now usually made to place children with special needs (sometimes referred to as 'difficult to place'), such as physical disability, mental handicaps, and so on. In this connection adoption is seen as a permanent family placement geared to meet the needs of the child at least as much as to provide a service for childless couples. The results of adoption have been investigated in a number of studies, Raynor's being the most recent. See also *Illegitimacy, Fostering*.

Home Office, (Houghton) Committee on the Adoption of Children *Report*, (1972) Cmnd 5107, HMSO.
Raynor, L. (1980) *The Adopted Child Comes of Age*, Allen & Unwin.
Tizard, B. (1977) *Adoption: a Second Chance*, Open Books.
Triseliotis, J. (ed.) (1980) *New Developments in Foster Care and Adoption*, Routledge & Kegan Paul.

Advice   Advice is an opinion backed by experience and/or expert knowledge indicating a preferable line of action or the provision of facts on which such action could be grounded. 'Advice in a welfare context is important for two reasons. First, a growing number of organisations are concerned that the citizen is well informed about possible remedial actions (e.g. through the Citizens' Advice Bureaux) or seeks to use 'advice centres' as a base for other services such as *intermediate treatment* or *community work.* A Home Office Circular (204/1963) asked local authorities to establish Family Advice Centres as a central point of reference for the public in need of advice or assistance in relation to the welfare of children. The provision of specifically legal advice is of growing importance, though Morris argued against any rigid separation of legal and social advice. By 1976 there were 120 consumer advice centres compared with 1 in 1970, but since 1976 the number has been considerably reduced. Second, advice has always had a place in the social worker's armamentarium, though until the late 1960s it was, outside the Probation Service, quite a low place: probation officers since the Probation of Offenders Act 1907 have been instructed to 'advise, assist and befriend'. Consumer studies in welfare indicate that users of social services place quite a high value on advice, though individual recipients of advice may understand very different things by the term.

Morris, P. *et al.* (1973) 'Public Attitudes to Problem Definition and Problem Solving: a Pilot Study', *British Journal of Social Work*, 3, 301-20.
National Consumer Council (1977) *Fourth Right of Citizenship: a Review of Local Advice Services.*
Reid, W. and Shapiro, B. (1969) 'Clients' Reactions to Advice', *Social Service Review*, 43, 165-73.

Advisers Advisers are specially appointed or recognised in some public manner to provide expertise in the appraisal of particular projects and of general policy direction. They work at many distinct levels, but of particular interest in social welfare are the appointment of academic and other experts to advise government, for example in relation to the Health Service, and the growth in the middle levels of the hierarchy of social services departments of a group of staff called advisers (or consultants, principal assistants, and so on). Such staff are usually not in direct contact with clients, neither are they in the direct management line. A recent study argues that the term 'adviser' is unhelpful and that four main kinds of role could be distinguished: specialist development officers, project officers, staff officers and consultant practitioners.

Billis, D. (1980) 'Advisers, Development Officers and Consultants in Social Services Departments', in *Organising Social Services Departments*, ed. D. Billis *et al.*, Heinemann.
Klein, R. and Lewis, J. (1977) 'Advice and Dissent in British Government', *Policy and Politics*, 1, 1-25.

Advocacy Advocacy originally concerned pleading another's case in court. This meaning obtains in welfare when social workers or others represent others before *tribunals* or to other organisations (e.g. the various utility services). In America in the late 1960s advocacy became one of the specialist roles in social work, particularly in relation to *welfare rights*, and in the process advocacy was widened to refer to groups as well as to individuals, and to include any attempt to obtain services from an initially unresponsive source. Rose criticises the 'middle-class' social work advocates and suggests claimants would be better advised to find advocates in their own ranks. Levy distinguishes three possible objectives in advocacy – procedural fairness, background fairness, corrective justice. Advocacy can also be of a cause: social provision (e.g. improved *community care*), and some social workers would now describe themselves as advocates of the poor or of the powerless. The notion, in either sense of advocacy, of the partisan respresentative poses problems in social work which as an occupation has always explicitly eschewed *manipulation*. See also *Representative*.

Brager, G.A. (1968) 'Advocacy and Political Behaviour', *Social Work*, 13, 5-15.
Levy, C.S. (1975) 'Advocacy and the Injustice of Justice', *Social Service Review*, 49, 39-50.
Rose, H. (1973) 'Up against the Welfare State', in *Socialist Register, 1973*, ed. R. Miliband and J. Saville, Merlin.

After-care After-care services are those offered or imposed following a period in a residential establishment such as a borstal, prison, or hospital; services consequent upon non-residential provision are usually described as 'follow-up'. At times in the development of a particular welfare service after-care receives special emphasis. For example, since 1964 the Probation Service has been known under the title of the *Probation and After-Care Service*. Older examples of specific roles and functions in the area of after-care would be the former approved school after-care officers and the work of such voluntary societies as the Mental After-Care Association founded in 1877 as the After-Care Association for the Female and Friendless Convalescent on leaving Asylums for the Insane (Roof). The separate idea of 'after-care' in the case of the physically and mentally ill has been largely absorbed into *community care*, and the ideal of a planned continuum of care or through-care is now fashionable. However, what follows a period of residential care or detention is always in danger of being an afterthought or, to extend Davies's description of prison after-care, an apology no one really wants.

Davies, M. (1974) *Prisoners of Society: Attitudes and After-Care* Routledge & Kegan Paul.
Monger, M. (1967) *Casework in Aftercare*, Butterworth.
Roof, M. (1957) *Voluntary Societies and Social Policy*, Routledge & Kegan Paul.

Agency This term usually refers to the organisation whose main programme is or includes social work provision of some kind: it used to be common to distinguish those agencies where the delivery of social work was a primary objective (such as a voluntary family casework agency) and those where it was secondary (such as a hospital). See *Functionalist School* for the systematic attempt to involve the notion and reality of agency in the description and the delivery of social work: for Functionalists, the agency was literally an agent of society. 'Agency' is also used in a more common sense. Voluntary societies can undertake work for the local authority as a result of agency agreements.

Aggression Aggression is not most usefully seen as a single phenomenon, though single theory explanations (for example, the death instinct in *Freudian theory* or the idea of aggression as always a response to frustration) have attracted support.

'Aggression' covers acts intended to worsen another's position or situation, but also acts required in the surmounting of difficulties; we speak of aggressive personalities and of aggressive *attitudes*, and of aggression as the summoning and use of energy to get something done. Not surprisingly, Storr believes that 'aggression is a portmanteau term which is fairly bursting at its seams.' The significance of aggression in welfare discourse derives from the place given to aggression/hate in explanations of human behaviour (see e.g. *Kleinian theory*); from interest in particular child-rearing practices or in features of the social environment as producing more or less aggression; and from explanations of the present state of social welfare as a product of the aggression of one social class against another. See also *Violence, Vandalism*.

Lorenz, K. (1936) *On Aggression*, Methuen.
Storr, A. (1970) *Human Aggression*, Pelican.
Swanson, H. (1976) 'The Biological Value of Aggression', in DHSS, *Violence*, ed. N. Tutt, HMSO.

Alcoholism   Alcoholism or the alcohol-dependence syndrome, see *addiction*.

Alienation   Alienation is a term originally used by Hegel and then substantially extended by Marx to refer to a social condition rather than to individuals in a psychological state of estrangement. The term is very loosely used in a welfare context to explain anything from suicide to relatively temporary disenchantment with life; it is frequently offered as an explanation for the persistence of hippies, drug addicts, etc. In Marx there are two central aspects to alienation: the notion of loss of meaning/connection with the product of one's work or with all other producers or with 'human nature' (in any use of alienation, it is important to ask 'alienated *from* what?') and systematic response to what has been 'lost' as if it were a 'foreign' and dominant force. Others have attempted to 'unpack' the notion along different dimensions. Seeman, for example, refers to powerlessness, meaninglessness, normlessness, isolation, and self-estrangement, and in this sense 'alienation' is used as an explanation of deviant behaviour. Attempts have also been

11

made to outlaw the term from discussions of social work and of social policy 'on the grounds that it does indiscriminate harm to users and victims alike' (Pinker) or, from a Marxist perspective, because it has 'been vulgarised beyond all use'. Usage of a very loose kind, however, is bound to survive.

Lukes, S. (1967) 'Alienation and Anomie', in *Philosophy, Politics and Society*, 3rd series. P. Laslett and W.G. Runciman, Blackwell.
Pinker, R. (1971) *Social Theory and Social Policy*, Heinemann, p. 154.
Seeman, M. (1959) 'On the Meaning of Alienation', *American Sociological Review*, 21.

Allocation   Allocation can be of work (as in allocation of new cases to a social worker's *caseload*) or of resources (as in the report of the Resource Allocation Working Party, 'Sharing Resources for Health in England', 1976). Resources can be allocated through different mechanisms, for example, through the *market* or through different kinds of policy decisions, including the selection of priority groups and priority areas and various devices of formal and informal *rationing*. Work in social services departments is allocated by team leaders or, less usually, through team allocation meetings. In consideration of resource allocation it is important to see that at a comparatively low organisational level social workers are in effective control of such crucial resources as their own time and attention. On the whole, these are not systematically allocated in terms of explicit priorities. See also *Caseload, Priorities.*

Hill, M. (1979) 'Social Work Teams and the Allocation of Resources', in *Planning for Welfare*, ed. T.A. Booth, Blackwell and Martin Robertson.
Judge, K. (1979) 'Resource Allocation in the Welfare State: Bureaucrats or Prices?', *Journal of Social Policy*, 8, 371-82.

Altruism   Altruism refers to acts and dispositions orientated to the alleviation of another's predicament or furtherance of their *interests*. The notion of helpful intention is essential, since behaviour that simply happened to improve another's situation would not count as altruistic. Usually altruism involves some cost to the altruist, but the idea of sacrifice (as opposed to willingness to incur cost) does not seem essential to the meaning of 'altruism'. The notion has gained importance in welfare discussion since Titmuss used the idea of *gift* to illuminate the Blood Transfusion Service. In that context the emphasis was on altruism to strangers. Pinker has recently argued that the unqualified use of that term (and of *egoism*), is 'largely irrelevant to the study of social welfare because they are inapplicable to the most characteristic forms of social behaviour ... for the egoist a social life is meaningless, and for the altruist it is impossible.' However, his use of the term 'family altruism' raises boundary questions concerning the obligation to 'altruism' within and beyond relationships already governed by certain expectations of 'help'. It is important to recognise that debate on altruism can be enriched from sources other than those of the study of social welfare. Debate concerning benevolence and the possibility or desirability of unselfish action has been active in philosophy since at least the eighteenth century; psychologists are interested in the study of altruistic behaviour and its motivation; whilst economists have become concerned with economics described as non-selfish.

Bryan, J.H. (1972) 'Why Children Help: a Review', *Journal of Social Issues*, 28, 87-104.
Collard, D. (1978) *Altruism and Economy: a Study of Non-Selfish Economics*, Martin Robertson.
Pinker, R. (1979) *The Idea of Welfare*, Heinemann, Ch. 1, 'Egoism and Altruism'.
Roberts, T.A. (1973) *The Concept of Benevolence*, Macmillan.

Ambivalence   Ambivalence is a disposition towards a person or situation marked by a persistent and unresolved 'contradiction' between positive and negative feelings and ideas. A good example of ambivalence is to be found in ordinary talk of a love–hate relationship. A term taken from *Freudian* and Kleinian theories and used in the attempts by social workers to understand present and past, usually family, relationships and relationships between clients and themselves. The *Functionalist School* of social work stresses the ambivalence of separation/union in personality development.' The idea is also used in wider analysis. Thus, Halmos argues that a major characteristic of all counselling is the implicit belief in 'love's prevalence in ambivalence'. It is possible to see the concept, though not the term, in Pinker's argument that the social sciences reflect 'our dispositions both to remember and to forget our social obligations' (helpfully discussed in some detail in Watson). 'Ambivalence' in ordinary professional discussion, however, seems often to represent the acceptable face of apathy.

Halmos, P. (1965) *The Faith of the Counsellors*, Constable, pp. 74-90.
Watson, D. (1978) 'Social Services in a Nutshell', in *Philosophy in Social Work*, ed. N. Timms and D. Watson, Routledge & Kegan Paul.

Anomie 'Anomie' was used originally by Durkheim and later developed by Merton in the study of deviance. Durkheim saw anomie as the main abnormal condition of modern industrial society: because of the increased division of labour there were insufficient contacts between members of society and an inadequate regulation of relationships. Anomie referred to a society characterised by absence of the moderating action of regulation. In his study of suicide, however, Durkheim referred to one kind of suicide as 'anomic'. Anomic suicide was the product of a state of mind of an individual with no effective restraints on aspiration. Merton used anomie to describe a disjunction between socially prescribed goals (like success) and the means by which these should be achieved. Such disjunction can be met in different ways depending on whether the means (innovation), or the goals (ritualism), or both (retreatism) are abandoned. This classification, sometimes extended, has been used in attempts to explain a range of conditions from delinquency to that of the *'problem family'*. Anomie does not provide a causal explanation of crime, but it does highlight a situation, found by many researchers into criminal behaviour, that a significant gap between aspiration and opportunity tends to generate deviation. More recently the idea of anomie has been used in discussions of *territorial justice*. It has not been much used in social work, though Hartman has attempted not very successfully to employ a distinction between societal anomie and psychological anomie.

14

Durkheim, E. (1952) *Suicide: a Study in Sociology*, Routledge & Kegan Paul.
Hartman, A. (1969) 'Anomie and Social Casework', *Social Casework*, 50, 131-7.
Merton, R. (1964) 'Anomie, Anomie and Social Interaction: Contexts of Deviant Behaviour', in *Anomie and Deviant Behavior*, ed. M. Clinard *et al.*, Free Press.

Anxiety Anxiety is a state of apprehension or fear. Obviously, 'clients' suffer all kinds of apprehension and fear as they approach and use social agencies and provisions, but the concept can mainly be found in a welfare context either in an elaborated form (as in anxiety neurosis in which a person suffers persisting free-floating dread; in separation anxiety or the results of shock following separation from a parent or parent figure) or in the context of psychoanalytic theory. In the latter context social workers have tried to understand people through the use of *Kleinian theory* and the polarities of depressive anxieties (or fears centred upon the safety of others) and of persecutory anxieties (or fears concerning the safety of self). Others have relied on more orthodox *Freudian theory*, but have not always systematically distinguished the different sources and kind of anxiety: objective anxiety concerning a 'real' threat, *super-ego* anxiety (or *guilt*), and ego anxiety that id impulses will be overwhelming (see also *ego*, *id*). In the study of social policy this last kind of anxiety is sometimes generalised across a social class and transformed into a major explanation, e.g. that Tudor social policy was governed by anxiety that labour would become so mobile that it escaped control.

Rycroft, C. (1968) *Anxiety and Neurosis*, Pelican.
Salzberger-Wittenberg, G. (1970) *Psycho-analytic Insight and Relationships: a Kleinian Approach*, Routledge & Kegan Paul.

Appeal It is normally decisions that are appealed; other kinds of behaviour are possible subjects of *complaint*. To appeal is to initiate a review by an independent body or person of a decision, adversely affecting the appellant, made by a 'constitutional' subordinate. Appeals are usually made through *tribunals*, though appeals against sentence or conviction are heard by superior courts. Decisions at one hierarchical level may, of course, be reviewed at a higher level, but this process is to be distinguished from that of appeal.

Area   A geographically or politically bound locality. Services of many kinds are administered from area offices, in the charge of area officers or controllers. Social services departments are normally divided into areas served by a number of *teams* of workers; sometimes a team is responsible for all work in a particular segment of the area (*patch system*). Area offices can be structured according to different models (Philipps and Birchall). At the central government level priority areas have been frequently used as a mechanism for the concentration of resources in housing, education, and community development. The proposed elimination of the Area Health Authority will mean that the boundaries of health authorities and local county authorities will no longer be co-terminous. See also *Priorities*.

Phillips, M. and Birchall, E. (1971) 'Structuring an Area Office to Meet Client Need', *Social Work Today*, 1, 5-11.

Assessment   An important part of the job of a social worker has to do with forming a view of what requires to be done in any particular situation; assessment is a *diagnosis* or an informed impression leading to action. There are also institutions which specialise in the detailed assessment of people thought to be in need of particular kinds of provision. Thus, the former approved school system was served by classifying schools, and the Children and Young Persons Act 1969 stipulated that each region's plan should contain proposals for the observation of children in care and the assessment of the accommodation most suitable for them. Such assessment is as desirable as meaningful observation connected to differential outcome is possible. In other words it is useless spending resources on assessment if, by and large, those emerging from the process are treated in the same way in the same kind of institution. Assessment provision has been criticised as 'artificial' and as conducive to '*labelling*'.

Hoghughi, M. (1980) *Assessing Problem Children*, Burnett Books.

Attachment   This term has two distinct uses in a welfare context: it refers to a method of organising work through the allocation of workers, and to a psycho-social process of some complexity and importance. In the work sense attachment may generally be seen as the allocation of a worker from one occupation or specialism to supplement the work of another occupation or specialism away from the worker's 'natural' base; managerial control may be shared between the 'host' and the worker's normal base or may be retained by the latter. The Seebohm Report recommended the attachment of social workers to schools, *health centres*, hospitals, and so on, but few social workers have been withdrawn from hospitals to an area office base, and attachment of social workers outside the Health Service is not common. The attachment of *health visitors* to general medical practices has been increasingly common.

In personality development 'attachment' refers to bonds of varying intensity established reciprocally between an infant and significant adults; it refers also to behaviour through which proximity to significant adults is promoted or sought. Bowlby has argued that the bond to one person (usually the mother or mother figure) is of crucial importance in personality development, but others argue for the normality of multiple attachment and the reversibility of failure in early bonding. See also *Loss, Deprivation.*

Abel, A. (1969) *Nursing Attachments to General Practice: Advantages and Problems*, DHSS Social Science Research Unit Study no. 1, HMSO.

Ainsworth, M. *et al.* (1974) 'Infant-mother Attachment and Social Development; Socialization as a Product of Reciprocal Responsiveness to Signals', in *The Integration of a Child in a Social World*, ed. M. Richards, Cambridge University Press.

Bowlby, J. (1969) *Attachment and Loss:* vol. I, *Attachment*, Hogarth Press.

Attendance centres   Attendance centres were established by the Criminal Justice Act 1948, S.19. A juvenile found guilty of an offence which in the case of an adult is punishable with imprisonment may be ordered to attend an attendance centre, if one is available. The aggregate number of hours must not be less than 12, unless he is under fourteen years of age, or more than

ATTITUDE

24. A juvenile cannot be sentenced in this way if he has previously been sent to prison, borstal or detention centre. Centres are often run by the police, and activities commonly involve physical exercise and handicrafts.

Attitude This term, bridging sociological and psychological discourse, refers to a learned, stable disposition, general or specific, negative or positive towards classes of behaviour, people, or things. Attitudes are often seen in terms of affective, cognitive, and behavioural dimensions. Within a welfare context 'attitude' is used in two main ways. First, changing attitudes is often cited as an objective of social policy (as in modifying or removing prejudicial attitudes of certain kinds or educating people to adopt different attitudes towards drink, smoking, etc.) or as a goal of social work with an individual (to modify a mother's attitude to her child). Second, public attitudes are offered as reasons why particular policies are either justified or rendered impracticable. Certainly, general attitudes are very hard to change and the complex relations between attitudes and behaviour may suggest the effort towards change in attitudes is scarcely worth while: 'behaviour changes can be as much the precursor as the result of changes in verbally expressed attitudes' (Eiser).

Davey, A. (1976) 'Attitudes and the Prediction of Social Conduct', *British Journal of Social and Clinical Psychology*, 15, 11-22.
Eiser, J. (1979) 'Attitudes', in *Psychology Survey*, no. 2, ed.
  K. Connolly, Allen & Unwin.
Warren, N. and Jahoda, M. (eds) (1973) *Attitudes: Selected Readings*, 2nd ed., Penguin.

Authority Public bodies are often referred to as 'authorities' – the local authority, the port authority, and so on. More importantly, authority can be seen as legitimate *power* and hence a feature of most social arrangements and relationships. Weber distinguished three sources of this legitimation – personal charisma of particular individuals ('he speaks with authority'); tradition (or rules and customs established over time); and the rational-legal (rules justified in terms of the law or of reason). Thinking about 'authority' can be assisted by discussion of such related ideas as 'authorisation', 'author', and 'authentic'. The subject of 'authority has attracted social work interest in terms of the justification of *intervention* and of certain aspects of social work behaviour in relation, say, to reluctant clients. The notion of the 'authoritarian personality' was at one time in vogue in social work circles, and this perhaps compounded the confusion that to be in authority or to be an authority was necessarily to behave in an authoritarian manner. Another common confusion is between accepting a situation through the operation of simple force and accepting it as part of rule-governed behaviour in which authority plays a necessary, not a merely contingent, part.

Adorno, T.W. *et al.* (1950) *The Authoritarian Personality*, Harper & Row.
Foren, R. and Bailey, R. (1968) *Authority in Social Casework*, Pergamon.
Tuck, R. (1972) 'Why is Authority such a Problem?', in *Philosophy, Politics and Society*, 4th series, ed. P. Laslett and W.G. Runciman, Blackwell.

Autism A severe disorder arising in infancy and characterised by failure to develop social relationships, severe delay in speech use and speech understanding, and compulsive and ritualistic behaviour. Kanner first described infantile autism as a separate disorder in 1943. Autistic children present considerable treatment problems. Theories to explain autism have emphasised family psychopathology or organic factors.

Rutter, M. and Schopler, E. (1978) *Autism: a Re-appraisal of Concepts and Treatment*, Plenum Press.
Tustin, Frances (1981) *Autistic States in Children*, Routledge & Kegan Paul.

B

Battered baby See *Family violence.*

Battered wife See *Family violence.*

Behaviour modification A form of psychological treatment based on the application of principles and research findings of learning theory to the study and change of maladaptive behaviour (rather than, for example *attitudes* or intra-psychic problems). The treatment involves the identification of the discrete behaviours that constitute the problem (e.g. specific fears, failure in the achievement of particular tasks); identification of the conditions controlling those behaviours in the present; specification of the modification of behaviour required; and formation of a programme that will lead to the modification. Programmes are built on the systematic use of particular techniques, including positive and negative reinforcement, extinction (as, for instance, in a programme of systematic desensitisation), imitative learning, penalising measures, and so on. The modification of specific behaviours may be undertaken by the therapist, social worker or by others in the 'patient's' environment. Behaviour modification was initially resisted as an approach in social work, mainly because it challenged the dominance of a psychodynamic approach and because it presented moral and possibly political problems. The latter are still voiced, but behaviour modification also challenges social work by its systematic and rigorous search for results and also for clear descriptions of *intervention*. Its use in conjunction with other approaches has been reported. See also *Conditioning.*

Epstein, I. (1975) 'The Politics of Behaviour Therapy: the New Cool-out Casework', in *Towards a New Social Work*, ed. H. Jones, Routledge & Kegan Paul.

Hudson, B. (1975) 'An Inadequate Personality: a Case Study with a Dynamic Beginning and a Behavioural Ending', *Social Work Today*, 6, 505-8.

Jehu, D. (1967), *Learning Theory and Social Work*, Routledge & Kegan Paul.

Benefit This term is used in an income-maintenance context as cash or the reduction or waiving of some form of 'charge' (rate *rebate*, rent rebate). Payments are based on national insurance contributions (e.g. death grant, sickness benefit, retirement pension) or on ability to meet certain conditions (e.g. child benefit, and family income supplement, though in other respects these are very different). Benefits in the first group are not subject to a test of means, though in certain cases earnings-related additions depend on previous earnings, and 'earnings rules' can abate some benefits specifically intended as earnings substitutes. Benefits in the second group may be based on a means test (e.g. *supplementary benefit* is, but child benefit is not). Means-tested benefits may be in relation to centrally provided services or those administered by local authorities (e.g. school meals, adaptations to homes, and personal aids are provided through locally administered assessments). Benefits can also be divided into those that are taxable and those that are not, though the extent of taxability is currently (1981) under discussion by government (e.g. widows' benefits are taxable, but maternity benefits are not). 'Benefit' raises a large number of questions in welfare, including level, complexitty of benefit systems, basis (e.g. the considerable criticism of costs, under-use, and social divisiveness of means-tested benefits), and relationship with the tax system. The assumptions of the benefit system as a whole are under increasing criticism (e.g. the assumption of an insurance principle, of a contribution test). Arguments are advanced that the conception of benefit should be extended to include tax, occupational and various private 'benefits' (Field).

Allbeson, J. (1981) *National Welfare Benefits Handbook*, Child Poverty Action Group.

Child Poverty Action Group (1981) 'Disability Benefits', *Poverty*, no. 48.

BRIEF TREATMENT

Field, F. (1981) *Inequality in Britain: Freedom, Welfare and the State*, Fontana.

Fimister, G. and Lister, R. (1981) *Social Security: the Case Against Contribution Tests*, CPAG.

National Consumer Council (1976) *Means-Tested Benefits*.

Rowland, M. (ed.) (1981) *Rights Guide to Non-Means-Tested Social Security Benefits*, CPAG.

Brief treatment This, sometimes called brief focused treatment, refers in a social welfare context to a particular approach in social work; the description 'brief' contrasts with treatment extended over a long time, measured perhaps in years rather than weeks. At one period in the history of social work it was assumed, because of the influence of psychoanalytic thought, that an ideal form of treatment was both long term and generally rather than specifically focused. Social work and indeed psychoanalytic practice have changed since then. In social work, *interventions* are now described as brief in three distinct ways: the brevity is not intended and the client simply ceases contact with the social worker; short-term contact between social worker and *client* is imposed through the exigencies of the situation (for example, a patient is in hospital for a limited period); brief treatment is deliberately and explicitly planned as such, it is within agreed limits of time and works towards specified objectives judged to be feasible. Work of this last kind has been usefully compared with more extensive treatment. Brief treatment often involves the making of a social *contract*. (See also the *Functionalist School*, which made explicit use of limits of time.)

Hutten, J. (1977) *Short-term Contracts in Social Work*, Routledge & Kegan Paul.

Reid, W.J. and Shyne, A. (1969) *Brief and Extended Casework*, Columbia University Press.

Bureaucracy Bureaucracy as a term has lived rather dangerously since the second half of the eighteenth century, and today it is often used pejoratively within a social welfare context, or as a synonym for a large organisation, or for part of the state apparatus of *social control*. Albrow has helpfully identified several distinct concepts of bureaucracy – as rational organisation, organisational inefficiency, public administration, administration by officials, as the organisation, or as modern society. 'Bureaucracy' in welfare talk refers both to a particular form of organisation and also to a way of operating. Social workers, and other groupings in large governmental organisations, are sometimes described as torn between their 'true' professional orientation and an administrative orientation imposed by the bureaucracy or by a bureaucratic way of working, since they inevitably work in public and publicly accountable organisations.

Albrow, M. (1970) *Bureaucracy*, Macmillan.
Glastonbury, B. *et al.* (1980) *Social Work in Conflict: the Practitioner and the Bureaucrat*, Croom Helm.

B

C

Care 'Care' is a term with wide-ranging reference. It is used in an occupational sense (as in care staff in residential work or as in 'caring professions', though this latter usage suggests that there are also non-caring ones); it is used to describe a status (a child may be in the care of a local authority – see *care order*); it describes an intention (to care) and an achievement (as a result of being in care and of caring efforts, someone flourishes and describes themselves as 'cared for'). The term is also used in the welfare argument concerning the possibility and/or desirability of combining 'care' with 'control' (see also *social control* and *care and control*). More recently the term social care has been coined, but it is unclear whether it is synonymous with all that is done towards *rehabilitation* or whether it marks out one kind of care from other kinds, such as medical, direct cash support, or the 'economic ways in which people look after each other directly or indirectly' (Barnes and Connelly).

Harris, R. J. (1980) 'A Changing Service: the Case for Separating "Care" from "Control" in Probation Practice', *British Journal of Social Work*, 10, 163-84.
Barnes, J. and Connelly, N. (eds) (1978) *Social Care Research*, Bedford Square Press.

Care and control This expression is used to point the debate about the function of the social services and of social work – to care through control or control through care (see *Social control*). More narrowly as a term, 'care and control' is used in relation to one of the main conditions to be met if a court order is to be made in respect of a child or young person. The court has to find not only that he or she is beyond control or guilty of an offence or describable in a number of other specific ways, but also that he or she is in need of care and control which is not likely to be given unless the court makes an order. 'Care and control' is also used in relation to divorce proceedings (Matrimonial Causes Act 1973 (SS. 424) deals with 'children of the family'). One parent may be given custody, care, and control, or a split may be made so that custody is given to one spouse and care and control to the other.

Care proceedings/Care order These belong to the *juvenile court*, which is a court of criminal jurisdiction, and refer to any child or young person from birth to 17 years of age. Care proceedings may be initiated by the local authority, police or NSPCC, if it is believed that there are grounds: i.e. neglect or ill-treatment, exposure to moral danger, being beyond control, failure to attend school, commission of an offence other than homicide. The court may make an order committing the child or young person to the care of the local authority if it is also satisfied that without such an order the child or young person is unlikely to receive the care and control required. Care proceedings suggest the likelihood of intensive social work with the child or juvenile, and the desirability of some measures of physical control (e.g. over where he resides). The care order combines earlier orders that no longer exist: the fit person order and the approved school order. It is now the local authority's responsibility to decide the best form of treatment in each case, though the present government (1981) may introduce a residential care order when resources allow.

Case conference A case conference is a formal meeting to discuss a case (i.e. a person or a family in a particular situation) with a view to reaching a joint decision; for instance the pattern of and responsibility for future work. Participants may all belong to the same discipline or come from the same organisation or the meeting may be of an inter-disciplinary nature (as, for instance, in relation to a possible case of a non-accidental injury to a child). Case conferences may be a feature of some kinds of social intervention or may be likely to be called at certain points in a person's 'career' in a particular service (e.g. a pre-discharge from residential care conference). Controversial questions arising from the widespread employment of case conferences include their effectiveness as joint decision-making or as decision-points, and the extent to which the client/s ought to be present.

Case history   The case history, often known in a welfare context as the social history, attempts to report the historical understanding of a person or a family and their problems. The case history summarises what are seen as the influential events and relationships of a life with a view to contributing to a *diagnosis* and to decisions in relation to preferred forms of treatment or disposal. The case history was first systematically developed in welfare in relation to psychiatric diagnosis and care. At one stage psychiatric social workers saw themselves and were regarded by others mainly as compilers of case or social histories, often of a detailed kind. Wide-ranging historical exploration receives much less emphasis today, and in some forms of therapy and of social work intervention historical grasp of a case is not considered to be necessary (e.g. *crisis* work). The methods and the rationale of the case history have reflected by and large an emphasis on psychological or psychobiological 'causation'; the long-standing sociological technique of the life history presents an unused source of insight.

Faraday, A. and Plummer, K. (1979) 'Doing Life Histories', *Sociological Review*, 27, 773-98.

Case review/Case review system   Cases are sometimes formally reviewed at regular intervals (as in the case of children in *foster care*) and in the course of staff and student *supervision*. The case review system is a means of the monitoring of social work developed as a piece of *action research*. It provides for the systematic use of designed records which show characteristics of the client and the problem, the social work activity and the aims, and the practical services provided. It also provides data that can be aggregated for management and research purposes. It is an important instrument in the development of priorities and of social work accountability.

Goldberg, E.M. and Warburton, R.W. (1979) *Ends and Means in Social Work*, Allen & Unwin.

Caseload   A caseload consists of those cases (individuals or families in particular, problematic situations) for which a worker or a *team* or an organisation carry responsibility. There is not an established convention concerning the point at which a contact or *referral* is to be regarded as a case or whether non-active or infrequently visited cases should be counted as part of the caseload. Sometimes a selection of the total of cases is referred to as the active caseload. Neither is it always certain who the case is – the individual or the household or the immediate family. Attempts have been made to establish case-weightings, so that all cases do not count as the same unit of 'load', and caseload management systems. Vickery's model of caseload management is a combination of decisions (e.g. definition of problem, goal to be achieved, people to be interviewed), specification of methods of influence, and a set of visiting frequencies (e.g. if the goal is change in behaviour, weekly contact is indicated). The term 'caseload' originated in the context of individual practitioner responsibility, but reference is now made to the potential load of a team's *'patch'* and to caseloads shared between social workers and others.

Vickery, A. (1977) *Caseload Management*, National Institute for Social Work Papers, NISW.

Casework   Originally, in the late nineteenth century, the term casework (and its related case-paper work) was work on individual situations, work case by case, as contrasted with statutory provision for categories of people or, as the pioneer American social worker Mary Richmond put it, retail rather than wholesale social provision. Grafted to this method and perspective, first in America and later in Britain, was the idea of a kind of specialised social work therapy. This conception was carried forward by what has been termed the *psychiatric deluge*. Casework is now seen less as a distinct therapy but as one of the methods constituting *social work* which includes *treatment* in its strong sense, and is usually described in brief as social work with individuals and families. Casework has been dominant in social work and most workers have been trained in casework but it is increasingly faced with problems and questions. These include its effectiveness as treatment, its place in effecting change in those social conditions that produce *social problems*, and its intellectual coherence. It is sometimes incorrectly assumed that a radical casework is not possible. One recent feature of social casework has been the multiplication of different modes of work (e.g. *crisis intervention*) and distinct theoretical approaches.

Fischer, J. (1976) *The Effectiveness of Social Casework*, Charles C. Thomas.

Strean, H. (ed.) (1971) *Social Casework: Theories in Action*, Scarecrow Press.

Timms, Noel (1964) *Social Casework: Principles and Practice*, Routledge & Kegan Paul.

Central Council for Education and Training in Social Work (CCETSW) This council was created in 1971 through the amalgamation of the Council for Training in Social Work (concerned with workers in what were then the local authority health and welfare services), the Central Training Council in Child Care, and the Advisory Council for Probation and After-Care. It is an independent statutory body concerned with the promotion and validation of training of salaried staff in the personal social services. Students who have successfully completed courses approved by the council are recognised as holding the Certificate of Qualification in Social Work (the CQSW) or the more recent Certificate in Social Service (the CSS). Among other developments are the post-qualification programme and the study of several important aspects of the social work curriculum (e.g. Legal Studies in Social Work Education, CCETSW Paper 4). In 1974 the council was made responsible for day-care training, including that for teachers for the mentally handicapped.

Cypher, J. (1979) 'Training', in *Seebohm Across Three Decades*, ed. J. Cypher, BASW Publications.

Younghusband, E. (1978) *Social Work in Britain: 1950–1975*, Allen & Unwin, vol. 2, pp. 93-103.

Central Policy Review Staff This small, inter-disciplinary, staff group in the Cabinet Office was established in 1970 (Cmnd

4506). Its aims include the establishing of *priorities*, helping to work out the implications of basic strategy in particular areas of activity, and identifying areas in which new options could be exercised. Of special interest in a welfare context are two reports: 'A Joint Framework for Social Policies', 1975; 'Population and the Social Services', 1977. The former argued for greater attention to the inter-connectedness of social policy seen as 'the distribution of resources and opportunities among the community, and ... ways of changing that distribution'. The latter concluded that the public has not always taken account of demographic change particularly in relation to foreseeable reduction in the size of client groups and to the desirability of early switches of resources between policy programmes.

Centre An increasingly popular way of describing the place at which non-residential services are available – day centres; nursery centres, which combine nursery education and day care; law centres, which provide legal advice; housing aid and advice centres, run by local authorities. The term is also used of *attendance centres* and of detention centres (penal institutions for offenders aged 14 to 21 years).

Ferri, E. *et al.* (1981) *Combined Nursery Centres: a New Approach to Education and Day Care*, Macmillan.

Change Change is an alteration of some durability in a positive or negative direction. It has not always been recognised that alteration brought about through social provision of many kinds, including social work, can result in a change for the worse as well as for the better. From the point of view of welfare, change is important both as alteration in an individual's situation and as social change. There has been argument whether social work should aim at changes in the individual and/or his circumstances or whether the aim is to deliver services simply as requested by individuals. Sometimes a distinction has been drawn between social work as directed at change and social work as *supportive*. When change has been intended, this has been seen as concerned with present behaviour, with a person's self-image, or with his 'growth' along identified phases towards *maturity*. Social change can be a deliberate objective of social policy, as, for instance, in the attempt to redistribute life chances. Sociologists see change as the normal condition of society, but in a social welfare context 'change' figures primarily in explanations of the development of social policy and legislation (as in the *social conscience* explanation), of the genesis of *social problems*, and the inadequacy of policy and practice that falls short of change in the basic social structure. Recent explorations of *systems theory* have led to a view of social workers as essentially 'change-agents', but Davies argues that social workers are social maintenance mechanics. See also *Elite*.

Davies, M. (1981) *The Essential Social Worker*, Heinemann.
Hall, P. *et al.* (1975) *Change, Choice and Conflict in Social Policy*, Heinemann.

Character disorder   The term 'character disorder' originated in psychoanalytic theory. It was used by social workers with a clinical orientation. It is difficult to pin down with any confidence and it is often used synonymously with behaviour disorder, *acting-out* of a persistent kind, neurotic character, character-neurosis, personality disorder (the preferred term in published psychiatric classifications). Moreover, there are disputed divisions within the disorder (e.g. the oral character disorder, the anal, and so on). At least three aspects appear important: it is the person's behaviour that continuously produces problems, mainly for others; the disorder stems from the personality, but is neither neurotic nor psychotic; the condition, therefore, requires special treatment of a nurturing and ego-building kind. See also *Ego*.

Pollak, O. (1976) 'Treatment of Character Disorders: a Dilemma in Casework Culture', in *Differential Diagnosis and Treatment in Social Work*, ed. F. J. Turner, Free Press.
Reiner, B.S. and Kaufman, J. (1959) *Character Disorders in Parents of Delinquents*, New York: Family Service Association of America.

Charity Organisation Society   This was founded in 1869; its name was changed in 1946 to Family Welfare Association. It was the dominant volunteer welfare organisation in the late Victorian era, exercising an international influence, and in the present century continued to innovate in social work practice, e.g. the Family Discussion Bureau (later the Institute of Marital Studies) and the Family Centre Project (Roof). The Charity Organisation Society is credited with an important role in the genesis of *casework* and criticised as the exponent of an individualistic idealist philosophy which gave insufficient weight to sheer material circumstances. It is connected in the minds of many with the distinction between the deserving and the undeserving poor, but through its most famous general secretary, C. S. Loch, it contributed to the start of *medical social work* and the consideration of important social reforms (as in the Royal Commission on the Poor Laws and Relief of Distress, 1905-9).

Mowat, C.L. (1961) *The Charity Organisation Society*, Methuen.
Roof, M. (1972) *A Hundred Years of Family Welfare*, Michael Joseph.

Child care service   This service was provided in the form of *fieldwork* and *residential care* by Children's Departments of local authorities in 1948-71, and by voluntary children's societies which in the nineteenth century offered mainly residential care. In the second half of the present century the voluntary societies have increasingly diversified and experimented with their services. The statutory work of local authorities in relation to children was subsumed in the new social service departments. Some Children's Departments had provided high quality service and their passing *specialisation* has been mourned, not always realistically.

Packman, J. (1975) *The Child's Generation*, Blackwell.
Younghusband, E. (1978) *Social Work in Britain: 1950-1975*, Allen & Unwin, vol. 2, pp. 36-97.

Child guidance   Child guidance clinics began to be established in Britain from around 1930, offering diagnostic and treatment services for disturbed children and their parents. The main element in provision consisted of the inter-disciplinary work of psychiatrist, psychologist (responsible for psychological testing), and social worker. The history of such clinics has been outlined until 1962. They should be seen as part of the general provision of psychological and psychiatric services for children which also include school psychological services, staffed by educational

31

psychologists and remedial teachers, child psychiatric clinics in certain hospitals, and the child health service, where an increasing number of clinics are held jointly by consultant paediatricians and child psychiatrists. Since that date and particularly since the Seebohm Report of 1968 the function and continued existence of 'the team' has been questioned. Seebohm wished to see much more time given to consultation with other staff. A government circular (DES 3/74) seems to commit clinics to provide treatment and assessment, and also help and general guidance to people ranging from health visitors and general practitioners to residential social work staff. The circular states somewhat vaguely: 'Rather than a self-contained, highly specialised child guidance service ... the concept of child guidance that now appears appropriate is of a network of services.' The most recent factual description of the service dates from 1975.

Child Guidance Special Interest Group/British Association of Social Workers (1975) *The Child Guidance Service*.

McPherson, I. and Sutton, A. (eds) (1981) *Reconstructing Psychological Practice*, Croom Helm.

Timms, Noel (1964) *Psychiatric Social Work in Great Britain, 1939-1962*, Routledge & Kegan Paul.

Child-minders   Child-minding is non-residential care of another's child, by a 'lay' person, for reward. Local authorities maintain registers of (a) premises and (b) persons undertaking child-minding. Anyone paid, in cash or kind, to mind children under 5 years of age for more than two hours a day for other people is legally obliged to register with the local authority social services department. Some authorities have schemes for the support and training of child-minders, but many remain unregistered. Of concern are: the vulnerability of those who require *day care* for their children (for example, one-parent families); the standards of care provided; how they can be improved or what alternatives should be sought and provided; controversy in the case of very young children over the comparatively long periods of separation from parents; the place of child-minding in the spectrum of child care.

Jackson, B. and Jackson, S. (1979) *Childminder: a Study in Action Research*, Routledge & Kegan Paul.

Children's Hearings   The Children's Hearing was introduced in Part III of the Social Work (Scotland) Act 1968 as a diversionary system to keep children in trouble out of court. The Hearing, a unique device, replaced the *juvenile court*, but it is not itself a court. A hearing consists of a chairperson and two other panel members: panels are established for each local authority and members are appointed by the Secretary of State from names submitted by the Children's Panel Advisory Committee. Panels are staffed by an executive officer (called a Reporter), who investigates any case of a child who may be in need of compulsory measures of care. The Reporter decides either that no action is required or that the local authority be asked to help on a voluntary basis or that the child should be brought to a Children's Hearing. The Hearing can discharge the referral or make a supervision requirement, which may include residential care. The Hearings have been criticised, but they represent an important development in the evolution of the juvenile court and in attempts to involve families in the future disposition of children. By 1977 the majority of Reporters were social workers.

Bruce, N. and Spencer, J. (1976) *Face to Face with Families: a Report on the Children's Panels in Scotland*, Macdonald.
Martin, F. *et al.* (1981) *Children out of Court*, Scottish Academic Press.
Parsloe, P. (1978) *Juvenile Justice in Britain and the United States*, Routledge & Kegan Paul, pp. 168-78.

C

Citizen   Citizenship is a status with rights; it involves allegiance and some form of residence. In welfare it is important for two distinct reasons. First, it is at the heart of much discussion of immigration, particularly black immigration. So the Nationality Bill (1981) seeks to create three new categories of citizenship. Second, the notion of citizenship played a crucial part in the beginning of social work and social reform at the end of the nineteenth century. More recently, Marshall argued that welfare rights were a crucial aspect of citizenship. This re-connection of citizenship and social welfare is best seen as a revival of a nineteenth-century view of the life of citizenship, associated with T. H. Green and Bernard Bosanquet.

Richter, M. (1964) *The Politics of Conscience: T.H. Green and his Age*, Weidenfeld & Nicolson.

Rose, E.J.B. (1969) *Colour and Citizenship: a Report on British Race Relations*, Institute of Race Relations/Oxford University Press.

Class   See *Social class*.

Client   Client, in a welfare context, is the general name for someone receiving non-casual help, willing or unwilling, from a social worker. It is reserved, on the whole, for those receiving some form of *casework*. *Community workers* do not usually wish to refer to client groups or client neighbourhoods. The term has often been described as inflating the professional stature of social workers ('client' goes with 'professional', unlike the suggested alternatives of 'customer' or 'user') or as misdescribing the enforced nature of much social worker–client interaction. No generally acceptable alternative has been found. The term, as used, can convey a general notion that users of welfare have some 'rights'. Important phases in the history of health visiting revolve around the change from 'patient' to 'client' as the preferred description of those to whom the health visitor ministers.

Tropp, E. (1974) 'Three Problematic Concepts: Client, Help, Worker', *Social Casework*, 55, 19-29.

Code of ethics   A set of rules and normative aspirations that is in some sense publicly 'available', even though there may be no explicit machinery for attending to behaviour that may be in violation of the code. It has been said that as far as social work is concerned misconduct is undefinable, but attempts have been made to define explicitly both particular behaviour (see *confidentiality*) and also to articulate a more general code. A Code of Ethics for Social Work was adopted by the British Association of Social Workers in 1975, and all members are required to uphold it. This code consists of a statement of general principles (e.g. 'Concerned with the enhancement of human well-being, social work attempts to relieve and prevent hardship and suffering'), and a list of twelve principles of practice (e.g. 'He will not reject his client or lose concern for his suffering ...'). Such codification enhances professional status, provided it avoids the ridiculous, and offers some protection to clients and workers alike. Both are often in vulnerable and 'private' situations which demand more than administrative *appeal* or *complaint*. Attempts have also been made to draw up a code of ethics for social researchers.

Communication   Communication is a social process involving an emitter (someone conveying a message of some kind), the message (verbal or non-verbal), a channel through which the message is conveyed, and a receiver. The source and the receiver may be more or less skilful in translating the message into appropriate codes (at encoding and decoding). The study of communication is important in welfare because social workers are required to be skilled communicators with clients and others; special measures are often taken with the specified intention of 'improving communication' because social services are often criticised for failure in the communication of information to staff and clients; poor communication has often taken complete blame for social service failure; and because clients can suffer from particular communication difficulties (e.g. the deaf).

Day, P. (1977) *Methods of Learning Communication Skills*, Pergamon.

C

Community   A large number of definitions of community are available in the sociological literature, referring in different ways to ideas of territory, social relations on the basis of a shared interest or of a locality, or simply to social groups. Students of welfare are interested in what Stacey refers to as two kinds of locality study: social institutions as manifested in a locality and the inter-relations of institutions in a locality, whether or not these are called community studies. The term is important in welfare vocabulary because of the range of expressions which refer to 'community'; the range of conditions to which 'community' is a remedy (e.g. *anomie*, rootlessness, etc.); and the notions of sharing, membership, and cohesion which seem to be implied in 'community'. In a welfare context, it is important to distinguish between community as a source of help, as describing help of a particular kind, and as a target for services. Plant has argued that in social welfare 'community as fact and value' can only be understood as part of a tradition of thought which goes back to the end of the eighteenth century.

COMMUNITY ACTION

Plant, R. (1974) *Community and Ideology: an Essay in Applied Social Philosophy*, Routledge & Kegan Paul.
Stacey, M. (1969) 'The Myth of Community Studies', *British Journal of Sociology*, 20, 134-47.

Community action   It is difficult to distinguish this term from 'social action'. 'Community action' probably originated in the American War on Poverty, but the term is also used in Britain. A wide or a rather more narrow definition has been offered. The first would 'include almost any movement by any minority groups using any methods to achieve change, and no doubt this use of the term will continue' (Community Work Group, p. 40). A definition of less wide scope would see community action as collective action on the part of the poor or those socially deprived in some way to overcome from a neighbourhood base some part of their general powerlessness. Leonard believes that community action is a possible alternative to the dominant welfare ideology, but suggests that it is seen differently by different groups: 'by some as a disruption and unhelpful challenge to effective planned change; by some as a more sophisticated means by which working class areas are manipulated by a new group of bourgeois professionals; by yet others as an effective way of increasing local control over bureaucracy and developing a consciousness of the possibilities of collective power.'

Community Work Group (1973) *Current Issues in Community Work*, Routledge & Kegan Paul.
Leonard, P. (ed.) (1975) *The Sociology of Community Action*, Sociological Review Monograph no. 21, University of Keele.
Marris, P. and Rein, M. (1967) *Dilemmas of Social Reform: Poverty and Community Action in the United States*, Routledge & Kegan Paul.
Moynihan, D. (1969) *Maximum Feasible Misunderstanding*, Free Press.

Community care   'Community care' was originally the general name of a programme offering a preferred alternative to long-stay residence in an institution (care in the community); it has now also come to be used to describe a particular response to a variety of problems (almost care by the community). The term was first widely used in relation to mental illness following the

Report of the Royal Commission, 1957. In 1961 the Minister of Health proposed the run-down of mental hospitals, and published in 1963 *Health and Welfare: the Development of Community Care*. Since then the term has been applied to provision for other groups, so that, for example, we speak of caring for children in the community. 'Community care' raises a number of questions: the extent to which institutional provision is or is not regarded as part of 'community care' or whether any provision that is non-institutional is simply as such an instance of community care; the assumption that because a programme is called 'community care' it is thereby effective as care; and, finally, the highly persuasive use of the term (as in such phrases as 'the caring community') which conceals the fact that the major costs of non-institutional care are carried by family members. Some argue that care in and by the community should be seen as an interweaving of formal and informal services; others that caring relationships should not be seen along a single continuum (from statutorily provided to neighbourly), but that there is a principled antithesis between formal and informal *care*.

C

Abrams, P. (1977) 'Community Care: Some Research Problems and Priorities', *Policy and Politics*, 6, 125-51.
Bayley, M. (1973) *Mental Handicap and Community Care*, Routledge & Kegan Paul.

Community development 'Community development' started as a post-World War II response in the under-developed parts of the world to help and to stimulate people to improve their own local way of life. Such improvement was believed to depend on the active co-operation of people themselves. Dominant at that time were ideas of the great benefits to be derived from a policy and programme of non-directiveness, of the essential element of popular *participation*, and of developing the skills of 'ordinary' people. Community development has since been identified as one of the interwoven strands of community work (the others being *community organisation* and community planning/policy formulation). It involves direct, face-to-face action directed towards mobilising people in a locality or *neighbourhood* around one or more issues or concerns.

COMMUNITY DEVELOPMENT PROJECT

Community Work Group (1978) *Community Work and Social Change*, report of Calouste Gulbenkian Foundation, Longman.

Community Development Project   This was launched by the Home Office in 1969 in the form of twelve *action-research* projects in areas of high social *deprivation*. The experiment was neighbourhood-based and designed to find new ways of meeting needs, partly through closer co-ordination of existing agencies and partly through citizen involvement and community self-help. Thus the experiment, supported by a significant research effort, can be seen as a combination of *community development* and *community organisation*. The Project is important as an organisational innovation ('an elaborate and ill-articulated structure that sought to hold together a coalition of action teams, research teams, local authorities, universities and government departments.' S. Hatch, 'Between Government and Community', *Social Work Today*, 5, 1974). It has been criticised as assuming that the source of problems as opposed to their location was in relatively small urban areas. Several local projects became convinced that the problems they discovered and encountered in working were due to elements in the social structure: local community problems might be found in special areas (and it was important whether these areas were declining or 'improving'), but their solution was not community-bound. The Community Development Project should also be viewed in the light of subsequent policies for the *inner city*.

Agpar, M. (ed.) (1976) *New Perspectives on Community Development*, McGraw-Hill.
Higgins, J. (1978) *The Poverty Business*, Blackwell.
Lees, R. (1975) *Research Strategies for Social Welfare*, Routledge & Kegan Paul.

Community group   Any group that is formed 'spontaneously' or through social workers and/or others, with a non-treatment purpose, but to take concerted action. Sometimes such a group is best seen as part of a *social movement* – as in the case of claimants' unions. Groups vary in size, continuity, internal cohesion, objectives, and so on. It has also been suggested that distinct phases in the life of each group can be identified.

Baldock, P. (1974) *Community Work and Social Work*, Routledge & Kegan Paul, pp. 66-82.

Community Health Council   Community Health Councils were established under the National Health Service Re-organisation Act 1973. A circular of 1974 clarified their role: to represent in their districts (England has 205 such districts) the interests of the public in the Health Service. Councils have between 18 and 36 members, half nominated by local authority, one-third by voluntary organisations, and the rest by the Regional Health Authority.

Levitt, R. (1980) *The People's Voice in the National Health Service: Community Health Councils after Five Years*, King's Fund.

Phillips, D. (1975) 'Community Health Councils', in *Year Book of Social Policy, 1974*, ed. K. Jones, Routledge & Kegan Paul.

Community home   The Children and Young Persons Act 1969 introduced this term to cover former approved schools – community homes with education on the premises (or CHEs) – detention centres, remand homes, and assessment centres. The residential needs of quite large areas (England and Wales were divided into twelve regions) were to be established by *Regional Planning Committees* for the whole range of problems, from those requiring residential nursery provision to those requiring treatment for disturbed adolescents. The term 'community home' indicated the legitimisation of the institution (it 'belonged' to the community), the operational boundaries (work should be undertaken by residential staff and fieldworkers with the child's family), and the preferred style of life (a planned environment leading to free communication).

Home Office, Advisory Council on Child Care (1970) *Care and Treatment in a Planned Environment* (Report on the Community Homes Project), HMSO.

Community organisation   'Community organisation' was originally used to describe efforts towards the greater *co-ordination* of voluntary organisations. It is now used more widely, sometimes as another way of referring to a highly generalised objective of community work (as in the idea of organising the community). A number of models of community organisation have been explored: for instance as locality or neighbourhood development (as in the work of the *settlements*); as social action to effect a redistribution of power; and as participative social planning. Sometimes community organisation, with an emphasis on increasing participation in existing organisations, is seen as a specific response to the social disorganisation of an area.

Brager, G. and Specht, H. (1973) *Community Organising*, Columbia University Press.

Community relations 'Community relations' is another term for untroubled race relations, and the promotion of such became an official object of social policy in the 1968 Race Relations Act. A central Community Relations Commission was established to assist in and to encourage the establishment of 'harmonious community relations'. It could vet the appointment of, and contribute towards the cost of, local Community Relations Officers and had some power to subsidise Community Relations Councils which were 'non statutory, multi-representative, and multiply-financed voluntary bodies' (Jones). The main objective of what has been termed the community relations movement was ambiguous. 'Was it intended simply to be a social service for Blacks ... or was it intended as a service for everyone with a public grievance or handicap who happened to reside in an "immigrant infested" area, and even, potentially for those with "community" grievances not resident in immigrant areas?' (Jones). But, of course, in a welfare context any label containing 'community' runs substantial risks of ambiguity. In the Race Relations Act 1976 the Commission for Racial Equality replaced the Community Relations Commission (and the Race Relations Board).

Jones, C. (1977) *Immigration and Social Policy in Britain*, Tavistock, pp. 157-69.

Community service order This order was introduced in the Criminal Justice Act 1972 for offenders aged 17 and over (other than murderers) found guilty of offences punishable by imprisonment. The idea of the order was based on one of the recommendations of a sub-committee of the Home Secretary's Advisory Council on the Penal System (1970). Courts may sentence to a period of unpaid work in the community of not less than 40 but not more than 240 days under the supervision of a community service organiser appointed by and subject to the local *Probation and After-Care Committee*. After a pilot, the scheme was extended nationally in 1975, though each local scheme had to be approved. The period of community service (CS) must be completed in one year. The community service order owes something to notions of the importance of reparation, of the 'failure' of imprisonment, and *rehabilitation* into the community. The present government in a White Paper on Young Offenders (1980) has expressed its intent to reduce the age of offenders able to be sentenced to community service to 16 years. The CSO scheme has been described as 'the most radical departure made by the British penal system since the introduction of probation and borstal at the turn of the century ...' (Davies, p. 6).

Davies, M. (1981) *The Essential Social Worker*, Heinemann.
Young, W. (1979) *Community Service Orders*, Heinemann.

Community work Community work 'seems to cover making delinquents pick up toffee papers, digging old people's gardens, helping tenants form an association of their own, and organising demonstrations. The literature does not make clear what it is and what it is not' (Baker). It has been claimed as a method of social work, or as a distinct mode of operation and philosophy independent of other occupations. The term is post-World War II, but interest in a social context wider than that of the family and in facilitating indigenous efforts rather than treating individually-defined ills owes something to earlier American interest in *community organisation* and to the application to advanced, industrial societies of ideas of *community development* originally designed for the encouragement of self-determination in the former British colonies. More recently community work has been seen as the systematic attempt to help 'the poor and the powerless' move towards changing the structure of society. There are, however, many perspectives on community work which are not always radical in intent or always in undying contest with social casework. Essentially it should be seen in terms of a widening of worker activity (e.g. involvement in local politics), of the objects of change (e.g. not so much the treatment of individual cases of depression but the unjust allocation of resources to single-parent families), of the 'unit' of work (people in a common plight), and a reiteration of the significance of what people can achieve on their own, given support.

Baker, J. (1978) *Neighbourhood Advice Centres*, Routledge & Kegan Paul.
Baldock, P. (1974) *Community Work and Social Work*, Routledge & Kegan Paul.
CCETSW (1975) *The Teaching of Community Work*, Report of a Working Party.
See also the series of collected essays *Community Work, One, Community Work, Two*, and so on, published by Routledge & Kegan Paul.

Compensation To compensate someone is to make justified and specific amends for a particular loss or harm. In welfare monetary awards in recognition of some loss or harm sustained are made in a number of circumstances. For example, the Criminal Injuries Compensation Board may make lump-sum payments to those who have sustained a personal injury which is directly attributable to crimes of violence or which has been received in the attempt to prevent a crime or in assisting the police. More generally, the idea of compensation or making up for a range of particular deficits can be seen in operation in various priority area policies and in the belief that one major justification of the *Welfare State* is to be found in compensation for diswelfares created by particular social changes (e.g. in kinds of employment). Some would argue that even in this extended sense compensation is too limited an idea: more resources should be channelled to particular groups in affirmation of their need and not simply to bring them to a non-compensatable level.

Bolderson, H. (1974) 'Compensation for Disability: the Social and Economic Objectives of Disability Benefits', *Journal of Social Policy*, 3, 193-211.
Day, P. (1981) 'Compensatory Discrimination', *Philosophy*, 56, 55-72.
Walker, A. and Townsend, P. (1979) 'Compensation for Disability: the Wrong Course', in *Year Book of Social Policy in Britain, 1978*, ed. M. Brown and S. Baldwin, Routledge & Kegan Paul.

Complaints Since the development of the Parliamentary

Commissioner (*Ombudsman*), a number of formal complaints procedures have been statutorily established. The 1974 Local Government Act, for instance, created the Commissions for Local Administration in England, and in Wales. (A commissioner for Scotland was appointed in 1975.) The commissioners have the task of investigating complaints of injustice arising from maladministration by local, water, or police authorities. Other people can complain, of course, on behalf of others, but, as Beardshaw indicates, this is often a difficult and daunting process.

Beardshaw, V. (1981) *Conscientious Objectors at Work; Mental Hospital Nurses*, Social Audit Ltd.

Hyde, M.R. (1977) 'The Commission for Local Administration', in *Year Book of Social Policy in Britain, 1976*, ed. K. Jones *et al.*, Routledge & Kegan Paul.

Compulsion   In a welfare context 'compulsion' has two distinct meanings. First it can be used in a psychiatric sense: a person can be subject to a disorder whereby he engages without apparent deliberation in repetitive behaviour, often of a ritualistic character. In this sense we speak of an obsessional-compulsive neurosis or of a personality that is of a compulsive (or driven) nature. Second, compulsion refers to particular measures taken to reduce a person's freedom of action. In welfare, compulsion refers usually to non-voluntary admission to a residential institution, to enforceable elements of a probation order, or to submission to regimes of treatment or control. For example, sections of the Mental Health Act refer to different kinds of admission to hospital through compulsion. The issues raised and those concerning compulsory treatment, especially where this is irreversible or hazardous or of an experimental nature, have been discussed in a wide-ranging review of the 1959 Mental Health Act. A Bill at present (1982) before the House proposes various changes, including the creation of a Mental Health Commission. It is important to recognise that compulsion may take rather non-specific forms in welfare: Charles Booth, for example, stated in relation to labour colonies for the casual poor: 'The only form compulsion could assume would be that of making life otherwise impossible' (quoted G. Stedman Jones, *Outcast London*, Clarendon Press, 1971, p. 365).

CONCILIATION SERVICE

Bean, P. (1980) *Compulsory Admission to Mental Hospitals*, Wiley.
DHSS (1978) *Review of the Mental Health Act, 1959*, Cmnd 7320, HMSO.

Conciliation service Provision of a conciliation service is a new development in divorce court welfare stemming from one of the recommendations of the Committee (Finer) on One-Parent Families. The report of this committee defined conciliation in terms of assisting the parties to deal with the consequences of the established breakdown of their marriage 'by reaching agreements or giving consents, or reducing the area of conflict ... in every matter arising from the breakdown which requires a decision on future arrangements.' Such matters included *custody*, support, access to and education of the children, and disposition of the matrimonial home. The first conciliation service was established in Bristol in 1978 and similar schemes are now being organised by statutory and voluntary agencies in other parts of Britain.

Fraser, D. (1980) 'Divorce Avon Style: the Work of a Specialist
    Welfare Team', *Social Work Today*, II, 12-15.
Murch, M. (1980) *Justice and Welfare in Divorce*, Sweet & Maxwell.

Conditioning A set of techniques for establishing change in behaviour without use of insight. Several kinds of conditioning have been identified: classical conditioning on a simple stimulus–response model, whereby responses are elicited by stimuli with which they were not originally associated (as in Pavlov's salivating dog experiments), or counter-conditioning (reciprocal inhibition), whereby a response incompatible with the maladaptive response is established, and the maladaptive response is eliminated. Operant or instrumental conditioning rewards the desired behaviour, perhaps through the reinforcement of successive approaches to it or through reward in a token economy system which immediately reinforces the behaviour with tokens that may later be exchanged for such primary reinforcers as food, privilege, etc. See also *Behaviour modification*.

Confidentiality This concerns the protection of information given by 'a client' or acquired by 'a professional' in the course of giving a service and the right to privacy. It is considered that confidentiality is a right of a client and imposes a duty on the professional. It has also been suggested that service could not be given unless the client assumed that the professional would not make irresponsible use of the information entrusted. In welfare, questions of importance arise concerning safeguards, the extent to which 'the matter is being communicated not merely to the individual caseworker but also to the social agency' (Biestek) and the circumstances under which confidential information may be disclosed. When a 'client' says, 'I want this treated as confidential', or a social worker says, 'This interview is entirely confidential', it is not always clear what is being requested and what disclosure is being given what kind of guarantee.

Biestek, F. (1961) *The Casework Relationship*, Allen & Unwin, pp. 120-33.
British Association of Social Workers (undated) *Confidentiality in Social Work*.
Wilson, S. J. (1978) *Confidentiality in Social Work: Issues and Principles*, Free Press.

Conflict Conflict figures in welfare as explanation and as strategy. It is suggested that students of welfare and practitioners understand society in terms either of a conflict between the powerful and the powerless (or between old and potentially new social forms) or of a consensus or implicit agreement that requires vigilance and correction but no radical change to ensure the continuation of society as we know it. Some see social conflict as limitless, but others, while recognising the importance of social conflict between social groups and/or interests, see no reason to assume unbounded conflict (Rex and Moore). 'Conflict' also figures in different explanations of the development of the social services (as the result of an increasingly refined *social conscience* or as gains the working class has been able to wrest from the possessing class). As a strategy, 'conflict' is to be found more usually in *'community work'* (though it is part of *'confrontation'* in work with individuals). It refers to a disposition to face conflicts of interest between, say, service-users and service-providers, and to take the implications of this into explicitly political struggle at the local or central government level. See also *Change*.

Rex, J. (1981) *Social Conflict: a Conceptual and Theoretical Analysis*, Longman.
Rex, J. and Moore, R. (1967) *Race, Community and Conflict*, Oxford University Press.

Confrontation   This is a term used to describe a social work technique involving 'facing' someone and facing them with a particular description of their behaviour and/or its likely effects with a view to evoking a direct response from them. So, a community worker (*community work*) may decide to meet a local authority housing official and face him with the consequences of a re-housing policy. Or a caseworker (*casework*) may tell a client that he apparently has no intention to carry out their *contract* or that continuing a certain line of behaviour will have certain consequences in reality. Systematic use of confrontation as a direct questioning of someone's *defences* is a feature of certain therapeutic programmes for people who abuse drugs and drink. Confrontation is frequently used in *reality* therapy.

Conscience   See *Social conscience*.

Consumer/Customer   In a welfare context these terms describe someone who uses a social service. Some see the term as preferable to '*client*', while others object to the implication of 'consumer sovereignty' and 'shopping around for the best buy'. A significant recent research development has been the study of the consumer's viewpoint in relation to services approached and/or help received. The importance of consumer research so that services can be better adapted to users has also been emphasised in the Health Services, as, for example, in the (Court) Report on Child Health Services, 1976.

Shaw, I. (1975) 'Consumer Opinion and Social Policy: a Research Review', *Journal of Social Policy*, 5, 19-32.

Contract   'Contract' is a term increasingly used by social workers, but it covers a number of different situations. In social work it is a formal agreement (not necessarily written) between social worker (and the agency?) and client which specifies the objectives to be achieved within a given period and the work each will do, and when, as their particular contribution towards agreed objectives. However, some social workers refer to the making of the contract as if the main work had been accomplished once an agreement had been reached; others talk of contract work if a plan has been shared at a very late stage in contact or if they have simply set objectives, whether or not these have been shared with the client. Corden has argued that a contractual model should be grounded on values rather than any claim to therapeutic effect, and that the fundamental value is *reciprocity* rather than the unilateral *gift*. Short-term work on a contractual basis can be seen as a way of increasing the client's autonomy.

Corden, J. (1980) 'Contracts in Social Work Practice', *British Journal of Social Work*, 10, 143-62.
DHSS (1978) *Social Service Teams: the Practitioner's View*, Olive Stevenson and Phyllida Parsloe, Introducers, HMSO, pp. 116-20.

Control   Refers to measures to regulate behaviour (through the use of certain drugs in the case of disturbed children – Taylor *et al.* – or through locking-up of children) and to over-all function: social workers are only/partly agents of *social control*.

Millham, S. *et al.* (1978) *Locking up Children: Secure Provision within the Child-Care System*, Saxon House.
Taylor, L. *et al.* (1979) *In Whose Best Interests— the Unjust Treatment of Children in Courts and Institutions*, Cobden Trust/Mind, pp. 80-4.

Convergence theory   Convergence theory refers to the ideas that in advanced industrial societies common patterns of behaviour emerge and that these evoke a common commitment to social welfare. Critics of 'the theory' argue that it does not give appropriate weight to political differences between such societies and to the different ways in which welfare benefits are distributed.

Castles, F. and McKinlay, R. (1979) 'The importance of Politics: an

CO-OPERATION

Analysis of the Public Welfare Commitment in Advanced Democratic Societies', in *Social and Educational Research in Action*, ed. M. Wilson, Longman/Open University Press.

Robertson, A. (1980) 'The Welfare State and Post-industrial values', in *Social Welfare: Why and How?*, ed. N. Timms, Routledge & Kegan Paul.

Co-operation Co-operation consists in working together towards mutually acknowledged and agreed goals. It is often assumed that co-operation occurs as a result of exhortation, that it invariably produces economy of effort and increased effectiveness, and that the co-operation of organisations or of welfare workers is in the best interest of service-users. Co-operation is also seen as a necessary condition for effective social work, and 'non-co-operative' has sometimes been used to describe reluctant clients or those reluctant to become clients.

Co-ordination This term has much the same meaning as co-operation except that the joint working of organisations is envisaged rather than a co-operative relationship between client and worker. Moreover, the idea of 'ordering' contained in 'co-ordination' suggests some over-arching machinery or dominant idea that sets agencies to work to secure common objectives. Co-ordination of effort and agreements about diagnosis is often the explicit objective of *case conferences* and review committees. The Wolfenden Report on the Future of Voluntary Organisations thought that the term co-ordination was not always appropriately applied to certain voluntary societies and instead suggested the term 'intermediate body' – intermediate with other organisations and intermediate between them and statutory authorities. See also *Councils of Voluntary Service*.

Councils of Voluntary Service These were formerly known as Councils of Social Service or what were termed local co-ordinating (*co-ordination*) bodies for voluntary societies. The Wolfenden Report on the Future of Voluntary Organisations suggested that such councils had five main functions: development and initiation; providing services (e.g. secretarial) to other voluntary organisations; liaison or the exchange of information and opinion between organisations; representation; and, in the case of some councils, providing direct service to individuals (e.g. through Citizens' Advice Bureaux). Following Wolfenden and the reorganisation of local government in 1974 there was a sustained effort to develop councils with boundaries co-terminous with the appropriate local authority area.

Lansley, J. (1974) *Voluntary Organisations Facing Change*, Report of a Project to Help Councils for Voluntary Service Respond to Local Government Reorganisation, Calouste Gulbenkian Foundation.

Counselling   Counselling is hard to define but there is a great deal of it about. One of the most significant recent developments in welfare has been the extension of counselling to an increasing number of situations (e.g. bereavement counselling, rape counselling, and so on). Counselling in these circumstances is often provided by non-professionals and/or by those who have undergone the same or a similar experience to those seeking comfort. Sutherland saw counselling as 'a personal relationship in which the counsellor uses his own experience of living to help his client to enlarge his understanding – and so make better decisions'. Counselling originated in public consciousness in relation to marriage (the Marriage Guidance Councils and the Roman Catholic Marriage Advisory Councils). The aim of the counsellor is to establish a relationship with the person in difficulty which enables him to describe his pressing situation and to discuss and try out various solutions. The counsellor is bound to respect confidences and is usually assumed to be non-directive. See also *Debt Counselling*.

Blackham, H.J. (1974) *Ethical Standards in Counselling*, National Council of Social Service.
'Proposed Definition of Counselling' (1978) *British Counselling News*, December, 7-10.
Sutherland, J. D. (1972) *Some Reflections on the Development of Counselling Services*, National Council of Social Service.

Counter-transference   A term used in psychodynamic therapy to refer to certain aspects of the therapist's unconscious response to the patient. Sometimes what is described are precisely those responses evoked by the patient's *transference*, but Winnicott talked more generally of those 'neurotic features which spoil the professional attitudes'. Again, some see counter-transference as exerting a negative effect on the analyst's technique, while others suggest that reflection on what the patient has come to represent from the therapist's past and the past wishes and feelings that the therapist is projecting onto the patient can be positively used in treatment.

Winnicott, D. (1960) 'Counter-transference', *British Journal of Medical Psychology*, 33, 17-22.

Crisis/Crisis theory 'Crisis' describes at least three different sets of events. First, when social workers speak of crisis work they may refer to work at a speed, dealing with the most pressing problem, rushing to the next situation with no time for reflection. Second, they may refer to a comparatively long critical phase in psychological development, as in 'the middle-age crisis'. Finally, 'crisis' can be viewed within the context of a theory of *intervention* as a significant disturbance in social/personal equilibrium which has particular implications for *brief treatment*. Rapoport argued that crisis was the product of three interrelated factors: hazardous events posing a threat to current or past instinctual needs, the threat is symbolically linked to earlier threats which results in vulnerability or conflict, a failure of adequate coping mechanisms. A crisis is seen as of a particular duration and as consisting of phases; it is argued that early and informed social work can have far-reaching positive effects. Crisis intervention is usually seen in terms of casework, but some attempts have been made to extend it to groupwork and community work.

Lukton, R.C. (1975) 'Crisis Theory: Review and Critique', *Social Service Review*, 49, 384-402.
Rapoport, L. (1970) 'Crisis Intervention as a Mode of Brief Treatment', in *Theories of Social Casework*, ed. R. Roberts and R. Nee, University of Chicago Press.

Culture of poverty This term was first used by Oscar Lewis to refer to a way of life developed and perpetuated by poor people in order to give their existence some meaning and to help them to cope with their problems. Lewis argued that the cycle of poverty was self-perpetuating and that by an early age the children had adopted the characteristic values and attitudes. The thesis has been criticised and in response Lewis has argued that poverty cultures tend to develop in particular societies, namely those characterised by a cash economy, high unemployment, a bilateral kinship system, and sparse social and economic provision for low-income groups. The idea of a culture of poverty probably influenced the recent social policy initiative in Britain concerned with transmitted *deprivation*.

Lewis, O. (1968) 'The Culture of Poverty', in *On Understanding Poverty*, ed. D. Moynahan, Basic Books.

Valentine, C. (1968) *The Culture of Poverty: Critique and Counter Proposals*, University of Chicago Press.

Custodianship order When Part II of the 1975 Children Act is implemented, any person caring for a child (e.g. a foster parent) may apply for a custodianship order which will vest legal custody in the custodian. Custodianship orders are revocable and do not entail the legal severance of child–parent ties, as in *adoption*.

Custody The Matrimonial Causes Act 1973 gave courts wide powers to make such orders as they saw fit concerning the custody and education of any child in the family under 18. The Proceedings and Magistrates' Courts Act 1978 introduced the custody and access order.

D

Dangerous   A person can be described as constituting a danger
to other people or to themselves, and by this we mean that they
are likely to do other people or themselves serious physical
harm, to inflict personal *violence*. Those at risk of causing other
kinds of harm are referred to as a menace. The general notion of
dangerousness is fairly easily grasped; more problematic are the
signs for recognising when a person is becoming dangerous and
the measures that can legitimately be taken once recognition has
been established, including the differential response towards
those at risk of violence directed towards the self and those likely
to be violent towards others. The Butler Committee saw
dangerousness as a propensity to cause serious physical injury
and lasting psychological harm; they judged that very few
people were 'unconditionally dangerous', but proposed, among
other remedies, a new form of indeterminate sentence for
dangerous offenders presenting a history of mental disorder
which could not be dealt with under the Mental Health Act and
for whom the life sentence is not appropriate.

Home Office, (Butler) Committee on Mentally Abnormal Offenders
(1975) *Report*, Cmnd 6244, HMSO, Ch. 4, 'Dangerous Mentally
Disordered Offenders'.
Prins, H. (1975) 'A Danger to Themselves and to Others', *British
Journal of Social Work*, 5, 297-309.

Day care   Day care is often provided in day centres, which
originated in the idea of day hospitals. Day care is now a
provision offered to a wide range of client groups – children (in
local authority or voluntary society children's centres), old
people, and so on. Day care provides at least an alternative,

52

temporary, 'roof' and, in addition, it is hoped, services of various kinds. It is defined mainly in terms of contrast with *residential care*, and sometimes seen as a part of *community care*. Provision under this description varies widely within and between client groups. For research purposes, Carter defined a day unit as 'a non-profit-making personal service which offers communal care and which has care-givers present in a non-domiciliary and non-residential setting for at least three days a week and which is open at least four to five hours each day' (p. 2).

Carter, J. (1981) *Day Services for Adults: Somewhere to Go*, Allen & Unwin.

Death   Death is marked by the cessation of life, and medically this is viewed in terms of brain death. The criteria by which brain death is established are of importance since these are used as the basis for the discontinuance of remedial effort. Of greater significance from a social welfare viewpoint are attitudes towards and social provision for death, and the fact that death is a social process involving the termination of membership of different social groups. The historical provision of the pauper's funeral indicates one way in which loss of membership can be symbolically reinforced. Societies differ in the way the process of death is defined and managed, but recently welfare interest has been awakened in a number of aspects, including the taboo character of death in contemporary Britain. So the process of mourning has been studied and bereavement counselling developed. Attention is also being given to special problems in relation to death in children and death in a child's world, and to the care of the terminally ill, particularly in connection with the hospice movement.

Burton, Lindy (ed.) (1974) *Care of the Child Facing Death*, Routledge & Kegan Paul.
Cartwright, Ann *et al.* (1973) *Life before Death*, Routledge & Kegan Paul.
Prichard, E. *et al.* (1977) *Social Work with the Dying Patient and the Family*, Columbia University Press.
Stoddard, S. (1979) *The Hospice Movement: a Better Way of Caring for the Dying*, Cape.

Death instinct   This is a Freudian formulation; one side of the

D

dichotomy between Eros and Thanatos, the life and the death instincts. Thanatos aims not at the reduction of tension but at a return to the inorganic state. *Libido* is the name of the energy available to the life instincts, but no name was given to the energy used through the death instincts. *Kleinian theory* views the notion of death instinct as active aggression against the self, and as extremely important in the dynamics of personality development.

Debt counselling A form of advice in relation to debts of different kinds (e.g. hire purchase, weekly credit accounts, check trading, loans, etc.) pioneered by the Birmingham Settlement Money Advice Centre.

Blamire, J. and Izzard, A. (1975) *Debt Counselling*, Birmingham Settlement.

Defence mechanisms/Mental mechanisms 'Defence mechanisms' have a place in *Freudian theory*, and the idea of human action deriving from 'machinery' described somehow as defensive is a good illustration of psychoanalytic innocence concerning the impact of language. The term is a collective name for systematic and habitual responses of the personality geared to warding off particular threats (e.g. from *id* or *super-ego*) and to advancing certain interests. Defence mechanisms are operated by the *ego* in order to preserve its functioning. The use of any particular mechanism should not be considered sufficient evidence of pathology: pathology depends on the way in which mechanisms are used, how efficient they are, and whether they make a net positive contribution to the total individual psychological economy. One problem concerns the number of defence mechanisms that can be separately identified. Laughlin has identified twenty-two major mental mechanisms and twenty-three minor responses.

Freud, A. (1966) *Normality and Childhood*, Hogarth Press.
Laughlin, H. (1963) *Mental Mechanisms*, Butterworth.

Defensible space This refers to personal territory with clearly identifiable status and lay-out which it is considered all humans need. It can be thought of as both physical and psychological space. The concept is used by those looking for causes for psychiatric 'breakdown', family breakdown, and crime in high-density, multi-storey living areas. Personal overcrowding is considered to be the cause of much psycho-social stress as evidenced by social work clients. The idea of defensible space is obviously applicable in residential provision.

Jephcott, P. (1971) *Homes in High Rise Flats: Some of the Human Problems Involved in Multi-storey Housing*, Oliver & Boyd.
Newman, O. (1973) *Defensible Space*, Architectural Press.

Delinquency In a welfare context delinquency refers primarily not to a peccadillo but to offences against the law or what would count as such on the part of juveniles. The term is often used as a negative stereotype to describe young people who break the law: most written material refers to adolescent males. Special treatment of the non-adult derives from the nineteenth century and is presently governed as far as court action is concerned by the Children and Young Persons Act 1969. The main issues arising from any special consideration of non-adults include: the (rising) age of criminal responsibility, theories concerning the 'causation' of juvenile delinquency (ranging from psychoanalytic explanations to sociological notions of sub-culture, 'drift' and so on), responses in terms of excluding larger numbers of 'delinquents' from the operation of legal agencies and possibly including them within a so-called treatment perspective, the changing official response to delinquency (e.g. the Criminal Justice Act 1961 reduced the minimum age of borstal training to 15).

Parsloe, P. (1978) *Juvenile Justice in Britain and the United States*, Routledge & Kegan Paul.
Schur, E. (1973) *Radical Non-intervention: Re-thinking the Delinquency Problem*, Prentice-Hall.

Dependency Dependency is a state of 'enforced' reliance on another for necessary psychological or material resources. It was, and remains, an objective of social work and of social policy to avoid the creation of a dependent class and to offer help without creating a state of dependency. On the other hand, temporary dependence on the goodwill or sustenance of a helper seems to be an element or phase in help that is effective. What is important in this context is the distinction between reliance on another for the attainment of specific objectives and a more generalised surrender. Restored independence signifies both the objective of social work/social service relationships and an 'ideal' state, but the notion of essential human inter-dependence requires more intensive exploration in welfare. Also of importance in social policy is the idea and classification of dependants and of the dependent relatives in relation to income maintenance services.

Depression Used in welfare discussion in a variety of ways. In *Kleinian theory* the so-called 'depressive position' (the infantile realisation that the loved mother and the mother who is attacked in phantasy are one and the same) is assumed to be part of everyone's normal development. In ordinary language 'to be depressed' is to be in a dejected mood, but this usage differs from psychiatric nomenclature which distinguishes between various kinds of psychiatric illness; e.g., the neurotic and the psychotic depression, the reactive depression compared to the endogenous whose onset appears to be connected with no discernible event. In a welfare context the conceptualisation of depression is important (as in Seligman's significant notion of learned 'helplessness'), as are ideas about the causation of the condition. Brown and Harris have recently suggested a model for the understanding of the causation of depression, consisting of a combination of provoking agents (severe life events and major difficulties), vulnerability factors, and symptom-formation factors. Vulnerability is significantly influenced – in the case of women – by social class factors.

Brown, G. W. and Harris, T. (1978) *Social Origins of Depression: a Study of Psychiatric Disorder in Women*, Tavistock.
Seligman, M. (1975) *Helplessness: on Depression, Development and Death*, Freeman.

Deprivation Generally 'deprivation' refers to a state of loss or of lack of that which is considered to be an important part of human welfare. The term is applied in social welfare in two different ways: an individual may suffer the consequences of emotional deprivation; particular areas may be characterised in terms of urban deprivation or particular groups in the population described as socially deprived. Since the 1950s, special attention has been paid to those psycho-social processes which lead to an individual state of deprivation through loss or failure of parenting: maternal separation was seen as leading invariably to emotional deprivation in the case of infants and young children, and to intellectual and emotional 'shortfalls'. Towards the end of the following decade the idea of urban deprivation began to be used to refer collectively to problems previously seen somewhat separately as slum housing, poverty, and so on. Norris argues that three separate concepts are involved in this change: deprivation, multiple deprivation, and urban deprivation. Recently, action and research have been directed towards the idea that deprivation shared by families or localities is transmitted across the generations. See also *Loss*.

Coffield, F. *et al.* (1980) *A Cycle of Deprivation?*, Heinemann.
Norris, G. (1979) 'Defining Urban Deprivation', in *Urban Deprivation and the Inner City*, ed. C. Jones, Croom Helm.
Rutter, M. (1972) *Maternal Deprivation Reassessed*, Penguin.

D

Deserving The distinction between the deserving and undeserving poor or between those who might be restored to a non-dependent status and those for whom remedial help could effect no lasting improvement was central to the *Charity Organisation Society* at least in the nineteenth century. The COS used the distinction to mark out respective responsibilities of charity or non-statutory provision and the Poor Law. However, a distinction between those deserving of charity and those who were not is part of the longer history of Christian almsgiving. Beatrice and Sidney Webb were wrong in asserting that the tradition of Christian philanthropy always emphasised a non-discriminating response and the exclusive value of the gift to the giver. The terms 'deserving' and 'undeserving' have long since been abandoned as explicit descriptions of those eligible for or constituting a priority for social welfare, but it has been argued strongly that notions of moral desert still play a part in the perceptions of those seeking help and in the judgments of those offering it (Rees).

Rees, S. (1978) *Social Work Face to Face*, Edward Arnold.
Tierney, B. (1959) *Medieval Poor Law*, University of California Press.

Detention centres Detention centres were introduced in the Criminal Justice Act 1948, partly as a response to the abolition of corporal punishment: a period of residential training aimed to provide what came to be known as a 'short, sharp shock'. These centres are part of the Prison Service and receive offenders aged between 14 and 21 years. Residential training is for three months (by a magistrates' court) or for six months (by a higher court). Detention centres have always been controversial. Intentions to phase them out (after the 1969 Children and Young Persons Act) have not materialised: 'Nearly everyone these days ... likes detention centres' (Taylor). The present government (1981) is experimenting with a tougher regime in some detention centres, but emphasis has always been on hard physical exercise and army-like drill.

Hall, P. *et al.* (1975) *Change, Choice and Conflict in Social Policy*, Heinemann, Ch. 12, 'Detention Centres: the Experiment which Could not Fail'.
Taylor, L. *et al.* (1979) *In Whose Best Interests?*, Cobden Trust/Mind.

Determinism Determinism is concerned with what in a strict sense is seen as the causes of human behaviour, and with asserting that no sense can be given to such sentences as 'He could have done otherwise'. Questions of freedom of the will are, of course, exceedingly complex. Spinoza, for example, said, 'A drunken man thinks that he speaks from the free will of the mind, those things which, were he sober, he would keep to himself.' In a welfare context theories that are arguably deterministic (*Freudian theories* or *Marxist*) are espoused by practitioners and by analysts at the same time as full recognition is given to human agency and the significance of personal intention. Both Freudian and Marxist theories appear to be capable of a deterministic and a liberational interpretation. Notions of desert and responsibility, of liability and collective responsibility which are important in understanding social provision and social response can find a place in a fully determined universe only with great difficulty. See also *Social engineering, Self-determination.*

Davidson, D. (1973) 'Freedom to Act', in *Essays on Freedom of Action*, ed. T. Honerich, Routledge & Kegan Paul.
Feinberg, J. (1970) *Doing and Deserving*, Princeton University Press.
Stalley, R. (1975) 'Determinism and the Principle of Client Self-determination', in *Self-Determination in Social Work*, ed. F. McDermott, Routledge & Kegan Paul.

Deviance Behaviour is described as deviant when it departs from the norms of a particular society at a particular time. Such departure usually invokes negative social sanctions, but it is not always the case that behaviour that is defined as deviant constitutes a serious threat to prevailing beliefs and the existing social order. There is no single, accepted, theory of deviance, and what is often described as the 'new deviancy theory' contains a range of insights from such distinct perspectives as Marxism, ethnomethodology, and so on. Recent studies of deviance do, however, suggest that the processes and procedures whereby individuals and classes of behaviour are socially defined as deviant are crucially important. Increasing attention is being given to the role of public agents in the amplification of deviance and the implications of deviance and controlling responses for questions of societal order. See also *Adjustment, Labelling.*

D

Hills, S. (1980) *Demystifying Social Deviance*, McGraw-Hill.
Pearson, G. (1975) *The Deviant Imagination*, Macmillan.

Diagnosis The term derives from medical usage, but since Mary Richmond's *Social Diagnosis* (1917) it has been extensively used in social work. Richmond's work is frequently championed as the model legitimising the sociological contribution, but a closer examination suggests that it 'reads much as might a legal text book on the collection, classification and admissibility of evidence' (Berleman). 'Diagnosis' as such has been seen largely in terms of the necessary precursor to casework treatment, as investigation or study by client and social worker together, though one of the widely accepted maxims of casework indicated that 'treatment' started as soon as contact was established. Diagnosis in casework has been explored in terms of increasing differentiation as increasingly sophisticated psychodynamic classifications have suggested themselves, but 'diagnosis' in the sense of assessment of the present situation with a view to specific action and the future is now considered a part of any social work or social planning. Diagnosis refers both to a process of discovery of the points in a situation salient for treatment and to the description of these points in a diagnostic statement. See also *Diagnostic School, Functional School.*

Berleman, W. (1968) 'Mary Richmond's Social Diagnosis in Retrospect', *Social Casework*, 49, 395-402.
Sainsbury, E. (1970) *Social Diagnosis in Casework*, Routledge & Kegan Paul.
Turner, F. (ed.) (1976) *Differential Diagnosis in Social Work*, Free Press.

Diagnostic School This was the name, loosely applied, to a large group of social work educators and practitioners in America from the late 1930s to the mid-1950s who were contrasted with the much smaller *Functionalist School.* The debate between the former (e.g. Gordon Hamilton) and the latter (e.g. Jessie Taft) is one of the few controversies in social work. It has long ceased to be active, but the issues are of historical and contemporary significance. The Diagnostic School held to the necessity of an encompassing *diagnosis* of the client's problem, with considerable emphasis on inner psychological factors: this was the worker's responsibility and alone ensured that appropriate service was given. Members of this school espoused a Freudian psychology, whereas the Functionalists held to the views of the schismatic Otto Rank. A diagnostic perspective tended to produce greater protectiveness towards the client and some scepticism about the necessity of pain for emotional growth. The Diagnostic School did not share the conviction of the Functionalists that the differences between the Schools involved fundamental moral and political questions.

Hamilton, G. (1950) 'The Underlying Philosophy of Social Casework', in *Principles and Techniques in Social Case Work: Selected Articles,*

1940–1950, ed. C. Kasius, New York: Family Service Association of America.
Taft, J. (ed.) (1944) *A Functional Approach to Family Case Work*, University of Pennsylvania Press.
Keith-Lucas, A. (1953) 'The Political Theory Implicit in Social Casework Theory', *American Political Science Review*, 47, 1076-91.

Disability Physical or sensory disability refers to the loss or the significant reduction of the functional ability of a part or the whole of the body; emotional or psychological disability refers to the loss or reduction of mental functions. Such disabilities commonly lead to disadvantages or restrictions in activity (*handicap*). Topliss argues: 'The concept of disability is a very slippery one, gliding imperceptibly into disadvantages or deviance unless somewhat arbitrarily limited'. In addition, we must also consider the social meaning of disability (the views and related behaviour of the disabled and those in regular or infrequent interaction with them concerning impaired functioning and the resulting social handicap). The disabled have become a subject of political importance since the Chronically Sick and Disabled Persons Act 1970 (see Topliss and Gould), which has emphasised the importance of local surveys of the disabled and of concrete help such as communications equipment, personal aids, and property adaptation. Such services should be seen in the context of older, specialised, often voluntary, services in relation to particular disabilities (e.g. the blind) and to particular functional aspects (e.g. at least one Disablement Resettlement Officer or DRO is located in each employment area with special responsibility for the disabled in the labour force).

Blaxter, M. (1976) *The Meaning of Disability*, Heinemann.
Topliss, E. (1979) *Provision for the Disabled*, Blackwell.
Topliss, E. and Gould, B. (1981) *A Charter for the Disabled*, Blackwell and Martin Robertson.
Walker, A. and Townsend, P. (1979) 'Compensation for Disability: the Wrong Course', in *Year Book of Social Policy in Britain, 1978*, ed. M. Brown and S. Baldwin, Routledge & Kegan Paul.

Discretion 'Discretion' consists in a certain liberty in the

61

exercise of judgment or in the application of rules. Its importance in social welfare is twofold. First, discretion is seen as an essential element in the decisions of professionals, though research on *ideology* suggests, in the case of social workers, that decisions may be highly routinised. Second, debate about the dominance of discretion as contrasted with the application of public rules of entitlement has played an important part in the devlopment of thought about supplementary benefits. Titmuss argued in favour of administrative discretion, but more recently Donnison stated: 'Growing reliance on discretionary additions makes it increasingly difficult for officials to discriminate between one equally needy case and another without resorting to moral judgments of the kind which we constantly try to exclude from our decisions.' Hill has usefully distinguished between the elimination of discretion through a process of legalisation and its control and review through judicialisation *(Welfare rights)*. Discretion can also be used to describe an attitude to information. The sociologist Simmel observed: 'discretion consists by no means only in the respect for the secret of the other, for his specific will to conceal this or that from us, but in staying away from the knowledge of all that the other does not expressly reveal to us.' See also *Confidentiality*.

Adler, M. and Asquith S. (1981) *Discretion and Welfare*, Heinemann.
Bull, D. (1980) 'The Anti-Discretion Movement in Britain: Fact or Phantom?', *Journal of Social Welfare Law*, March, 65-83.
Donnison, D. (1976) 'Supplementary Benefits: Dilemmas and Priorities', *Journal of Social Policy*, 5, 337-58.
Giller, H. and Morris, A. (1981) *Care and Discretion: Social Workers' Decisions with Delinquents*, Burnett Books.
Hill, M. (1974) 'Some Implications of Legal Approaches to Welfare Rights', *British Journal of Social Work*, 4, 187-200.
Titmuss, R. (1971) 'Welfare Rights, Law and Discretion', *Political Quarterly*, 42, 113-32.

Discrimination 'Discrimination' refers to behaviour and to judgment: the behaviour is based on the appreciation of certain distinguishing characteristics of an object or person. In a welfare context reference may be made to the importance of the social worker's discriminatory response to a client, but more significant reference is to negative and positive discrimination. People can be discriminated against; i.e. treated unfairly on the basis of an irrelevant distinguishing mark, such as skin colour or gender. It has been successfully argued that legislation at least contributes to the reduction of negatively discriminating behaviour, and three laws in the 1970s were enacted: Equal Pay Act 1970; Sex Discrimination Act 1975; Race Relations Act 1976 (see *race relations*). Central bodies were created to help to enforce the legislation and to assist individuals – the Equal Opportunities Commission, the Commission for Racial Equality. See also *Positive discrimination, Community relations.*

Divorce court welfare   The (Denning) Committee on Procedure in Matrimonial Causes, 1947, recommended the appointment of court welfare officers in divorce courts. The first experimental appointment was made in London in 1950, and in 1959 the Probation Rules were changed to make divorce court work a statutory duty for probation officers, taking the form of social inquiries connected with children of the marriage, at the request of the judge.

The preparation of divorce court welfare reports now represents a considerable addition to the workload of the probation officer. Similar reports are often requested by magistrates when deciding custody and access issues in the magistrates' courts.

Murch, M. (1980) *Justice and Welfare in Divorce*, Sweet & Maxwell.
Wilkinson, M. (1981) *Children and Divorce*, Blackwell.

D

Double bind   To be in a double bind, according to Evans, is to be subject to a contradictory communication from a person with whom one is in an intense relationship which has high survival for at least one partner in the relationship. The communicator asserts something and also makes or implies a comment on the assertion, and the recipient of the double bind is unable to step outside, as it were, the framework of the message. An example of a double bind can be found in the assertion of a mother saying to her child: 'Let Mummy comfort you', but behaving in a rejecting manner. Bateson in America first drew attention to the possible significance of repeated double binds in the aetiology of *schizophrenia*, but it has proved difficult to substantiate this possibility since double binds are very difficult to identify unambiguously. The idea of double bind can be used in a positive and ironic manner in therapy: it is termed in that context the therapeutic paradox, and it is used to reveal and study *ambivalence*.

Bateson, G. *et al*. (1956) 'Towards a Theory of Schizophrenia', *Behavioral Science*, 1, 251-64.

Evans, J. (1980) 'Ambivalence and how to Turn it to your Advantage: Adolescence and Paradoxical Intervention', *Journal of Adolescence*, 3, 273-84.

Watslawick, P. (1963) 'A Review of the Double-Bind Theory', *Family Process*, 2, 132-53.

Drugs See *Addiction*.

E

Education Welfare Officer This description (of what was originally the School Enquiry Officer) became common after 1944, partly as a recognition of the growing welfare functions of education departments, including work in relation to school attendance, free school meals, shoes and clothing, and child employment. The report of a working party established by the Local Government Training Board (Ralphs Report, 1973) referred to the neglect and undervaluation of the work of the EWO, and a more recent research report stated: 'The relative lack of integrity or clarity of function of the role of the EWO raises such questions as what is distinctive about the role, how far is the EWO able to practise particular skills as an individual practitioner, what are the adjacent roles and what are the necessary relationships between these roles?' (Johnson *et al.*, p. 135). Dominant issues in relation to the EWO concern the wide variation in duties and organisational structure, the extent to which the EWO should be seen as an education social worker (a specialisation developed in America), and the degree to which the potential of the role is being fulfilled in the interests of parents, child, and school.

Johnson, D. *et al.* (1980) *Secondary Schools and the Welfare Network*, Allen & Unwin.
Robinson, M. (1978) *Schools and Social Work*, Routledge & Kegan Paul, pp. 165-90.

Educational Priority Area The idea of an Educational Priority Area was first formulated as such in the Plowden Report. It encapsulated the argument that in order to compensate for the deprived social conditions which adversely affected the

65

educational progress of many children and to enable them to contribute to economic progress, priority should be given to poor areas which should go far beyond the achieving of equality of resource distribution: 'The first step must be to raise the schools of low standards to the national average; the second quite deliberately to make them better' (Plowden, p. 54). The concept of the EPA raised important questions concerning the unit towards which the special intervention was aimed (individual child, school or area); the possibility of creating a workable index for the designation of areas; and the class basis of the distribution of educational disadvantage. In 1968 a three-year programme of *action research* was established, 'cautiously open-minded on the capacity of the educational system to reform itself, dubious about an educational approach to the abolition of poverty, but at least as optimistic as Plowden about the primary school and pre-schooling as points of entry for action-research aimed at inducing changes in the relation between school and community' (Halsey, p. 5).

Central Advisory Council (England) (1967) *Children and their Primary Schools* (Plowden Report), HMSO.
Halsey, A.H. (1972) *Educational Priority* (Reports sponsored by DES and SSRC): vol. 1, *EPA Problems and Policies*, HMSO.

Egoism/Ego Egoism or the systematic tendency in decisions actively to prefer one's own interests is contrasted, in welfare discussion, with *altruism*. A foundation for at least a minimal social policy has been sought at least since the nineteenth century in the idea of enlightened egoism. Ego is a term featuring in psychoanalytic theory which has exercised, as part of a dynamic conception of personality, a considerable influence on the development of social casework: the American school of ego psychology has inspired a number of influential social work texts. The ego is best seen, in psychoanalytic terms, as essentially part of a dynamic triad which includes *id* and *super-ego*. Ego is perhaps most helpfully described in terms of a number of important functions. Thus, Alexander states: 'The adaptive, integrative function of the ego consists in gratifying needs and releasing emotional tensions in such a way that the integrity of the ego is maintained' (p. 89). A whole set of related terms has developed (ego strength/weakness, ego split, ego instinct (i.e. all non-sexual instincts). *Jung* distinguishes ego from the self.

Alexander, F. (1949) *Fundamentals of Psychoanalysis*, Allen & Unwin.
Parad, H.M. (ed.) (1963) *Ego-Orientated Casework: Problems and Perspective*, New York: Family Service Association of America.

Elderly See *Old People.*

Elite An elite is a minority group who exercise power and influence on the basis of recognised or assumed superiority in some respect. Elites are socially defined in relation to a whole society, as in the idea of a ruling elite, or in relation to particular organisations, as, for example, the elite of a political party. Elites may be highly conspicuous or they may operate on a more implicit basis through shared values, common background experiences, and so on (as in Wright Mills's *Power Elite*). Elitism is the assumption of generalised deference to people in particular social positions. Policies criticised as elitist do not necessarily originate from elite groups but are productive of status distinctions. Thoenes has argued that within the existing democratic order it is possible for an elite to act as a catalyst of significant social *change.*

Thoenes, P. (1966) *The Elite in the Welfare State*, Faber.

E

Emotion Social workers often talk about feelings (of anger, fear, love, hate, and so on) – their own and those of others. Biestek lists, as two of the seven principles of social casework, the purposeful expression of feelings (sometimes he refers to this misleadingly as their 'release'); and controlled emotional involvement. In welfare discourse emotions and feelings are often spoken of as if they were forces somehow operating independently 'within' a person, and insufficient attention is paid to what has been called the intentionality of emotions (they have an object to which they are directed) and to their close connection with appraisals of different kinds (for example, fear is inseparable from judging a situation to be dangerous). Ragg argues that 'the description of feeling is not simply the realisation of a pre-existing thing. It is a creative act' (p. 62).

EMPATHY

Recently, philosophers have given consideration to the place of feeling in moral judgment and to the role of morality in the education of feelings. Such considerations are likely to have significance in both social work and social policy.

Biestek, F. (1961) *The Casework Relationship*, Allen & Unwin.
Ragg, N. (1977) *People not Cases*, Routledge & Kegan Paul.
Williams, B. (1973) 'Morality and the Emotions', in *Problems of the Self*, ed. B. Williams, Cambridge University Press.

Empathy   This term has early association with aesthetics and with the idea of losing oneself in a work of art in such a way that one's appreciation is deepened or quickened. More generally, to emphasise is to make contact at a deep emotional level with a person or situation so that particular aspects may be configured. The term is frequently used in social work and therapy, and some argue that 'empathy is the key ingredient of helping' (Carkhuff, p. 173). A distinction is sometimes made between empathy and sympathy in terms of the difference between 'being one with a person' and 'being with a person'. Empathy is a very generalised term and it is preferable to follow Scheler's suggestion and start not with global terms like love but with such social processes as 'rejoicing with' and 'commiserating'. Carkhuff identifies levels of empathy from ability to express the same affect and meaning as 'the other' to the deepest level which 'involves filling in what is missing rather than simply dealing with what is present' in communication (p. 204).

Carkhuff, R. (1969) *Helping and Human Relations*, vol. 1, Holt, Rinehart & Winston.
Scheler, M. (1954) *The Nature of Sympathy*, Routledge & Kegan Paul.

Employment services   These were last basically reorganised in the Employment and Training Act 1973, which established an independent Manpower Services Commission to operate the three divisions of Employment Service (e.g. through Job Centres), Special Programmes (e.g. Youth Opportunities Programme), and Training Services (e.g. training for the disabled, working through the statutory Industry Training Boards). The Act also imposed on local education authorities a duty to provide a vocational guidance service and an employment service for those leaving educational institutions. Full employment as an objective of social policy – as a background assumption without which many services would lose public support, and as arguably the most important element in the Welfare State – is a subject of considerable importance. See also *Unemployment*.

Beveridge, W. (1944) *Full Employment in a Free Society*, Allen & Unwin.
Showler, B. (1976) *The Public Employment Service*, Longman.

Environment   In one sense 'environment' is boundless, like clean air which has recently been recognised as an important constituent of a healthy environment. In welfare particularly environment is often used in the attempt to conceptualise everything outside the intra-psychic structure of the personality, though sociologists would argue that the social environment does not stop, as it were, at the circumference of a person's skin. Three more restricted usages can be identified in welfare. First, post-World War II discussions of the *Welfare State* often attempted to distinguish social from environmental services in terms of direct concern with an individual's particular well-being: such a distinction may lie behind the more recent idea of *personal social services*. Second, 'environment' figures in accounts of early *socialisation*: it is argued, for example, that much of a person's social environment is engendered by his own immediate environment which in turn fosters consistency of behaviour. Third, reference used to be made in social work to 'environmental manipulation' as a method of work distinct from the attempt to increase someone's *insight*. The term is used less now, partly because the growing awareness that a person's environment is other people draws attention to the possibility of *manipulating* them. It appears that little progress has been made in the conceptual grasp of 'environment' from the point of view of social work action, and in practice systematic attention is not always paid to those most influential in the client's immediate social environment. Social work on environmental aspects of a situation has seldom enjoyed high status.

Davies, M. *et al.* (1974) *Social Work in the Environment*, Home Office Research Unit Report no. 21, HMSO.

Equality   Equality is the state of being equal in relation to some quality (equal as human beings), or to some treatment (no priority is given in the allocation of scarce resources), or to the distribution of benefits (for instance constitutional rights and liberties, social status, and economic welfare). Runciman has used the work of Rawls (see *social justice*) to argue that 'the test of inequalities is whether they can be justified to the losers; and for the winners to be able to do this, they must be prepared, in principle, to change places' (p. 273). Equality of procedure, of opportunity, and of outcomes play important parts in welfare discussion and provision. Equality as an objective of social policy in terms of benefits considered not at any particular point in time but over a person's life-span received eloquent support in the work of Tawney. Welfare arguments have also been developed concerning the justification of unequal treatments in relation to need or hardship, desert or merit, natural capacity and public benefit (in order to render people 'equal' to others).

Runciman, W. (1966) *Relative Deprivation and Social Justice: a Study of Attitudes to Social Inequality in Twentieth-Century England*, Routledge & Kegan Paul.
Tawney, R.H. (1964) *Equality* (Introduction by R.M. Titmuss), Allen & Unwin.
Weale, A. (1978) *Equality and Social Policy*, Routledge & Kegan Paul.

Ethnic minority   'Ethnic' is a complex term which refers both to the sense of being a distinct people and being treated as such and to a participation in a shared culture or distinctively patterned way of life. An ethnic minority is a group within a numerically and socially dominant society which is treated as distinct and conceives of itself as distinct in terms of a connected set of characteristics, such as language, sense of homeland, skin colour, and so on. Ethnicity and race are sometimes distinguished, sometimes not, but it is important to identify separately racialism, as a systematic way of organising social relations, and racism, or a set of beliefs used to justify such organisation. Within welfare, 'ethnic minority' is important as a way of talking about race relations in which emphasis is as much if not more on

70

'minority'. In the history of social work, contact between social caseworkers and such ethnic groups as Poles, Italians, and so on in America marked the origins of the attempt to use ideas of cultural and sub-cultural difference in understanding human behaviour. See also *Race relations*.

Bowker, G. and Carrier, J. (eds) (1976) *Race and Ethnic Relations: Sociological Readings*, Hutchinson.
Ellis, J. (ed.) (1978) *West African Families in Britain: a Meeting of Two Cultures*, Routledge & Kegan Paul.
Peach, C. *et al.* (eds) (1981) *Ethnic Segregation in Cities*, Croom Helm.
Simon, R. and Alstein, H. (1977) *Transracial Adoption*, John Wiley.

Evaluation An evaluation is a measurement or assessment of the extent to which a project or programme or particular *intervention* has achieved its objectives. Welfare activity of all kinds (social work by professionals or by volunteers, special action programme in relation to poverty, and so on) has recently been subject to evaluation of different kinds (see *action research*). A strict experimental design is not always feasible, but its requirements are as follows: measurement of 'the dose'; reliable and valid measures of the condition before and after treatment; a representative group of subjects and a control group similar to that group in all relevant respects except that it does not receive 'the treatment'; the establishment of criteria of success; and some means of 'connecting' outcome to resource input. Alternative approaches to evaluation of innovations relying more on description and interpretation and less on measurement and prediction include illuminative evaluation (Parlett and Hamilton). More recently, attention has been given to the evaluation of different alternative responses to the problems of particular groups, e.g. the old.

Goldberg, E.M. and Connelly, N. (eds) (1981) *Evaluative Research in Social Care*, Heinemann.
Mullen, E. and Dumpson, J. (1972) *Evaluation of Social Intervention*, Jossey-Bass.
Parlett, M. and Hamilton, D. (1976) 'Evaluation as Illumination', in *Curriculum Evaluation Today: Trends and Implications*, ed. D. Tawney, Macmillan.

Existentialism A philosophy expressed in the writings of

EXISTENTIALISM

Kierkegaard, Sartre, and others, which emphasises the significance of human decision and choice for what is called an authentic life (as opposed to one based on bad faith). It has been used as a basis for psychotherapy and social work partly because of its elaborate explanation of ideas of human freedom. Existentialist therapy views *anxiety* as an unlived possibility and emphasises the immediate concrete experience which has to be made authentic, and the notions of person-in-situation (or man as being-in-the-world) and of value (by which is meant that the next step is implicit in what the present experience can carry forward in just so many ways).

Krill, D. (1978) *Existential Social Work*, Free Press.
May, R. (1967) *Psychology and the Human Dilemma*, Van Nostrand.
Ragg, N. (1967) 'Personal Philosophy and Social Work', *British Journal of Psychiatric Social Work*, 9, 8-17.

F

Family 'It would seem ... very difficult to avoid having the family as a social institution even if one wanted to' (Harris, p. 91) but, of course, the family takes a number of different forms. For example, the nuclear family, characterised by relationships of parent–child and of mates, differs in respects important for welfare considerations from the extended family, with its significant kin network. Generally speaking, we can think of the family as a group related by marriage, blood, or adoption constituting (at least for a period) a single household. In a welfare context the family assumes importance for a number of reasons: it is the locus for distribution of care obligations; it is the matrix for much *socialisation* of young and old; it is the scene and source of many troubles (e.g. *family violence*); services sometimes seek to provide a substitution for the scale and care of the family (as in the idea of the Family Group Home in child care provision). In addition the family is protected by notions of privacy; and arguments about how households are constituted and which grouping should be recognised *as* a family are common in social policy discussion. The controversy surrounding the so-called co-habitation rule in relation to supplementary benefit is a good illustration of the last two factors.

Bell, N. and Vogel, E. (eds) (1961) *A Modern Introduction to the Family*, Routledge & Kegan Paul.
Clayton, P. (1981) *The Cohabitation Guide*, Wildwood House.
Donzelot, J. (1977) *Policing Families: Welfare versus the State*, Hutchinson.
Harris, C.C. (1969) *The Family: an Introduction*, Allen & Unwin.

Family aides Employed as a way of avoiding the necessity of residential care in the case of children. They do not undertake

FAMILY INCOME SUPPLEMENT

domestic tasks, as would a home help, but work in co-operation with the social worker to develop the client's own capacity.

Family Income Supplement A benefit marking the first direct subsidy to low earners to be introduced since the Poor Law Amendment Act 1834 abolished what became known as the Speenhamland system of allowances in aid of wages. The Family Income Supplement is a means-tested benefit for families (including one-parent families) with one or more children where the head of the family is in full-time work but the gross income of the family falls below a certain level.

Family policy It is perhaps better to consider family policy not as a single intention or a particular set of outcomes but rather as a grouping of policies, even though family policy was first ventured in relation to specific anxieties over the replacement of the population. Family policy may be explicit or implicit. In the former case there can be specific programmes and services designed to achieve explicit goals in relation to the family or there can be programmes aimed at serving families but without the articulation of over-all goals. Implicit family policy concerns government actions which have indirect consequences for the family but which are not specifically or primarily addressed to the family. Britain has not so formulated an explicit family policy, but social policies over a wide range (income maintenance, services for children, old people, and so on) make and enforce crucial assumptions about relationships between the sexes and the generations. Land argues that these assumptions form a distinctive set and that they persist over time.

Kamerman, S. and Kahn, A. (1978) *Family Policy: Government and Families in Fourteen Countries*, Columbia University Press.
Land, H. (1978) 'Who Cares for the Family?', *Journal of Social Policy*, 7, 257-84.
Moss, Peter and Sharpe, Don (1980) 'Family Policy in Britain', in *Year Book of Social Policy in Britain, 1979*, ed. M. Brown and S. Baldwin, Routledge & Kegan Paul.

Family therapy Family therapy is a distinct mode of intervention aimed at helping the family to become a better functioning group through the application of specific procedures of treatment. Walrond-Skinner has defined family therapy as 'the psychotherapeutic treatment of a natural social system, the family, using as its basic medium, conjoint interpersonal interviews' (p.1). Family therapy first developed in America in the 1950s and interdisciplinary interest on the part of psychiatrists and social workers has been maintained. Several theoretical frameworks have been used, but the most common are general *systems theory* and psychoanalytic theory. Social workers referred to working with or treating the family as a whole long before the invention of family therapy, but usually they were speaking of treating individual problems in a family context. Family therapy can be seen as part of a larger movement from exclusive concern with individual problems and towards a recognition of the crucial role of social relationships, but it has been criticised for what it takes for granted in terms of social culture (Pearson).

Minuchin, S. (1974) *Families and Family Therapy*, Tavistock.
Pearson, G. (1974) 'Prisons of Law: the Reification of the Family in Family Therapy', in *Reconstructing Social Psychology*, ed. N. Armistead, Penguin.
Walrond-Skinner, S. (1976) *Family Therapy*, Routledge & Kegan Paul.

Family violence   This term is increasingly used to refer to two problems, not always occurring together in the same situation, i.e. 'baby battering' and 'wife battering'. The first term is quite frequently replaced by the wider term 'child abuse' or the more neutral 'non-accidental injury'. The 'battered child syndrome' was first named by Kempe in America in 1962, though more general concern over problems of child neglect and cruelty are of much longer duration, peaking at particular times; for example, over anxiety about 'problem families' manifested in the late 1940s and 1950s in this country. In 1968 the NSPCC in Britain established a special unit to carry out a comprehensive treatment and study programme, but the main factor in focusing public attention and that of local authority social services departments on the systematic physical abuse of children in their own homes was the DHSS Report of the Committee of Inquiry into the Care and Supervision Provided in Relation to

Maria Colwell (1974), HMSO. Since then, 'fear of another Colwell case' has been a continuous and acknowledged anxiety for local authority social workers. Violence to children is an important problem for a number of reasons. First the size and significance of the problem in terms of understanding family relationships: a special DHSS Committee on Child Health Services indicated that, in cases of non-accidental injury to children, 'from 7% to 8% die – the fourth commonest cause of death in the first five years – and that of those who survive 11% have residual brain damage and 5% visual impairment ...' (*Fit for the Future,* Court Report, Cmnd 6684, 1976, HMSO, vol. 1, p. 43). Second, the problem has been socially defined through the interaction of local and central government (see e.g. The First Report from the Select Committee on Violence in the Family, *Violence to Children,* Cmnd 7123, 1978, HMSO), professional groups, and the public at large. Third, the problem has been responded to by the creation of new organisations (e.g. NSPCC Special Units) and of new training and procedures (see *registers*). Violence against adult women of the household is probably as old as violence against children, but it has only recently come to be defined as a social problem rather than a private misfortune (Timms). Public interest has increased since the Report of the Select Committee of the House of Commons on Violence in Marriage (1975) and research efforts are beginning to produce fruits (R. E. and R. P. Dobash, for example). In a welfare context innovatory services have made an appearance, in particular the refuges for battered women (Pahl), but perhaps of greater importance is the growing realisation of the disadvantaged position of women legally, socially, and psychologically and the effects of this on the legitimisation of male rights to physical violence against them.

Dobash, R. E. and Dobash, R. P. (1979) *Violence against Wives: a Case against the Patriarchy,* Free Press.
Pahl, J. (1978) *A Refuge for Battered Women: a Study of the Role of a Women's Centre,* DHSS, HMSO.
Timms, N. (1975) 'Battered Wives', in *Year Book of Social Policy in Britain, 1974,* ed. K. Jones, Routledge & Kegan Paul.

Feelings   See *Emotion.*

Fieldwork/ Fieldworker Fieldwork describes either the main work of those who are not residential social workers or a major element in the social work training course. The distinction between residential social work and field social work (as, for example, in the expression 'field team') is not easily summarised and is beginning to give way before a certain flexibility of role (e.g. staff in a children's home helping in the selection of, and introduction of children to, foster homes); fieldworkers in hospitals have always worked mainly with hospital residents and their families. In social work education the term fieldwork has come to replace 'practical work' to describe the periods of supervised practice in a service agency – in contrast to study at the academic centre (see *supervision*). CCETSW has for some years been seeking to emphasise the value and place of fieldwork learning.

Younghusband, E. (1978) *Social Work in Britain: 1950–1975*, Allen & Unwin, vol. 2, pp. 61-74.

Financial aid Financial aid and what is known as material relief have a very long history in welfare, going back to the idea of alms (discriminate or indiscriminate) in the Middle Ages and, more recently, to the more exacting ideas of the *Charity Organisation Society* that a grant of money was justifiable only to the extent that it secured a permanent improvement in the situation. Argument has often arisen concerning the relative importance of the giving of financial (and material) aid or its weight compared to the 'counselling' aspects of social work. Jordan has recently argued that it 'is the mixture of public assistance and social work that is so fatal to the social worker's professional task, and to the interests of their clients in need of either service' (pp. 180-1). At other times social workers have supported such provisions as is contained in Section 1 of the 1963 Children and Younl Persons Act which as part of preventive measures allows the local authority to give 'assistance in kind or, in exceptional circumstances, cash'. Social workers have also at different times advocated the definition of material problems as real and 'deserving' of response as such or, alternatively, as manifestations of psychological difficulties which have to be understood. In the latter perspective they are

F

FOSTERING

seen as *presenting problems*.

Jackson, M.P. and Valencia, B. (1979) *Financial Aid through Social Work*, Routledge & Kegan Paul.
Jordan, B. (1974) *Poor Parents*, Routledge & Kegan Paul.

Fostering   Fostering or the care of children in households of which neither parent is a member is an old form of child-rearing. It was adopted as public policy in England towards the end of the nineteenth century with the practice of boarding-out, compared to the boarding-in of destitute children in the workhouse. Fostering or boarding-out (as in the Boarding-Out Regulations, 1955) has a long policy history, with legislation concerning the selection and supervision of foster homes going back to 1782 at least. The core of the contemporary idea of the fostering of children are the two notions of placement in a family (for a short or a long period) and the provision of monitoring of some kind by a recognised authority. (Private fostering has particular problems and is covered by separate legislation; see Holman.) Fostering covers a wide range of situations: quite a high proportion of children who are fostered are with relatives; special kinds of foster parents, so-called 'professional' foster parents, are from time to time recruited for, say, disturbed adolescents (Hazel). Questions of difficulty in skill and in conception arise concerning the role of the social worker in the selection, maintenance, and development of foster-care resources and relationships between foster parents and natural parents. The 1975 Children Act has been seen as providing a strengthening of the former's position. Other problems concern the criteria of successful placement in so far as the child's sense of identity is concerned and also the role of foster parents, particularly as interpreted by the National Foster Care Association, and by central government guidelines and local practice. It is now usual to group foster care and adoption together as forms of family placement. See also *Adoption*.

DHSS (1976) *Foster Care: a Guide to Practice*, HMSO.
Hazel, N. (1981) *A Bridge to Independence*, Blackwell.
Holman, R. (1973) *Trading in Children*, Routledge & Kegan Paul.
Triseliotis, J. (1980) *New Development in Foster Care and Adoption*, Routledge & Kegan Paul.

Fraternity In a welfare context or in a broad political sense this refers to a kind of fellowship marked by interpersonal affection of some intensity and a sharing of values and goals. It has come, with equality and with liberty, to be a conception linked with the goals of welfare services and with the description of welfare, though it has been much less extensively explored in this connection. This may be due in part to a moral ambiguity in the application of 'fraternity' to welfare. It can be taken as the foundation of a general obligation to humanity (under the skin all men are brothers) or as a means of distinguishing some men from others because they belong to a special band of brothers or to the fraternity. Donnison has drawn attention to kinds of fraternity much less attractive than the one espoused by R. H. Tawney: 'There is a cosy, conservative brand, which seeks protection from new ideas, disturbing people and competition of all kinds; and there is a harsh, authoritarian brand ...' Halsey has argued that the ethical value of the fraternity of the monk or the party member depends on the treatment meted out to those who by choice or circumstance do not belong to the brother-hood.

Donnison, D. (1976) 'Liberty, equality and fraternity', in *Talking About Welfare*, ed. N. Timms and D. Watson, Routledge & Kegan Paul.

Halsey, A. H. (1978) *Change in British Society*, Oxford University Press, Ch. 8. 'Fraternity as Citizenship'.

McWilliams, W. C. (1973) *The Idea of Fraternity in America*, University of California Press.

Freudian theory 'Freudian theory' refers to a complex set of theories (people refer, for instance, to Freud's *libido* theory or to his instinct theory) which underwent a considerable modification in Freud's own lifetime and expansion and development afterwards. Freud and those described as post-Freudians together account for a great deal of the psychology that has actually or by repute informed social work (see *psychiatric deluge*). However, psychoanalysis is first and foremost a technique which led to a range of theoretical formulations, such as the structural model of personality as *id, ego* and *super-ego*, or the idea of crucial phases of development (such as the resolution of the *Oedipus* complex), or the notion of unconscious wishes. Yelloly has identified four major postulates: the unconscious, psychic determinism, infantile sexuality (or sensual stirrings and satisfactions), and the inevitability of mental conflict. She notes that it 'is often the case [that] the social worker's knowledge of psychoanalytic concepts is gained through secondary sources rather than from first-hand acquaintances with Freud's own work' and that as a consequence 'distortions the more readily occur and can easily be perpetuated and disseminated through the literature' (p.6). She also correctly observes that 'it is extremely doubtful whether psychoanalytic techniques (dream analysis, free association, *transference* interpretation) have ever been employed to more than an inconsiderable extent in social work (if indeed at all) ... ' (p. 73).

Peters, R. (1956) 'Freud's Theory', *British Journal for the Philosophy of Science*, 7, 4-12.
Wisdom, J. (1956) 'Psycho-analytic Technology', *British Journal for the Philosophy of Science*, 7, 13-28.
Yelloly, M. (1980) *Social Work Theory and Psychoanalysis*, Van Nostrand Reinhold.

Friendship Telfer suggests three necessary conditions for 'friendship': shared activities (rather than reciprocal service), the passions of friendship (such as desire for each other's company), and an acknowledgment and consent to the special relationship. Friendship is important in welfare partly because it is a term sometimes used by clients and social workers to describe what is established between them, because it is at other times used in contrast to an appropriate professional relationship (as in the suggestion that a social worker has ceased to *be* a person's social worker if their relationship has become one of friendship). It is also closely connected to 'befriending', which has for long been associated with *probation* – to advise, assist, and befriend – and more recently has been consistently employed to describe the work of the Samaritans. In the case of both 'friendship' and 'befriending' it has been argued that welfare usage debases the language in so far as it conceals the two-faced notion of using a friendship to achieve particular objectives rather than to establish enjoyment. One wonders how Octavia Hill's nineteenth-century social welfare maxim, 'not alms but a friend', would have survived such criticism of the use of a relationship for the pre-ordained objectives of one member of 'the friendship'.

Telfer, E. (1970–1) 'Friendship', *Proceedings of the Aristotelian Society*, S, 223-41.
Timms, N. (1968) *Language of Social Casework*, Routledge & Kegan Paul, pp. 76-82.

Functionalist School   This distinctive approach to social work, not to be confused with the functionalist school in sociology, was developed in America from the late 1930s, largely in the Pennsylvania School of Social Work. In contrast to the dominant *Diagnostic School*, Functionalists relied on the psychology of Otto Rank with its heavy emphasis on the will, and on the polarities of unification and diversification in relationship – and of yielding and resistance to help. They stressed the significance of process in helping and of what they defined as the function of the agency. This function has two inseparable aspects: the potential of helpfulness is inherent in the entity of the service rather than in the social worker's intervention guided by a full diagnosis; the given service provides a form of experience psychologically characteristic of the giving and taking of help in terms of that specific service (e.g. the experience of having a child placed in a foster home is very different from the experience of bringing the same child to a child guidance clinic, even though the use of either service may be motivated by the same emotional rejection on the part of the parent; Kasius). A review of the ideas of the Functional School and the Diagnostic in 1950 concluded that the two were incompatible, but the significance of agency function seems to have been widely accepted since then. Writing from a Functionalist perspective continued into the 1960s (Smalley), but the sharpness of controversy has been blunted long since.

Kasius, C. (ed.) (1950) *A Comparison of Diagnostic and Functional Casework Concepts*, New York: Family Service Association of America.
Smalley, R. (1967) *Theory for Social Work Practice*, Columbia University Press.

F

G

Gatekeeper This term is used in urban sociology to refer to a kind of informal patron who can connect those he or she knows in the locality to powerful others in larger social networks. In social policy the term seems to be used in a more negative sense to refer to those who control access at the boundaries of organisations. People who work as receptionists are typically described as gatekeepers. They work at a point at which role ambiguity and confusion of information on the part of the applicant are particularly significant. More recently, in socio-legal studies the police have been referred to as 'gatekeepers' to the penal process. This emphasises the place of *discretion* in decision-making at this 'entry point' to the legal system.

Hall, A. (1974) *Point of Entry: a Study of Client Perception in the Social Services*, Allen & Unwin.

Generic 'Generic' as a welfare term was introduced into a social work training to point a contrast with 'specialist' and to refer to a social worker not trained according to one of the then recognised specialisations (child care, psychiatric social work, probation, medical social work). The idea was connected to a conviction that social work was a single profession, that the difference in practice in different sorts of agency were not so great that 'social work' was a more or less happy grouping of occupations, and that it was one *profession* (that a common training would demonstrate that more often than not social workers were dealing with much the same problems in the same general ways). The first 'generic' social work training courses started at the London School of Economics in 1954, but 'generic' training is now less rapturously embraced, partly because a

82

distinction has slowly emerged between 'basic' common training irrespective of future career prospects and more advanced training in *specialisation* and partly because the content of 'basic' training has been increasingly enlarged. A distinction has also been gradually forged between generic training and general practice to the same level regardless of any particular client group.

Timms, N. (1968) *Language of Casework*, Routledge & Kegan Paul, pp. 26-44.
Vickery, A. (1973) 'Specialist: Generic: What Next?', *Social Work Today*, 4, 262-6.

Geriatric   A geriatrician is a medical specialist concerned in the study and treatment of diseases common to old age, but the term 'geriatric' is often applied to patients, hospitals, nurses, and so on. The medical specialism (not one of the most popular among medical students or practitioners) helps to ensure that the illness complaints of the old are investigated and treated (rather than dismissed as inevitable consequences of an intractable old age). The Report of the Royal Commission on the National Health Service (1979) called attention to the tendency of other physicians to leave all aspects of health care of the elderly to the geriatricians. In a social policy perspective the idea of the 'geriatric' thus poses two general questions: how can workers, of all kinds, be attracted to a specialisation; how can the specialisation be defined so that all workers in other specialisations do not thereby cease to hold any responsibility at all towards the conditions in question?

British Council for Ageing (1976) *Research in Gerontology*, Bedford Square Press.

G

Gestalt therapy   This school of therapy was developed by Perls from the psychological work of Kohler, Westheimer, and Koffka, though the emphasis on holism or the whole can be found in Adler and others; L. T. Hobhouse, for example, termed the natural interdependence of parts with the whole 'consilience'. A gestalt is a total configuration, a unified 'whole' not apprehensible through its parts separately considered. Gestalt therapy aims to bring discordant elements, either within an individual or between individuals, into a confrontation characterised by mutual self-disclosures. *Diagnosis* is seen as an undesirable escape from the process of participation in which therapist and patient are engaged. Emphasis is placed on the distinction between experience (e.g. of confusion) and awareness ('I am confused'), and experiencing the fullest possibilities (e.g. of confusion, etc.) is one of the objects of gestalt therapy.

Gift relationship The giving and/or the exchange of presents has been a feature of many societies, and the French sociologist Marcel Mauss called attention to the ways in which such transfers are bound up with the regulation of one's conduct towards others and with the achievement of social cohesion. Since R. M. Titmuss's *The Gift Relationship* (Allen & Unwin, 1970), the idea of the unilateral transfer to strangers has gained an important place in discussion of social policy generally, though the idea of relationship through non-reciprocated gift was used primarily to describe and justify a particular provision within the British Health Service (blood transfusion by volunteers). Plant has argued that the arguments 'are not persuasive in the case of blood and are difficult to generalise from that case to medical care generally'. He argues that the objective of social integration which may be achieved through opportunities to give to strangers '*can* threaten personal freedom'. The notion of giving is of obvious importance in welfare as is the consideration of the different motives for doing so. The idea of the stranger is also worthy of exploration in social welfare but, equally, consideration must be given to the social implausibility of 'gift' without any notion of *reciprocity* at all, at any time. Similarly, we should examine the idea of 'gift' as offering an explanation of those who are meeting obligations to their own family and friends who are far from strangers. See also *Altruism*.

Plant, R. (1977) 'Gifts, Exchanges and the Political Economy of Health Care, Part I', *Journal of Medical Ethics*, 3, 166-73.

Groupwork/Social groupwork Groupwork or social groupwork is usually described as one of the main methods of *social work*, contrasted with smaller scale intervention on an individual or family basis (*casework*) and with locally based neighbourhood or *community work*. It is applied to situations in which social relations in specially formed groups is the medium through which social work is undertaken or where the fact and consequences of grouping make a significant difference to the objectives and approach of the work. Many situations in which social workers transact business are group situations (those of committees, team meetings, case conferences, etc.), but the social worker would not be undertaking groupwork in them, though knowledge of group interaction might well be used. Groups which are the direct object rather than the context of social work activity can be classified in a number of different ways. Douglas suggests a classification by purpose (to appreciate and act on certain information; to serve as an instrument of treatment), by activity (e.g. recreation), by field of endeavour (for instance, groups are formed in hospitals, hostels, etc.) and by theory (e.g. gestalt theory, or Bion's theory of group assumptions).

Bion, W. (1961) *Experiences in Groups*, Tavistock.
Davies, B. (1975) *The Use of Groups in Social Work Practice*,
    Routledge & Kegan Paul.
Douglas, T. (1978) *Basic Groupwork*, Tavistock.

Growth   In welfare, 'growth' is used in two main senses: we speak of economic growth in terms of increase in gross domestic product, and apply this idea in arguments concerning the necessity of growth for any significant increase in resources allocated to welfare. We also speak of 'growth' in social work students and/or clients, but reference here is to some advance in social skills and/or *insight* or to progress through a particular stage towards psychosocial *maturity*. Of course, many things not only grow but can be seen to grow – plants, crystals, cells, cities, cultures, wealth, organisations, and so on. This has suggested to some bold spirits used to the atmosphere of high abstraction the possibility of a general theory of growth covering all of these developments.

Boulding, K. (1953) 'Toward a General Theory of Growth', *Canadian Journal of Economics and Political Science*, 19, 326-40.

G

Guilt   Guilt refers to the sense of having assented in some way to wrongdoing. It is used mainly in connection with attempts to understand behaviour (for example, Freud suggested that a sense of guilt transformed sadism into masochism), with court findings concerning legal guilt, and also with explanations of individual or group welfare activity (as in suggestions that the middle classes towards the end of the last century were driven or moved by class guilt). Rank (a psychologist associated with the *Functionalist School*) distinguished moral guilt, arising from action against a moral code, from ethical guilt, arising from any assertion of will against 'the other'. A more important distinction is between guilt as an appropriate response to doing what one believes to have been wrong and guilt as a response to unconscious threats (see *super-ego*). Moral guilt entails the idea of action in recognition of a moral judgment; psychological guilt is simply carried or paraded.

Gypsies For long, gypsies were not seriously considered in the study or practice of welfare, but they are now beginning to receive attention, partly because of the Caravan Sites Act 1968, which made local authority site provision mandatory. They are also seen, largely because of their usual lack of a settled abode and their not easily articulated but distinct culture, as 'a uniquely deviant minority' (Adams). They are not simply a social but an *ethnic group* with membership based primarily on descent. The descent is 'from a varied set of groups including tinkers, pedlars and Romanies' (Todd).

Adams, B. *et al.* (1975) 'Gypsies: Current Policies and Practices', *Journal of Social Policy*, 4, 129-50.
Todd, R. (1978) 'Social Policies towards Gypsies', in *Year Book of Social Policy in Britain, 1977*, ed. M. Brown and S. Baldwin, Routledge & Kegan Paul.

H

Halfway house A term not widely used now, but one usage describes residential provision (possibly as a base from which residents depart for daily work – see *hostels*) which offers service and conditions 'between' those of full residential life and life in the 'normal' community. Developed first as a provision in relation to mental hospitals, one of their serious organisational problems was to ensure the flow of residents into independent social life. The term has also been used in a housing context to refer to sub-standard council housing in which families live a waiting life until standard council housing is available. In relation to other groups it has become almost a synonym for the small hostel, different from the hospital or large institution and 'not quite like home'.

Handicap Adults and children are often called 'handicapped', but a preferable usage is 'people with a handicap'. A handicap (and some would see this as the same as a disability) refers to a disadvantage resulting from an impairment, and an impairment refers to defect or loss of part of the body. Wing has distinguished three types of handicap: primary or intrinsic, secondary or psycho-social, and non-clinical or extrinsic; and suggested that the classification should be applied to both psychiatric and physical handicaps. A variety of terminology is used, however, and the local surveys conducted in accordance with the historically significant Chronically Sick and Disabled Act 1970 refer to 'handicapped', 'disabled', 'handicapped/impaired', 'physically handicapped', and so on. The range and problems of services available are usefully discussed by Topliss (see also *mental handicap*). In terms of social work training an attempt is made to

87

balance understanding of and response to problems common to people with handicaps and the knowledge and skill required in relation to specific handicaps such as deafness and blindness.

Topliss, E. (1979) *Provision for the Disabled*, Blackwell and Martin Robertson.
Wing, J. (n.d.) Appendix on 'Teaching on Handicapping Factors', in *People with Handicaps need Better Trained Workers*, CCETSW, paper no. 5.

Health Advisory Service A Hospital Advisory Service was established in 1969 after a DHSS report (Cmnd 3975) on allegations of ill-treatment of mentally handicapped patients. Its two functions were to improve the management of patient care in individual hospitals (excluding matters of individual clinical judgment) and the hospital service as a whole by a process of constructive criticism and the propagation of good practice and new ideas; and directly to advise the Secretary of State for Social Services about hospital conditions. Annual Reports have been issued since 1969. In 1976 the Service became the Health Advisory Service and its remit was extended to include the community health services. The Health Advisory Service is independent of the DHSS and the Welsh Office, but does not investigate individual complaints or allegations against individuals. It works mainly through team units, with the Health Service professionals mainly seconded from the National Health Service and the social workers drawn mainly from the Social Work Service of the DHSS, the Welsh Office, or seconded from local authority or voluntary services. In 1978 the Secretary of State proposed a closer working relationship between the HAS and the Development Team for the Mentally Handicapped.

Health centre 'Throughout its history those involved with Health Centres have resisted attempts to categorise the particular combination of functions associated with it' (Beales *et al.*). Since the first exploration of the idea of a centre concerned with the more effective and efficient delivery of health care in the community, the conception has changed, as has the policy impetus behind any particular notion. The term was first used in a report on the Future of the Medical and Allied Services in

1920, but this contained no reference to a group of general practitioners working from the same premises. The National Health Services Act 1946 gave local authorities the duty 'to provide, equip and maintain' centres at which 'general medical services, general dental services, pharmaceutical services, local health authority services, specialist services, etc.' could be made available. However, the idea was grasped neither enthusiastically nor unambiguously; for instance, were these medical (treatment) centres or health (prevention of illness) services? The present preference is for health centres as specially planned premises for groups of general practitioners and other workers in the *primary health care* team. Financial incentives have been provided since 1967, and 1966–76 has been termed the years of the Health Centre Explosion.

Beales, J. *et al.* (1976) *The Microcosm: Health Centres in Practice*, Organisational Analysis Research Unit, Management Centre, University of Bradford.
Hall, P. (1975) 'The Development of Health Centres', in *Change, Choice and Conflict in Social Policy*, ed. P. Hall *et al.*, Heinemann.

Health Service   The National Health Service was established in 1948 under the Act of 1946. The basic structure remained unchanged until reorganisation in 1974, though criticisms of the tripartite division of services had been voiced much earlier: between 1948 and 1970 the Labour government produced two consultative papers on reorganisation. In 1974 the community health services (e.g. health visiting, school health) were amalgamated with the hospital services under fourteen regional boards and ninety Area Health Authorities (to be abolished in 1982); general practitioners were incorporated into the unified organisation through a special committee of each Area Health Authority. Areas were divided into districts, up to six in each area. The new bodies are served by management teams and professional advisory committees. The base of on-going relations between the central government regions and areas is the planning cycle. Local authorities and health authorities are required to establish machinery for joint consultation. From a welfare perspective the NHS represents a considerable achievement but also poses a range of problems, including differential access to and provision of services; management problems and the problem of managerialism, especially since 1974; the low priority given to prevention and the high regard for the disease model of health and for the dominant medical profession. The Report of the Royal Commission on the National Health Service (Chairman Sir Alec Merrison, Cmnd 7615, HMSO, 1979) 'stands as a useful source and reference book for all those with an interest in the well-being of the NHS' (Carrier, p. 113).

Carrier, J. (1980) 'The Merrison Report on the National Health Service', in *Year Book of Social Policy in Britain, 1979*, ed. M. Brown and S. Baldwin, Routledge & Kegan Paul.
Jaques, E. (ed.) (1978) *Health Services*, Heinemann.
Klein, R. (1974) 'Policy Making in the National Health Service', *Political Studies*, 22, 1-14.
Social Science Research Council (1977) *Health and Health Policy*, Report of an Advisory Panel.

Health visitor   A health visitor is a state registered nurse with additional specialist training in obstetric nursing or midwifery employed by Area Health Authorities (1981) to undertake a range of advisory, supportive and health education work. Health visitors were first appointed in 1862, and training for Lady Health Missioners started in 1890. Until the late 1950s health visitors usually worked in districts or areas, but *attachment* to general practitioners is now more common. Specialisation has also developed (e.g. in work with the elderly). The expertise and central task of the health visitor has often been a matter for debate: the health visitor is part social worker, part teacher, and part nurse. Some have wished to orientate the occupation to the family rather than any particular patient group; the Briggs Report on Nursing (Cmnd 5115, HMSO, 1972) referred to the health visitor as the family health sister. In an occupation so closely connected with medicine, attempts to define health visiting as a professional practice in its own right have not met with success. The approach to health visiting through the study of consumer reaction may help towards a more precise description of the actual impact of the health visitor. See also *Consumer/Customer*.

Orr, J. (1980) *Health Visiting in Focus: a Consumer View of Health Visiting in Northern Ireland*, Royal College of Nursing.

Wilkie, E. (1979) *A History of the Council for the Education and Training of Health Visitors*, Allen & Unwin.

Help 'Help' is a general term used to describe aid and succour given and taken in many different sorts of situation (from the rescue response to the cry 'Help' from a drowning person to people whose careers could be described in terms of helping the disadvantaged). It may seem unlikely that such a wide-ranging term would have a role in welfare discussion, but (a) 'help' has been contrasted with 'treatment' as a more appropriate description of social work aims and activity; (b) 'help' has been contrasted fundamentally with 'controlling' ('To conceive of help as prescription in fact reduces it to the level of a control process directed at nothing more radical than adaptive efficiency. It leaves no place for love or joy', Keith-Lucas, p. 29); (c) formal helpers (such as social workers) have been usefully distinguished from in-formal helpers (such as neighbours and friends), and the different behaviours adopted by those seeking help from either source have been identified as a problem for research which has also important implications for practice.

Bottoms, A. and McWilliams, W. (1979) 'A Non-treatment Paradigm for Probation Practice', *British Journal of Social Work*, 9, 159-202.
Brannen, J. (1980) 'Seeking Help for Mental Problems: a Conceptual Approach', *British Journal of Social Work*, 10, 457-70.
Keith-Lucas, A. (1972) *Giving and Taking Help*, University of North Carolina Press.

Hierarchy In a welfare context, 'hierarchy' is used in a psychological and an organisational sense. In psychological discussion, reference is made to Maslow's idea of human needs organised in an ascending order from physiological needs (for example, food and sleep) through safety needs, and needs for belonging to the need to actualise the self (Shaw). The organisational sense of 'hierarchy' is increasingly common in discussions of 'the life and hard times' of local authority social services departments. In this sense the hierarchy consists not simply of directors, as a kind of episcopal baron, but of a comparatively long chain of positions of differentiated responsibility from field social worker through senior social worker, area director, assistant director, and so on. It has been argued by social analysts of the Brunel School that a hierarchical aspect is inevitable in the organisation of social services departments; others argue for a very considerably reduced hierarchy and what is described as a flatter organisational structure.

Cooper, D. (1980) 'Salaries and Hierarchy', in *Social Work in Conflict*, ed. B. Glastonbury, Croom Helm.

Shaw, J. (1974) *The Self in Social Work*, Routledge & Kegan Paul.

Whittington, C. and Bellaby, P. (1979) 'The Reasons for Hierarchy in Social Service Departments: a Critique of Elliott Jaques and his associates', *Sociological Review*, 27, 513-39.

Home help   Since 1971 local authorities have had a duty to provide an adequate home help service. The most recent general survey of home helps is by Hunt. Issues of interest in considering the home help service include the question of charges and the distribution of home help time between the old, the chronic sick, cases of maternity and short-term illness, hospital discharges, problem families, and cases in which a disabled person in the household is not the housewife.

Howell, N. *et al.* (1979) *Allocating the Home Help Services*, Bedford Square Press.

Hunt, A. (1970) *Home Help Service in England and Wales* (Government Social Survey for the DHSS), HMSO.

Home visit   This is a social work term, compared to the medical terminology of the domiciliary visit. It indicates the location of an interview in a domestic rather than an office setting: the interview may be with a potential or actual client or one or more members of the family or it may be with members of the client's informal network. At one time social workers used to discuss the therapeutic potentials of home visits compared to office or clinic interviews: it was argued that home visits provided diagnostic information that could not be obtained in other ways. There seems to be little contemporary discussion of the effects of the location of social work interviews, or much consideration of the relative economic advantages of the home visit and the office interview. However, one of the main aims of a significant experiment in probation and after-care was to lessen reliance on the office interview.

Behrens, M. and Ackerman, N. (1956) 'The Home Visit as an Aid in
Family Diagnosis and Therapy', *Social Casework*, 37, 11-19.
Folkard, M.S. *et al.* (1974) *Impact: Intensive Matched Probation and
After-care Treatment*, vol. 1, Home Office Research Unit Report,
no. 24, HMSO.
Paterson, J. and Cyr, F. (1960) 'The Use of the Home Visit in
Present-day Social Work', *Social Casework*, 41, 184-91.

Homelessness At one time homelessness was seen as a problem confined to a particular, marginal group (see *vagrancy*) or as
the result of inadequate personality and consequent mismanage-
ment. The issue of definition is crucial and it is now argued by
certain pressure groups that the homeless are not a particular
group who are 'roofless' at any particular date but a whole range
of people from those without any accommodation to those who
are inadequately housed. The Housing (Homeless Persons) Act
1977 is the most recent legislation, and the only Act specifically
concerned with homelessness as a condition. It places homelessness within housing policy, and if a person claims to be homeless
the local housing authority has an initial duty to enquire if he is
homeless or threatened with homelessness; whether he is
unintentionally homeless; and whether he falls within certain
priority groupings (e.g. if a person has one or more dependent
children living with him or her). If the three conditions are met,
the housing authority has a duty to ensure that accommodation
is available. If the conditions are not met, the local authority
must offer advice and assistance. A code of guidance has been
issued to all local authorities on the discharge of their functions
under the Act. This points out, for example, that it is appropriate
for young homeless people at risk of sexual or financial
exploitation to be considered as a priority need.

Cuttings, M. (1979) *Housing Rights Handbook*, Penguin.
Robson P. and Watchman, P. (1981) 'The Homeless Person's Obstacle
Race', *Journal of Social Welfare Law*, January, 1-15; March, 65-82.
Stewart, G. and Stewart, L. (1978) 'Housing (Homeless Persons) Act,
1977: a Reassessment of Social Need', in *Year Book of Social Policy
in Britain, 1977*, ed. M. Brown and S. Baldwin, Routledge & Kegan
Paul.

Hostels Hostels developed as a variant of long-term residential
provision supplying needs over twenty-four hours of the day: the
hostel is a residential resource supplying a relatively short period

of care, often in a community context; hostels' residents may leave the residence for work or school 'in the community'. Increasingly, hostels are considered as small-scale provision, providing care that differs from that available in the large institution but is also 'not quite like home'. Sometimes reference is made to the need for 'secure hostels', for example in the case of so-called inadequate offenders. A secure hostel, however, is something of a contradiction in terms: as a judge once commented, such places are better known as prisons. Hostels possibly originated in wartime provision for 'unbilletable' children (emergency hostels for difficult children), but hostels now feature as part of the social provision for many different groups. Children's Dpartments were able to establish hostels for young people in care, and a DHSS report (*Hostels for Young People*, 1975) noted that 200 were provided in 1971. Hostels have been provided for psychiatric patients, people on bail, ex-prisoners, alcoholics, for the homeless, and so on. Sinclair has published a sensitive account of probation hostels which usefully distinguishes successful from unsuccessful regimes and emphasises the significance of the personality of the hostel warden.

Otto, S. and Orford, J. (1978) *Not Quite Like Home: Small Hostels for Alcoholics and Others*, Wiley.
Sinclair, I. (1971) *Hostels for Probationers*, Home Office Research Unit Report no. 6, HMSO.

Housing Since the first governmental intervention in matters of sanitation and the control of unfit housing in the nineteenth century, housing policy and provision is now a highly complex area of study and action. It covers three main kinds of housing tenure – council tenancy, owner–occupier, and tenancy in the private rented sector. Each of these has a legislative history and its own specific problems. For instance, should council house tenants be permitted to buy the houses they inhabit and, if so, under what conditions? Should governmental subsidy, an important mechanism in housing policy, be given to people in certain categories or to dwellings? Each kind of tenure produces problems with wide ramifications (e.g. the fall in supply of private rented accommodation produces *homelessness*, particularly in places like London). In addition the problems and provisions of the three housing sectors interact. Between 1919 and 1976 fourteen major pieces of housing legislation were passed covering finance, rent control, priority areas, and so on. Social work has been connected with housing, to varying extents, since the days of Octavia Hill. For some modern discussion of this relationship in a Scottish context, see the Morris Report.

Burke, G. (1981) *Housing and Social Justice*, Longman.
Cullingworth, J. (1979) *Essays on Housing Policy: the British Scene*, Allen & Unwin.
Harloe, M. (1978) 'The Green Paper on Housing Policy', *Year Book of Social Policy in Great Britain, 1977*, ed. M. Brown and S. Baldwin, Routledge & Kegan Paul.
Scottish Development Department (1975) *Housing and Social Work: a Joint Approach* (Morris Report), HMSO, Edinburgh.

Housing associations   These are now non-profit-making bodies concerned with building, converting or improving houses for letting. (Associations may also be called societies or trusts, and the former are defined in the Housing Act 1964.) The history of associations can be seen broadly in three phases: in the second half of the nineteenth century philanthropic associations established model regulated dwellings; in the 1920s housing associations were registered under the Provident Societies Act 1893 4, and later expanded into provision for special groups – the old, for example; in the 1960s central government showed considerable interest in housing associations: in 1974 the Housing Corporation became the dominant institution in the field. It administers a public fund advancing money to housing societies which conform to model rules for cost-rent and co-ownership schemes.

Burke, G. (1981) *Housing and Social Justice*, Longman, pp. 54-9.

Id A term in Freudian theory to describe that which 'contains' everything that is inherited, that is present at birth and laid down in a person's constitution; above all the instincts which Freud almost invariably polarised between what he finally formulated as those of life and death. After a child's birth *ego* and *super-ego* were gradually differentiated out from the id. It is not easy to be precise about the meaning of 'id' and Freud attempted at times an approximation through imagery – for example, of a cauldron seething with instinctual energy driven by impulses that demand satisfaction.

Nagera, H. (ed.) (1970) *Basic Psychoanalytic Concepts on the Theory of Instincts*, Allen & Unwin.

Identification In a general sense identification refers to the recognition of X or of an X as something, as a particular or as a certain kind of thing, person, quality, etc. So one can identify aspects of a social problem as leading to social policies of a particular kind. More specifically in social work 'identification' has a psychoanalytic reference: here identification is with someone or with a particular role (as in the notion of 'identification with the aggressor'). The child, as a result of affectional attachments, models his behaviour, usually without being aware of his behaviour under this description, on important figures in his environment or on aspects of them. In a psychoanalytic perspective 'identification' is of general importance as a mechanism of socialisation (e.g. in boys the *super-ego* is considered to arise from identification with the father at the time of the resolution of the *oedipal complex*). It is also used in the

96

explanation of specific problems (e.g. in melancholia it is assumed that the *ego* is identified with the lost object).

Identity   The term 'identity' is used in two main ways: to refer to how one is seen, 'placed', and categorised by others in relation to their behaviour towards one (one's identity is 'read off' an official document, one is 'given' a social place because of dress, accent, etc.) and to refer to how a person sees and regards himself – as a certain person with a particular biography, occupying a certain social space, and carrying particular value. It is possible, of course, that identity in the second sense is derived almost exclusively from identity in the first sense (from what Curle has described as belonging-identity compared with awareness-identity quoted in M. Yelloly, *Social Work Theory and Psychoanalysis*, Van Nostrand Reinhold, 1980, p. 171). Both senses, however, have significance in welfare. For instance, *stigma* in relation to social services is sometimes defined in terms of spoiled identity; again, certain stages in personality development are described as presenting a crisis of identity – Erikson has characterised adolescence as the stage at which the personality achieves identity compared to role diffusion; the early phase of marriage, and the mid-life crisis have also been characterised as posing problems to a person's sense of identity and of individual worth.

Erikson, E. (1951) *Childhood and Society*, Imago, Ch. 7.
Lynch, D.H. (1958) *On Shame and the Search for Identity*, Harcourt Brace.

Ideology   A term widely used in socio-political analysis of social welfare and recently in attempts to understand social work practice (as in Smith's categorisation of ideologies of need, in terms of unit, source, and assessor of need). The term was used by Marx of any form of thought deriving from vested interests, whilst Karl Mannheim saw ideology as directed either at the conservation or restoration of a social order or Utopia. Something of the notion of distortion or at least special pleading thus hangs over 'ideology'. Generally speaking 'ideology' in a welfare context refers to an interrelated set of ideas, not all of which are entertained in an explicit fashion, held with emotional conviction, and referring to general beliefs concerning man and society. In welfare discourse (and elsewhere) the term should be used with care, and some have suggested that whatever useful life it had has long since been exhausted. Recently an attempt has been made to resuscitate it so that it can be recognised as serving certain limited purposes: 'We have ideological beliefs in a world, not ideological knowledge of the world and, consequently to portray ideology as theory is radically mistaken ... What the ideologically committed affirm is an aspiration in life' (Manning, p. 130).

Manning, D. (ed.) (1980) *The Form of Ideology*, Allen & Unwin.
Smith, G. (1980) *Social Need*, Routledge & Kegan Paul.

Illegitimacy An illegitimate child is one born to parents who are not married at the time of the birth; if the parents subsequently marry, the child becomes legitimate from the date of the marriage. Illegitimacy is one of several possible outcomes of extra-marital pregnancy; others include *abortion*, marriage, and *adoption* of the child. Illegitimacy has been of interest in welfare for a considerable time, in terms of bastardy legislation and services for the unmarried mother and her child. The law in relation to the illegitimate child has been gradually reformed but even after the Family Law Reform Act discriminations remain. According to Hart, these include the facts that the only method by which a single mother can obtain legally enforceable maintenance is through the Affiliation Proceedings Act 1957; thus an illegitimate child cannot inherit a title nor can he or she inherit on the intestacy of grandparents, etc. The Law Commission favours the abolition of the status of illegitimacy. See also *One-parent families*.

Cheetham, J. (1976) 'Pregnancy in the Unmarried: the Continuing Dilemma for Social Policy and Social Work', in *Tradition of Social Policy*, ed. A.H. Halsey, Blackwell.
Gill, D. (1977) *Illegitimacy, Sexuality and the Status of Women*, Blackwell.
Hart, M. (1980) 'Illegitimacy: the Law Commission's Proposals for Abolition', in *Year Book of Social Policy in Britain, 1979*, ed. M. Brown and S. Baldwin, Routledge & Kegan Paul.

Immaturity   In general and rather haphazard usage 'immature' refers to a person or to behaviour that fails to meet expectations of a particular kind; the behaviour violates expectations concerning appropriate responsibilities. More specifically, 'immature' must depend on *'mature'*; that is on a conception of the fully mature person (or response) or of phase-specific maturity. By the latter we refer to the assumption that *growth* is not an 'all at once' occurrence, but should be seen in terms of stages; 'mature' behaviour is that which indicates the successful completion of whatever stage the person has reached. So we can speak of a 'mature' toddler, a mature resolution of the conflict between autonomy and shame, as well as of an adult as mature. One of the most used versions of stages of development is that of Erikson. At one point 'immaturity' was a controversial concept in the exploration of the 'problem family', and it has obvious implications for the role and authority of those who would describe their work with the aid of this concept, and the necessary implication that welfare activity should be directed towards helping people 'to grow' and 'to grow up'.

Erikson, E. (1951) *Childhood and Society*, Imago, Ch. 7.
Irvine, E.E. (1979) *Social Work and Human Problems*, Pergamon, pp. 95-155.

Immigration   An immigrant is someone who comes to live in a country different from his native land, probably with the intention of permanent settlement. Absorption into the 'host' community may or may not be desirable to the immigrant or to the society to which he has come, and 'host' may conceal the interests served in attracting what may be, initially and for a long time, cheap labour. Societies receiving immigrants on a large scale may adopt phased policies (moving from combating discrimination to fostering integration) or may distinguish sharply between first-generation immigrants and those of other generations. It is not uncommon for policies to be directed in contradictory directions – taking no special note of immigrants and 'ignoring' the 'special' services they use (e.g. private fostering, child-minding), providing services which compensate them and/or others in similar situations (e.g. urban poverty), or creating services designed to preserve cultural and religious differences. In recent British history three periods of immigration are of particular importance: the Irish 1800–61; East European Jews 1870–1911; and the New Commonwealth 1950–71.

Cheetham, J. (1972) *Social Work with Immigrants*, Routledge & Kegan Paul.
Jones, C. (1977) *Immigration and Social Policy in Britain*, Tavistock.

In-service training In-service training refers to training of employees (e.g. of a social services department) during their term of employment. The training is usually under the auspices of the employing body: it may be concerned with the induction of new staff, with new developments (e.g. *family therapy*), with aspects of legislation, with staff recruited to new posts (e.g. senior social workers), and so on.

Nicholds, E. (1966) *In-Service Casework Training*, Columbia University Press.
Ward, J. (1975) 'In-Service Community Work Training: a Job-Centred Approach', in *Community Work Two*, ed. D. Jones and M. Mayo, Routledge & Kegan Paul.

Individualisation Individualisation is one of the usually cited principles of social casework. Biestek defined it as 'the recognition and understanding of each client's unique qualities and the differential use of principles and methods in assisting each toward a better adjustment'. Individualisation was first espoused as a welfare principle by the *Charity Organisation Society* who were opposed to the general treatment of classified categories of people. Recognition of the principle seems to lead to client satisfaction at 'being treated as a person', but there are problems in the scope of the principle. Taken on its own it obscures the role of generalisation and of concept in understanding and grasping anything. It can embody a systematic failure or refusal to look beyond a case or series of cases to the underlying social causes of social problems. Lastly, radical social work critics argue that the aim of social work is not the development of the 'abstract' self-regarding individual but his growing appreciation of his group identity and of the ideological basis of his idea of 'individual' and of individual rights. See also *Individualism*.

Biestek, F. (1961) *The Casework Relationship*, Allen & Unwin, pp. 23-32.

Individualism   A very complex notion with a long, distinguished, and confused history. It is best seen, following Lukes, as a set of doctrines and a group of basic ideas. The doctrines are: political individualism, including the view of government as based on the individually-given consent of the citizen; religious individualism or the view that the individual belief needs no intermediary; economic individualism; epistemological individualism or the view that the source of knowledge lies within the individual; and methodological individualism or the view that social phenomena are ultimately to be explained in terms of facts about individuals. The basic ideas are: the supreme value or dignity of the individual; *autonomy* or self-direction; privacy; and self-development. Some or all of these doctrines and ideas have figured prominently in welfare policy and in social work practice. They have performed a number of important roles: justifying policies and actions, setting boundaries beyond which public action should not pass; acting as criteria against which welfare actually is judged. Radical critics, including Lukes, argue that the way of talking encapsulated in 'individualism' encourages a very abstracted, asocial idea of the individual, but it is easy to bolster such a straw man the more easily to dispose of more stubborn 'individualistic' ideas, such as the notion of individual rights. It is difficult to see how some Marxist demolitions of 'the individual' (as for example in the anti-humanism of Althusser) can find a place in welfare discourse.

Lukes, S. (1973) *Individualism*, Blackwell.

Industrial injuries/Industrial disablement/Death   Under each of these categories certain benefits are available: e.g. under industrial disablement benefit, constant attendance, hospital treatment, or exceptionally severe disablement allowances may be paid. In a welfare context interest centres upon the level of benefit, the identification of particular circumstances entitling additional help, and the principle of organising benefit around the concepts of industrial misfortune, and of compensation.

INEQUALITY

DHSS (1981) *Reform of the Industrial Injuries Scheme*, Cmnd 8402, HMSO.

Inequality This concept is perhaps easier to grasp than its opposite number *equality* in so far as discussions of inequality usually concern the lack of justification for the unequal distribution of a 'good' that is known (e.g. housing provision). Inequality has to do with unjustified variableness. In a welfare context 'inequality' figures in a number of ways, general and specific. Ideas of felt inequality are important, as in the notion of the visibility of unequal treatment. Inequality is often used in arguments related to particular services (e.g. some areas are judged to be 'under-doctored' or to employ fewer teachers, social workers, etc. than 'would be expected'). It is also used in relation to the 'uneven' distribution of problems – so people talk of the 'skewed' distribution of disease or of poor people's illnesses and those of rich people. Marxists also refer to the more basic source of all inequality, those structural disparities of wealth which stem from the division of labour and consequent relationship to the means of production. A Marxist perspective on welfare sees the inequalities of service distribution or access simply as manifestations of more basic inequalities. Others would see the basic source of unequal distribution in other ways.

Fenicks, C. *et al.* (1975) *Inequality: a Reassessment of the Effect of Family and Schooling in America*, Penguin.
Townsend, P. and Bosanquet, N. (eds) (1972) *Labour and Inequality*, Fabian Society.

Initial interview An initial interview is the first interview between a social worker and a client or clients or a group, though in the latter case it would be more usual to refer to initial meeting. Clients may not, of course, see it as 'initial', i.e. an introduction to a number of interviews, but it represents the first point at which they can test their expectations of potentially helpful persons and the occasion on which a change between the roles of 'applicant' and 'client' (or situation of contact and contract) can begin to be negotiated.

Perlman, H. (1960) 'Intake and some Role Considerations', *Social Casework*, 41, 171-7.

102

Thomas, E. *et al.* (1955) 'The Expected Behaviour of a Potentially Helpful Person', *Human Relations*, 8, 165-74.

Inner city Changes in the population and dominant uses of particular areas of a city have been common at least since the Industrial Revolution, and a differentiating social policy response in Britain probably starts with the zoning areas of the Town Planning Act 1909. Present interest in problems described as those of the 'inner city' is of more recent origin, but some of the problems described specifically as those of the inner city are not confined to such areas (e.g. housing), and differing emphasis can be given to the location of a number of, perhaps discrete, problems or to the causal links through which the problems are connected to each other. What may be called the new inner-city policy was launched in 1968, following a widely reported speech by Enoch Powell predicting the fatal consequences of black immigration, though the *Community Development Projects* suggested concern for certain inner-city areas. Under the Local Government Grants (Social Need) Act 1969 extra resources were made available for voluntary and statutory projects in areas with special needs. This policy was reviewed in the DoE White Paper, *Policy for the Inner Cities* (Cmnd 6845, July 1977), which, largely on the basis of inner areas studied by the Department of the Environment, placed special emphasis on the restoration of economic life in the inner city. A number of innovations were announced including Inner City Programmes and a Partnership Scheme between central government and local authorities. More recently, problems of urban violence have featured as a significant part of inner city problems. However serious these are, it is worth considering Lord Scarman's comment: 'Inner City areas are not human deserts: they possess a wealth of voluntary effort and goodwill' (Cmnd 8427, p. 101). See also *Urban.*

Butler, P. and Williams, R. (1981) 'Inner City Partnerships and Established Policies', *Policy and Politics*, 9, 125-36.
Deacon, N. and Ungerson, C. (1977) *Leaving London; Planned Mobility and the Inner City*, Heinemann.
Home Office (1981) *The Brixton Disorders* (Scarman Report), Cmnd 8427, HMSO.
Wicks, M. (1978) 'Social Policy for the Inner Cities', in *Year Book of*

INSIGHT

Social Policy in Britain, 1977, ed. M. Brown and S. Baldwin, Routledge & Kegan Paul.

Insight 'Insight' can be used in a general and a specialised sense. 'Insight' in relation to 'all human knowledge in mathematics, natural science, common sense, philosophy, human science, history, theology ... consists in a grasp of intelligible unity or relation in the data or image or symbol' (B. Lonergan, *Method in Theology*, Darton, Longman & Todd, 1972, pp. 212-13). The ideas of 'grasp' and of a coherence or connection of some kind are also evident in more specialised, psychoanalytic references. Psychoanalytic insight is the lively realisation of the specific influence of unconscious conflicts and their infantile roots; it derives from interpretation, particularly of the *transference*. Recognition of the source of phantasies and conflicts described as 'intellectual' is suspect, while the realisation that 'comes in a flash' may indicate insufficient assimilation. At one time it was thought possible to distinguish social casework from psychotherapy in terms of different levels of insight development. 'Insight' as the main objective of either social casework or psychotherapy has been criticised, but French has usefully distinguished between awareness of a repressed wish or fear, problem-solving insight, and practical understanding (p. 18).

French, T. (1958) *The Reintegrative Process in Psychoanalytic Treatment*: vol. 3, *The Integration of Behavior*, University of Chicago Press.

Lonergan, B. (1958) *Insight: a Study of Human Understanding*, Harper & Row (paperback, 1978).

Yelloly, M. (1980) *Social Work Theory and Psychoanalysis*, Van Nostrand Reinhold, pp. 134-41.

Instinct In so far as theories and ideas of instinct have been influential in welfare, one major source has been Freud's instinct theory. This is a complex set of ideas, but Freud clearly distinguished four major features of talk about instincts. In this context instincts are conceived in terms of: source, to be found in states of excitation within the body; impetus or a demand on energy; aim, to achieve satisfaction through extinction of the stimulation at source; and object, or that in and through which the aim of somatic modification is achieved. Freud grouped the several instincts into life instincts *(libido)* and *death instincts*. Others have viewed instincts rather differently. Lorenz, for example, saw instincts as stereotyped patterns of behaviour, inherited and specific, which are released in a complex way rather than guided by the environment (Fletcher).

Fletcher, R. (1957) *Instinct in Man*, Allen & Unwin.

Institution The term has two distinct meanings: a social institution can refer to a major unit in the analysis of society and the experience of participants in social action; it is an established set of ways of behaving, so that we talk of the family as an institution. In a more narrow sense an institution refers essentially to a place (e.g. the Poor Law Institution or institutional care). The wider sense of institution is relevant to social welfare in at least two ways. First, the major social institutions may generate welfare or diswelfare. Second, one general approach to the growth and place of social welfare stresses its institutional nature. In other words, 'welfare' is not a special function that will at some point cease or be reserved only for marginal groups; it is part of ordinary and ordered social life. The more restricted usage (institution as place rather than norm) is important because *residential care* features in programmes for many groups and also because it is believed that certain ways of managing life in institutions produce a particular deleterious condition known as 'institutionalisation', or the acceptance and incorporation by inmates of certain stereotyped responses to their predicament.

Intake team 'Intake' refers to the initial response of an organisation to possible instances of new work. In some social services departments all *referrals* and enquiries are the intital responsibility of a group, a specialised team, of *'gate-keepers'*. If work on the case lasts longer than a stipulated period of time or is judged likely to last such a period or longer, it is transferred to a long-term team. There are, however, interesting differences between the actual work of teams all called 'intake' (e.g. not all take on court reports or emergencies). The common problems are those of case assessment, decision-making, and transfer.

Lowestein, C. (1974) 'An Intake Team in Action in a Social Services Department', *British Journal of Social Work*, 4, 115-41.

INTEGRATION

Integration   This term has two main uses in welfare. First, it refers to a desirable state of social cohesion based on status equality. In this sense 'integration' is seen as the desired objective of social policy as a whole; social policy is social (as contrasted with economic) and is good policy if it seeks after and achieves social integration. Such a judgment is also made in connection with particular services when it is suggested that one group within a category should be treated differently from, or not 'in full association' (DES, *Special Needs in Education*, Cmnd 7996, 1980) with, others in the same category. So it has been argued that the confused elderly should not be treated in special 'segregated' homes or that maladjusted children should be integrated with other children in 'ordinary' rather than in 'special' schools. In sociological terms the integration we are concerned with is 'social integration' (orderly relationships between 'actors') rather than 'system integration' (relationship between parts of a social system). Second, integration is used to describe a very particular and desirable state of non-dividedness, as when in social work education reference is made to the 'integration' of theory and practice. No one has satisfactorily explained what this means or how such fine dovetailing could be recognised, and attempts to heal the split between 'theory' and 'practice' by use of some variant of the Marxist idea of praxis marks no noticeable improvement. See also *Segregation*.

Interaction   Interaction in groups or between individuals is a frequent topic of discussion in social work, social psychology, and sociology (Layder). Use of the term is at times extremely wide-ranging so that reference is made to any social exchange at all; i.e. no emphasis is given to *inter*-action or action responding to a perception of or the behaviour of another. The term can also be used in a more technical social psychological sense to refer to a distinctive research interest in the detailed, often non-laboratory-based, study of behaviour, to its biological base and its cultural setting. This research is concerned with 'various signals: verbal and non-verbal, tactile, visible and audible – various kinds of bodily contact, proximity, orientation, bodily posture, physical appearance, facial expression ... direction of gaze, timing of speech ... type of utterance and linguistic structure of utterance' (Argyle, p. 9). Interaction is also used as a shorthand for a particular approach, namely that of symbolic interaction, associated with G. H. Mead. For an account of the interactionist perspective that derives from this source, see Plummer, Ch. 2.

Argyle, M. (1973) *Social Encounters: Readings in Social Interaction*, Penguin.
Layder, D. (1981) *Structure, Interaction and Social Theory*, Routledge & Kegan Paul.
Plummer, J. (1975) *Sexual Stigma: an Interactionist Account*, Routledge & Kegan Paul.

Interest 'Interest' can have descriptive or normative weight. We can say that X is in A's interest if it is what he wants or we can say X is in A's interest because it promotes or ensures his good, his advantage, etc. In the former instance A is in the possession of privileged knowledge, since he is the best source of knowledge about what he wants, but he could easily be mistaken about what would promote his good. We tend also to refer to 'interest' in relation not so much to particular acts but to sequences of acts or policies. The central notion of interest in the descriptive sense is conveyed in the proposition that one policy is more in a person's interest than another if that person were to experience the results of both policies and to choose the outcome he or she would prefer. Interests in this sense refer both to what a person wants over a period of time and to the description under which it is wanted: a man may forgo certain material goods, which he had wanted for some time, in the interest of maintaining a relationship of trust with another. The idea of interest is important in social welfare for a number of reasons: social workers and others may act in someone's interest by, for example, acting as a *representative*; at times people will be struggling to grasp where their true interests lie (and some would argue that these cannot be grasped unless the cloud of false consciousness is pierced); at other times action has to be taken in someone's best interest (e.g. in relation to children). Finally, writers on social policy refer frequently to the sustained preferences of powerful groups or vested interests.

INTERMEDIATE TREATMENT

Swanton, C. (1980) 'The Concept of Interests', *Political Theory*, 8, 83-101.
Watson, D. (1980) *Caring for Strangers*, Routledge & Kegan Paul, pp. 116-32.

Intermediate treatment   Intermediate treatment is a sentencing possibility for juveniles, supplying care, control, and treatment to high-risk juvenile delinquents within a non-custodial context. Intermediate treatment or IT now receives considerable attention, but it has taken time for the concept to evolve and to gain popularity. The first description of forms of treatment called 'intermediate' is in the White Paper of 1968, *Children in Trouble*, which outlined ideas of treating the child as a member of the community, with his peers (not all of whom would be delinquent), and with some measure of compulsion. The first DHSS circular on IT in 1969 said the term could be used narrowly to describe treatment undertaken by a supervised person under the supervisor's directions or more broadly to describe arrangements for helping young people in trouble or at risk of getting into trouble. In the same year the Personal Social Services Council saw IT as action through a range of community-based programmes. The statutory framework for IT is the 1969 Children and Young Persons Act and in this context IT is a measure which can be added as an additional clause to a supervision order; the additional clause gives discretion to the supervisor (local authority or probation) to require the supervisee to attend a facility of intermediate treatment, but the facility has to be of a type approved by the Secretary of State and listed in the *Regional Planning Committee's* scheme for IT (Jones and Kerslake).

Billis, D. (1980) 'Intermediate Treatment: In Search of a Policy', in *Organising Social Services Departments*, ed. D. Billis *et al.*, Heinemann.
Jones, R. and Kerslake, A. (1979) *Intermediate Treatment and Social Work*, Heinemann.

Intervention   This has become a common name for social work action. It was probably adopted because it avoids the notion of treatment in a strong sense and does not assume that social work is principally treatment aimed at 'named' clients. It also conveys an idea of purposefulness over a period of time: an interminable psychoanalysis may or may not be desirable but it is more coherent than an interminable intervention. A distinction can be drawn between a strong sense of the term (intervening between a couple in conflict) and a weak sense (any purposeful action at all). This distinction is of importance in a consideration of a social worker's right to intervene: action in the former sense requires more precise authorisation than the competent goodwill implicit in the latter. 'Intervention' is also used as a general description for the activities of many other professionals, such as planners. Bailey has argued for the importance of viewing their intervention theoretically.

Bailey, J. (1980) *Ideas and Intervention*, Routledge & Kegan Paul.
Timms, N. and R. (1977) *Perspectives in Social Work*, Routledge & Kegan Paul, pp. 187-96.

Interview   An interview is a formal meeting to transact business of some kind between people occupying (temporarily or more permanently) different organisational positions. Friends, family members, neighbours, are not described as interviewing each other, but people such as headteachers, social workers, research workers are concerned with interviewing. The most extensive discussion of the social work interview is by Kadushin, who defines the interview too widely as 'a conversation with a deliberate purpose mutually accepted by the participants' (p.8). From this definition a number of characterisations of the interview are said to follow, including: the content of the interview is chosen to facilitate the achievement of the conversation's purpose; someone has to take responsibility for directing the interaction; the two separate roles (i.e. interviewer and interviewee) imply a non-reciprocal relationship; the actions of the interviewer should be planned and deliberate; the interview is usually a formally arranged meeting. Stipulative definition of this kind may mask the different ways in which in different contexts interviewers and those 'being' interviewed actually define roles and experience the relative distribution of power, etc. Ability to interview is considered a prime skill in social work and in many other 'social welfare' occupations.

INTROVERSION-EXTRAVERSION

Kadushin, A. (1972) *The Social Work Interview*, Columbia University Press.
Kuhn, M. (1962) 'The Interview and the Professional Relationship', in *Human Behavior and Social Processes: an Interactionist Approach*, ed. A. Rose, Routledge & Kegan Paul.

Introversion-extraversion This dichotomy has a long history in psychological thought (Eysenck has traced some of the more influential thinkers). Jung saw the distinction in terms of two fundamental attitudes of personality and argued that people could be typified in terms of the predominant attitude, though the less dominant attitude was developed unconsciously. Introversion is an established general tendency to direct attention inwards, and, as a consequence, the outer world suffers a kind of depreciation. Extraversion is the tendency to direct interest towards others and the external environment, and to attribute to this outer world essential value. The distinction between the two tendencies is sometimes made on the basis of interest, or of adaptation to the social environment, or of covert or apparent behaviour. For Eysenck introversion-extraversion is one of the two independent dimensions of personality, the other being neuroticism.

Eysenck, H. (ed.) (1970-1) *Readings in Extraversion-Introversion:* vol. 1, *Theoretical and Methodological Issues*, Staples Press.
Sinclair, I. (1974) 'The Relationship between Introversion and Response to Casework in a Prison Setting', *British Journal of Social and Clinical Psychology*, 13, 51-60.

Involvement This is seen as a necessary element in social work, but also one that contains dangers, as in references to 'over-involvement' and 'controlled emotional involvement'. 'Involvement' in social work refers to experienced and expressed interest in a person's situation and to closeness to what the situation means to that person. This closeness leads to and is expressive of a kind of understanding. A social worker is involved if his or her encounter with the client is both personal and professional. The involvement is partly a product of what the social worker feels as he or she responds to the client, but involvement is not 'loss' of self; it is 'directed by the over-all purpose of the case, by the client's changing needs in each interview and by the caseworker's

diagnostic ongoing thinking' (Biestek, p.66). Questions have
been raised concerning the possibility and the desirability of
such control. See also *Friendship*.

Biestek, F. (1961) *The Casework Relationship*, Allen & Unwin, pp.
48-66.

Irrationality Lukes argues that beliefs are irrational if they
suffer from certain kinds of inadequacy, among which he lists
inconsistency or self-contradictoriness, insufficient supporting
evidence, being held in a way that does not leave them open to
refutation, being nonsensical, and so on. Criteria for irrational
conduct and irrational belief are likely to be controversial, but
judgments of people's ends and actions in welfare are frequently
made in terms of irrationality/rationality, and not exclusively in
the consideration of *mental illness*. Particular questions are, of
course, raised by the relationship of *psychosis* and irrationality.
Brown, for example, suggests that two important and related
questions can be asked about the rationality of psychotic people:
does a psychotic person act and believe, to a significant extent,
on the basis of reasons, and did the agent have his reasons,
whether good or bad, for trying to become psychotic. See also
Rationality, Madness, Unconscious.

Brown, R. (1976) 'Psychosis and Irrationality', in *Rationality and the
Social Sciences*, ed. S. Benn and G. Mortimore, Routledge & Kegan
Paul.
Lukes, S. (1970) 'Some Problems about Rationality', in *Rationality*, ed.
B. Wilson, Blackwell.

Issue See *Social problem.*

J

Jung/Jungian theory The ideas of Jung have influenced a small school of psychoanalysts, that of analytical psychology, and a perhaps smaller number of social workers. (In 1927 Dr Jung wrote to the social work journal of the time: 'I must say I never would have expected so much appreciation from a sphere that seems to be so remote from my professional activity'.) However, Jungian theory has been influential in terms of a general orientation to, and recognition of, 'the social'. Major notions in Jung's theories are: the importance of the distinction between introversion and extraversion as a basis for the *typology* of personality; an imaginative grasp of the significance and role of image and symbol (a Jungian analyst once remarked that even the penis is a symbol); the idea of expressed and unexpressed polarities (for example, the good mother and the witch contained within the same personality); and the theory of the collective *unconscious* and of archetypes.

Fordham, F. (1966) *An Introduction to Jung's Psychology*, 3rd ed., Penguin.
Munroe, R. (1957) *Schools of Psychoanalytic Thought*, Hutchinson, Ch. 13.

Justice See *Social justice.*

Juvenile court Juvenile courts, as special sittings of magistrates' courts with criminal and civil jurisdiction, were established in the Children Act of 1908. Subsequent legislation of importance includes the two Children and Young Persons Acts of 1933 and 1969. Changes in law and the often sharp accompanying and lasting controversies are most economically

112

understood as the defence, expansion, and criticism of what Parsloe has described as three models of juvenile justice: these centre upon ideas of welfare (which see law-breaking as the expression of personal or social malaise), of criminal justice (the re-establishment of the rule of law over responsible offenders), and of the community approach (the offender is a social victim and the societal response ought to take the form of preventing further *labelling*). In Scotland *Children's Hearings* have taken the place of juvenile courts.

Parsloe, P. (1978) *Juvenile Justice in Britain and the United States*, Routledge & Kegan Paul.

K

Key worker/Key person Where the client of a social services department or a social worker is in contact with a number of welfare personnel (e.g. a child in a well-staffed children's home or a family receiving visits from voluntary and statutory services), one particular 'worker' may be designated by the superior or by case conference as the main resource, the worker of first contact for other agencies, and the bearer of the main therapeutic effort. He or she should act as the keystone of the over-arching treatment plan for the individual family or group.

Kleinian theory The psychoanalytical theories of Melanie Klein are sometimes seen within the context of *object-relations theories*. They have had an influence on psychotherapists and social workers, though Yellowly has noted: 'If social work is indeed about change, then the kind of change strategy implicit in Kleinian theory has little relevance to social work, and it has little to offer as a theory of change' (*Social Work Theory and Psychoanalysis*, Van Nostrand Reinhold, 1980, p. 163). Kleinian theory is based largely on the direct experience of applying and modifying psychoanalytic technique in the treatment of very young children. It places the dynamics of *ego* and *super-ego* formation in the first year of life; emphasises the intensity and complexity of infantile phantasy; gives structural importance to what are described as the depressive and paranoid positions; explores particular feelings (e.g. envy) and particular mechanisms (e.g. projection or unconscious attribution, and introjection or the absorption of 'external' feelings, etc.).

Salzberger-Wittenberg, I. (1970) *Psycho-Analytic Insight and Relationships: a Kleinian Approach*, Routledge & Kegan Paul.

KNOWLEDGE

Knowledge 'Knowledge' arises as a term in welfare in at least three different contexts. Social work educators refer frequently to the 'knowledge base' of social work, and mean by this theories, usually of psychology and sociology, which inform social work understanding and support social work activity, or should provide such underpinning. In this connection insufficient attention is paid to the different senses of 'knowing': one can know someone (i.e. recognise them), but one can also know how to do something and know that something is the case. Second, knowledge is used in the sense of information, and questions are continually raised about the ways in which agencies collect and store information (so that their activities may be the more 'knowing') and the extent to which changes, proposed or realised, are based on hard information or real knowledge. Third, those concerned with the development of *social administration* as an academic subject are aware of the necessity to develop its base in systematic research or publicly available knowledge: 'the attempts must be made (at present it scarcely is made) to develop theories specific to, and useful in, research both in and on social policy.' This research should, it is argued, seek to integrate the various social science disciplines (Blume).

Blume, S. (1979) 'Policy Studies and Social Policy in Britain', *Journal of Social Policy*, 9, 311-34.

Philp, M. (1979) 'Notes on the Form of Knowledge in Social Work', *Sociological Review*, 27, 83-111.

Rein, M. and White, S. (1981) 'Knowledge for Practice', *Social Service Review*, 55, 1-41.

L

Labelling Labelling theory, though Becker correctly denies that work in this area has the achievements or faces the obligations of 'theory', calls attention, within an *interactionist* framework, to the contribution that those other than the identified deviant make to the genesis and amplification of deviant acts and deviant careers. Obviously if we had no labels at all life would consist of bumping into 'things', but labelling theorists direct attention to 'name-calling', usually of an unfavourable kind, to orientation and activity towards the other on the basis of the name, and to the person's own assimilation of the name as part of his identity. Social policy has often categorised people on the basis of labels which were supposed to indicate special treatment of some kind: the effects of this have not always been beneficial, though they may have been far-reaching. Social workers are often at the point at which 'labels' (psychopath, disturbed, *dangerous*) are determined and applied or, in Lemert's terms, when primary deviation is publicly acknowledged and treated and hence becomes secondary.

Becker, H. (1974) 'Labelling Theory Reconsidered', in *Deviance and Social Control*, ed. P. Rock and M. McIntosh, Tavistock.
Lemert, E. (1967) *Human Deviance, Social Problems and Social Control*, Prentice-Hall.
Plummer, K. (1979) 'Misunderstanding Labelling Perspectives', in *Deviant Interpretations*, ed. D. Downes and P. Rock, Martin Robertson.

Learning theory See *Behaviour modification.*

Level In a general sense, social workers have used the term to distinguish different kinds of work (as in the expressions 'working at a deep level' or 'working at a superficial level'). Sometimes the distinction was made in psychoanalytical terms and so work was seen as at the conscious or the unconscious level. In either case it was for a time assumed that the deeper the work the more the services of an 'advanced' worker were required. The idea of level in a more specific sense can also be found in the classification of strata of work applied to the health and social services. In a recent analysis, five distinct levels of work have been identified in terms of responsibility for prescribed output, situational response, systematic service provision, comprehensive service provision, and comprehensive field coverage. See also *Hierarchy*.

Rowbotham, R. and Billis, D. (1978) 'The Stratification of Work and Organisational Design', in *Health Services*, ed. E. Jaques, Heinemann.

Liaison   See *Co-operation*.

Libido   A term in *Freudian theory* which describes the energies proceeding from what Freud called the sexual instinctive drives. *Jung* retained the term to describe a more general life energy. Freud distinguished between object libido and narcissistic libido, and argued for a hierarchy of erotogenic zones through which progressive libidinal development took place – from oral erotism through anal to phallic.

Nagera, H. *et al.* (1969) *Basic Psychoanalytic Concepts on the Libido Theory*, Allen & Unwin.

Life skills   See *Social skills*.

Long-term team   Used in relation to the idea of social work as divisible into long-term and short-term contact with a particular case. A long-term team is a group of social workers whose main responsibility is in relation to cases carried by the agency, or perhaps likely to be carried, for a period longer than that judged appropriate for work in the short term. For example, long-term work may be said to begin after a case has been with the agency more than three months, or is considered to be likely to require contact of more than three months' duration. See also *Intake team*.

Loss The notion of loss originally attained significance in welfare as a description of an assumed crucial consequence of maternal separation; i.e. loss of the prized love object. Response to psychological loss is assumed to follow clearly identifiable phases: those of protest, of despair, and of detachment. 'Loss' has been seen as a crucial concept in a range of situations – mourning and grief after the death of someone close, or reaction to amputation. It has also been extended to the understanding of change on the social scale (Marris). It is important that 'loss' on the psychological level or as an approach to understanding social change is not confused with 'lack': not all our problems are caused because we no longer possess a prized object or relationship – it may never have been numbered among our possessions. See also *Deprivation*.

Bowlby, J. (1973) *Attachment and Loss:* vol. 2, *Separation*, Hogarth Press.
Marris, P. (1974) *Loss and Change*, Routledge & Kegan Paul.

Madness At one time to speak of madness or the mad was considered to be an old-fashioned and retrograde way of referring to mental illness or the *mentally ill*. Now it is used in the attempt to rescue a particular range of deviant behaviour from the control, and the vocabulary, of the medical profession. 'Madness' is a term favoured by those who seek to oppose psychiatric imperialism and by writers such as Szasz, Cooper, and Laing. It is also a term of common lay usage and serves as a reminder of the long history of control and service of those judged to be leading irrational or potentially destructive lives.

Siegler, M. *et al.* (1969) 'Laing's Models of Madness', *British Journal of Psychiatry*, 115, 947-58.

Manipulation Manipulation is a special case of A getting B to perform, believe, or experience something. It is different from ordering or advising, and is best seen as a kind of powerful influence in which A usually does not disclose to B either the fact that he is exercising influence or the direction in which he is seeking 'to move' B. In some restricted instances, however, a person could be described as consenting to treatment that might be called manipulative (*behaviour modification* of certain kinds). More usually manipulation of clients is criticised by social workers because of the primacy of the client's ends and the importance of an open acknowledgment of the steps to be taken to relieve his problem. Manipulation of the environment, a kind of direct or indirect engagement with the material stuff of life on the client's behalf, has been seen as a possible way of conceptualising part of social work, but it has often been pursued as a strategy separated from consideration of the client as a whole person.

In a community work context manipulation of the environment may be said to include manipulation of 'powerful others' in the client's environment (e.g. local political leaders), and this produces its own problems. Brager and Specht state a controversial position that 'manipulation should be eschewed *except* when it clearly supports another, overriding, value. The magnitude of the need, the powerlessness of the constituent, and the rules of the game as played by adversaries dictate the conclusion that manipulation (which they see as involving exaggeration, distortion or lying) is sometimes justified' (p. 288).

Bibring, J. (1949) 'Psychiatric Principles in Casework', *Journal of Social Casework*, 30, 230-5.
Brager, G. and Specht, H. (1973) *Community Organizing*, Columbia University Press.
Ware, A. (1981) 'The Concept of Manipulation: its Relation to Democracy and Power', *British Journal of Political Science*, 11, 163-81.

Market 'Market' refers to a mode of exchange determined by such factors as price, supply, and demand. It has been argued that the market in capitalist societies is characterised by private ownership, the fact that the inputs and outputs of the economic process are for exchange and not use, and that the quest for profit is the main steering mechanism. Downie has indicated that it is inaccurate to describe the economic relation as one of self-interest or egoism, though he examines the plausible thesis that social welfare services exist in order to remedy some of the moral defects and consequences of a free market economy. For others the ideas of a choice and consumer sovereignty embodied in 'market' have led to arguments that social services should be distributed as market goods for which prices are paid. Others, such as Sleeman, believe that the distribution of social services as 'merit goods' would not be best achieved through market mechanisms.

Downie, R. (1980) 'The Market and Welfare Services: Remedial Values', in *Social Welfare: Why and How?*, ed. N. Timms, Routledge & Kegan Paul.
Sleeman, J. (1979) *Resources for the Welfare State*, Macmillan.

MARXIST THEORY

Taylor-Gooby, P. and Dale, J. (1981) *Social Theory and Social Welfare*, Edward Arnold, Ch. 6, 'The Market'.

Marriage counselling   What is now called marriage or marital counselling started as the offer of sympathetic guidance and advice by *volunteers* to people in marital difficulty. The Marriage Guidance Council was established in 1937, and the Catholic Marriage Advisory Council in 1946. Gradually counselling has become the preferred description of activities involving the establishment of a relationship of trust between lay counsellor and the client or clients, in which full disclosure of the marital problem is encouraged and the attempt made to develop *understanding* with a view to taking informed action. The most recent review of the development and of the financial and conceptual problems of the main agencies working in the field is to be found in *Marriage Matters*. Keithley has argued that 'Marriage Guidance Councils and the counsellors who work for them are currently in a state of flux: both with regard to the scope and with regard to the setting of their work.'

Home Office and DHSS (1979) *Marriage Matters* (Consultative
. Document by the Working Party on Marriage Guidance), HMSO.
Keithley, J. (1977) *Marriage Guidance Research: a Preview*, Working
Party in Social Policy and Administration, University of Durham,
Department of Sociology and Social Administration, paper no. 1.

Marxist theory   The writings of Marx and the Marxists have recently been explored by those seeking a new understanding of welfare history and of the present and the future direction of practice in social provision and social work. Thus, the development of the *Welfare State* has come to be seen in terms of the limited success of the working-class struggle against exploitation, the requirement of advanced capitalist societies for a highly productive labour force, and the price exacted for political security. The radical force of a Marxist approach is evident and it has recently been argued that it offers a special challenge to those engaged in the study and practice of social administration: 'To take materialism seriously would be to license on the one hand the view that needs may be systematically and socially produced by agencies beyond the control of the state in democratic welfare capitalism; and on the other hand that the state, a product of material relations, may be unable to meet them' (Taylor-Gooby and Dale, p. 28). On the other hand Mishra's generally sympathetic review of the Marxist perspective refers to Marxism as 'a theory pitched at a high level of generality and rich in ambiguity' (p. 83). Marxism is also characterised by deep internal controversy, often in areas relevant to consideration of social welfare such as the place and legitimacy of humanism. Such controversies are rarely reproduced in attempts to establish the Marxist approach to welfare.

Mishra, R. (1977) *Society and Social Policy: Theoretical Perspectives on Welfare*, Macmillan, Ch. 5.

Taylor-Gooby, P. and Dale, J. (1981) *Social Theory and Social Welfare*, Edward Arnold.

Material aid   See *Financial aid.*

Maternal deprivation   See *Deprivation, Loss.*

Maturity   This term in its psychological meaning refers to the final objective of growth or to the successful passage of a particular stage in development. Attempts to define maturity in detail lead inevitably to controversy, since notions of the normative are invariably built into description. The value-laden nature of a specific notion of maturity is clear from the following description of early, contrasted with late, maturity, as 'characterised by still further separation from the family into which the child is born, most often through the establishing of his own family or household. He continues the development and identification of himself as an individual through educational and vocational choice and pursuit and a more responsible relationship to society, and through his identification as an adult with a new role as 'maker and shaker' of his world (R. Smalley, *Theory for Social Work Practice*, Columbia University Press, 1967, p. 76). The notion of maturity can also be applied more widely than in psychology. So Lukacs argued in a Marxist context that the fate of the revolution would depend on the 'ideological maturity' of the proletariat, by which he meant its level of class consciousness (*History and Class Consciousness,* trans. R. Livingstone, Merlin Press, 1971).

Medical social work   Formerly the description of a particular branch of social work, originating in the role of hospital almoner created by C. S. Loch of the *Charity Organisation Society*. It came to be considered as social work undertaken by social workers in hospitals, in the then local authority health departments, or in connection with general medical practice. Medical social workers are no longer a distinct professional group, but the problems they faced in the course of developing a distinctive social work practice within organisations geared to treat people with illnesses and dominated by the medical practitioner are still relevant. Is the best operational base for social work that is medically orientated the hospital 'team', the general medical practice, or the local authority? Are social workers who see themselves as 'medical' most likely to be effective if they have a secure relationship with 'other' health personnel or if their community links are strong and predominant? Is the target for medical social work the smoother functioning of the health services, co-operation in the cure of specific illnesses, the social context of identified patients, or *prevention*?

Carter, D. (1976) 'The Social Needs of the Physically Sick and the Role of the Medical Social Worker', unpublished doctoral thesis, University of York.
Goldberg, E. and Neill, J. (1972) *Social Work and General Practice*, Allen & Unwin.
Snelling, J. (1962) 'Social Work within Medical Care', *The Almoner*, 15, 66-72.

Mental handicap   This is now the preferred term to describe sub-average general intellectual functioning and impaired adaptive behaviour. It replaces mental subnormality, though a distinction is still maintained between severe and mild mental handicap. Recent developments in provision have been concerned with incorporating the mentally handicapped within general services (e.g. in 1971 local education authorities were made responsible for the education and training of all mentally handicapped children), questioning the suitability of large institutions with the dominant character of hospital (White Paper, *Better Services for the Mentally Handicapped*, Cmnd 4683, HMSO) and the most appropriate form of staff training and of service, including the ingredients of an effective programme of community care.

Bayley, M. (1973) 'The Mentally Handicapped and their Helpers', *British Journal of Social Work*, 3, 319-63.
DHSS, (Jay) Committee of Enquiry into Mental Handicap Nursing and Care (1979) *Report*, Cmnd 7468, HMSO.

Mental illness Mental illnesses are listed in a number of authoritative publications (e.g. *Glossary of Mental Disorders,* World Health Organisation, 1974), but the idea of certain forms of behaviour as 'sick' and requiring treatment that is medical remains elusive and controversial. The idea of mental illness and the provisions made to cure and to prevent it raise a number of important questions in welfare. How do people reach 'official' psychiatric care and on the way how do they and others define their problems, and with what results? What is the effectiveness of particular treatments and programmes (such as *community care*)? How necessary are the elements of *compulsion* often considered to be an essential part of services for the mentally ill? How wide is the definition of mental illness drawn and what influence do social conditions and circumstances have on behaviour that is sooner or later *labelled* as mad? (See *Madness*) Where should the line be drawn between madness and badness? (See *Psychopath*).

Flew, A. (1973) *Crime or Disease?* Macmillan.
Goldberg, D. and Huxley, P. (1980) *Mental Illness in the Community*, Tavistock.
Miles, A. (1981) *The Mentally Ill in Contemporary Society*, Martin Robertson.

Mental welfare officer This description replaced that of the Duly Authorised Officer (authorised for certification procedures under the 1890 Lunacy Act) in 1960. The mental welfare officer makes an application for the admission of a mentally disordered person to hospital if the nearest relative does not wish to do so or there is no such relative. The Review of the Mental Health Act of 1959 agreed with the British Association of Social Workers that the term 'mental welfare officer' had now been outdated, and considered 'approved social worker' to be preferable. It proposed that the 1959 Act be amended to give approved social workers a statutory duty to interview the person concerned before making an application for compulsory admission and a responsibility to be satisfied that the care and treatment offered was in the least restrictive conditions practicable.

DHSS *et al.* (1978) *Review of the Mental Health Act, 1959*, Cmnd 7320, HMSO.

Motive In a welfare context, 'motive' is used to explain behaviour (that of an individual or group) or to establish a person's reasons for acting. Kelly (*Personal Constructs*) is one of the few psychologists to repudiate the idea of motivation. Others see it as goal-directed behaviour carried out in such a way that the present or future biological requirements of the individual or the species are met. For some, a motive is a drive or moving force which is a causative factor in every act. Peters stresses that we ask about someone's motives when his conduct is to be assessed in some way, when we want to discover the purpose of his behaviour, or when we wish to know *the* operative reasons why he acted as he did. Notions of motivation figure in social welfare in attempts to understand behaviour and in particular in recruitment to such occupations as social work.

Peters, R. (1958) *The Concept of Motivation*, Routledge & Kegan Paul.

Mourning 'Mourning' refers to a psycho-social process of accumulative response to and appreciation of loss of a valued object or relationship. The process is made up of a number of more or less distinct stages following bereavement or loss: from initial numbness through pining to *depression* and hence to recovery. It has been argued that the overall reaction to bereavement or serious loss is determined by the way in which the grief process has been negotiated, by the extent of *stigma* incurred in the form of changed behaviour and attitudes on the part of significant others, and by effects of deprivation or the absence of the necessary person.

Parker, C. (1975) *Bereavement: Studies in Grief in Adult Life*, Penguin.
Pincus, L. (1976) *Death and the Family*, Faber.

MULTI-DISCIPLINARY

Multi-disciplinary   This term refers to the presence and collective contribution of a number of disciplines; in practice the term refers more simply to the presence and contribution of more than one discipline. In a welfare context the reference is often doubly persuasive: that social work actually counts as a discipline (compared to medicine) and that the discipline of medicine actually stands for the range of occupations participating in health care. Many of the problems with which social policy and social work are concerned are frequently assumed to call for a multi-disciplinary approach, but successful attempts to execute the idea are hard to find. (*Child guidance clinics* were based on the idea and ideal of inter-professional collaboration, and it is perhaps mainly with regard to children that a multi-disciplinary approach is most insistently urged.) Thus, the Court Report on Child Health Services (*Fit for the Future,* Cmnd 6684, HMSO, 1976) was 'at pains ... to emphasise the inter-relationship of health, educational and social factors in a child's development ... Hence it is crucial that the balance between a child's health needs and his educational and social needs be understood, and effective co-operation between the three authorities and between their professional staff be established' (pp. 160-1).

Hallett, C. and Stevenson, O. (1980) *Aspects of Inter-professional Co-operation,* Allen & Unwin.

Needs The term is used very frequently in social welfare, and Plant *et al.* have argued that 'the concept of need is absolutely fundamental to the understanding of contemporary social policy and the welfare state' (p. 20). The term is also regularly used by social workers to understand the behaviour of clients (as under pressure from certain personality needs) or to legitimise certain requests for help (as really needed). 'Need' refers to that which is required in order to restore or create a valued state (a hungry man requires food to restore a valued physical/psychological condition); to the legitimacy of what is required (what is sought proceeds not from a whim); and to what is to be satisfied if the requirement is obtained (as in a human need for recognition). Thus 'need' is a complex notion, and statements using the term are often of different kinds. Bradshaw has usefully called attention to different ways of arriving at 'need' statements, through expert judgment, through experience, and through comparison of provision for one group as contrasted with another.

Bar-Yosef, R. (1980) 'The Social Perspective of Personal Needs and their Satisfaction', in *Welfare or Bureaucracy?*, ed. D. Grunow and F. Hegner, Oelgeschlager, Gunn & Hain, Cambridge, Mass.

Bradshaw, J. (1972) 'Taxonomy of Social Need', in *Problems and Progress in Medical Care*, ed. G. McLachlan, Oxford University Press.

Plant, R. *et al.* (1980) *Political Philosophy and Social Welfare*, Routledge & Kegan Paul, pp. 20-51.

Neighbourhood A neighbourhood is a small locality as much defined by common sentiment as by clearly acknowledged physical boundaries. The word is used in welfare to describe agencies (e.g. a *settlement*), a way of organising service delivery (on a local rather than a centralised basis), resources (as 'belonging' to or attracted by a certain locale), or a kind of community work. (Henderson and Thomas see neighbourhood work and community work as interchangeable terms.) In the last sense, neighbourhood work centres on work informed by a lively sense of local networks, though the groups worked with may not represent the totality of the neighbourhood: they are (like health action groups, mothers' groups, etc.) in and of the neighbourhood, but they do not constitute the neighbourhood. The idea of the neighbourhood community has also strongly influenced social planning but its context may well be vacuous from sociological and other points of view. Dennis persuasively argues that 'people seem to find it extraordinarily difficult to realise that mere living together in the same locality can result in a conglomeration of very little sociological importance'.

Dennis, N. (1968) 'The Popularity of the Neighbourhood Community Idea', in *Readings in Urban Sociology*, ed. R. Pahl, Pergamon.
Henderson, P. and Thomas, D. (1980), *Skills in Neighbourhood Work*, Allen & Unwin.

Neurosis   A functional disorder of psychogenic origin (e.g. an obsessional neurosis in which a person is preoccupied by certain images and compelled to repetitive, ritualistic behaviour) distinguished from *psychosis*. However, systematic differences between the two (in terms of insight, social adaptation, etc.) are not easily established. 'Neurosis' has to be understood in terms of the various theories that describe and explain it. Harry Stack Sullivan talks of the neuroses as substitutive processes (the disintegrative processes are the psychoses); Adler believed that neuroses developed through incompatibility between the ideal self and the environment; Freud saw their origins in repression, particularly repression of the *oedipal* wish. The term is significant in welfare as an attempt to classify mental disturbance used by workers in the mental health services which also has implications for the 'ordering' of the mentally ill. See also *Madness*.

Horney, K. (1951) *Neurosis and Human Growth*, Routledge & Kegan Paul.

NON-JUDGMENTAL ATTITUDE

Ryle, A. (1967) *Neurosis in the Ordinary Family: a Psychiatric Survey*, Mind and Medicine Monograph no. 15, Tavistock.

New towns The notion of establishing new urban centres or significantly and deliberately expanding existing small towns was put into practice in the town and country planning era following World War II through the New Towns Act 1946 and the Town Development Act 1952. However, this legislation relied on an inheritance of ideas of urban renewal and the relations between town and country which went back at least until Ebenezer Howard's Garden City Scheme. New towns, comprehensively planned by a development agency and with a balanced social structure, have been created for several different purposes: to accommodate metropolitan growth, to provide an urban centre for a rural area, to accommodate the growth of a particular industry. The coherence and success of the New Towns Programme and of its constituent ideas, such as the balance in social structure, has recently been seriously questioned (Aldridge). Others see the New Town Development Corporation as an innovation of wide significance in urban regeneration.

Aldridge, M. (1979) *The British New Towns: a Programme without a Policy*, Routledge & Kegan Paul.

Cresswell, P. and Thomas R. (1973) 'The New Town Idea', Open University, DT 201, Urban Development, Unit 26.

Heraud, B. (1975) 'The New Towns: a Philosophy of Community', in *The Sociology of Community Action*, ed. P. Leonard, Sociological Review Monograph no. 21, University of Keele.

N

Non-accidental injury See *Family violence*

Non-judgmental attitude Biestek defines the non-judgmental attitude as 'a quality of the casework relationship' and argues that it is 'based on a conviction that the casework function excludes assigning guilt or innocence ... but does include making evaluative judgements about the attitudes, standards, or actions of the client ...' Ramsey more helpfully seeks to grasp what 'judgmental' means, and discovers at least seven different contexts in which the notion is used: condemning behaviour

129

under a particular description (as sin), imposing a dogmatic interpretation on a situation, working with undue reliance on prior notions, imposing strict disciplinary rules, manipulating, uttering warnings, pronouncing absolution. Whatever else the principle of being non-judgmental does it certainly encourages the avoidance of something seen as unhelpful or as demeaning. It is important to note that being judgmental is different from judging something or someone, from persuading or from directing them.

Biestek, F. (1961) *The Casework Relationship*, Allen & Unwin, pp. 89-99.

Ramsey, I. (1976) 'On Not Being Judgmental', in *Talking about Welfare*, ed. N. Timms and D. Watson, Routledge & Kegan Paul.

Stalley, R. (1978) 'Non-judgmental Attitudes', in *Philosophy in Social Work*, ed. N. Timms and D. Watson, Routledge & Kegan Paul.

Object-relations theory Associated usually with the work of Klein, Fairbairn, Winnicott, and Guntrip. The term 'object' seems misleading, and Gregory has remarked: 'Perhaps only in psycho-analysis could such an inappropriate term be used to designate the essentially human.' 'Objects' in psychodynamic theory are people or parts of people (a mother's breast would be a part-object, and a mother in her completeness would be a whole object) existing in the outer world or as internalised occupants of a person's inner world. The theory assumes that *ego* not only reacts to and adapts to its objects but is also constituted by its object-relations: *libido* is seen as primarily not pleasure – but object-seeking. The emphasis on the inner world and on relationships has made this theory attractive to social workers seeking to explain and to describe human behaviour.

Gregory, I. (1975) 'Psycho-analysis, Human Nature and Human
    Conduct', in *Nature and Conduct*, ed. R. Peters, Macmillan.
Guntrip, H. (1973) *Personality Structure and Human Interaction*,
    Hogarth Press.

Oedipal complex The oedipal complex or conflict was original-ly a Freudian term describing the child's genital wish for the parent of the opposite sex. The term was first used in relation to male development and requires some elaboration in application to girls, though Jung's less exclusively sexual interpretation avoids this. In the ancient Greek legend in which Oedipus murders his father, marries his mother, and inherits the kingdom we can discern the most important aspects of Freud's theory: the idea of inevitability (the complex is an unavoidable phase in normal development) and of unconsciousness (Oedipus did

131

none of these things wittingly); and also the notion of reward or inheritance (according to Freud the complex leads to fears of castration on the part of the child but also directly to the *super-ego*).

Old people The 'old' are sometimes defined as those who live beyond the official age of retirement, 60 for women and 65 for men. Clearly, retirement does mark an important stage in life, for which people should be adequately prepared, but the problems of old age are more varied and more variable in their distribution. It can no longer be assumed that the adequate welfare response to old age is ensuring appropriate pensions. Provision and policy for the old raises and should seek to answer a range of important questions: how is old age basically seen (as a time of increasing disengagement, for example); which particular groups of the old require a special response (for example, the so-called old-old or those aged 75 and over, the aged mentally infirm, the severely incapacitated); how do we understand the problems differentially encountered by the old (for instance, how do we distinguish loneliness from isolation, and isolation from desolation)?

Davies, B. and Knapp, M. (1981) *Old People's Homes and the Production of Welfare*, Routledge & Kegan Paul.
Tinker, A. (1981) *The Elderly in Modern Society*, Longman.

Ombudsman What has been called the ombudsman idea (i.e. the appointment of an official to hear and 'adjudicate' complaints against the actions of governmental agents) originated in Sweden in 1713 when the Chancellor of Justice was appointed to investigate complaints against royal officials. The first 'ombudsman' in Britain was appointed under the Parliamentary Commissioner Act 1967 to investigate complaints of injustice through governmental maladministration referred by MPs. Acting as the Health Service Commissioner (1973), he has a wider brief in so far as he is able to investigate an alleged failure in a service or an alleged failure to provide a service, though not complaints in which clinical judgment of health service staff is in question. In 1974 Commissions for Local Administration were established to investigate possible cases of injustice caused by maladministration by local, water, or police authorities. See also *Complaints*.

Hyde, M. R. (1977) 'The Commission for Local Administration', in *Year Book of Social Policy in Britain, 1976*, ed. K. Jones, Routledge & Kegan Paul.

Stacey, F. (1978) *Ombudsmen Compared*, Clarendon.

One-parent families   A one-parent family consists of a father or a mother living without spouse (or not cohabiting) with his or her dependent child or children. The lone parent and his or her child or children may face special strains, whether the condition has arisen from death of the spouse, from break-up of the marriage or from the situation of unmarried motherhood. The Finer Committee on One-Parent Families (Cmnd 5629, HMSO, 1974) stressed that many one-parent families were able to cope well with their difficulties; an injustice would be done 'if an account of the disadvantages from which they suffer were to categorise them as a section of our society united in inadequacy, whether self-made or imposed'. None the less, children and their families tended to show symptoms of stress and the Committee took a serious view of the financial plight, recommending a guaranteed maintenance allowance. It is a sign of the changing social definition that in 1973 the National Council for the Unmarried Mother and her Child became the National Council for One-Parent Families: what was once seen as a discrete problem, that of the unmarried mother who did not give her child for adoption, has become recognised as a problem with much wider dimensions, and seeking a more diversified policy response.

George, V. and Wilding, P. (1972) *Motherless Families*, Routledge & Kegan Paul.

Leete, R. (1978) 'One-Parent Families: Numbers and Characteristics', *Population Trends*, HMSO, 13, pp. 4-9.

O

Organisation   In welfare this term is used not in the sense of social organisation (or the way in which parts of the social system are interdependent) but, less widely, to refer to groups of people established to fulfil certain social tasks (as in hospitals, schools, or voluntary agencies); in carrying out these tasks they evolve sets of interlocking roles and resulting patterns of behaviour. Social workers commonly refer to *agencies* when

speaking of social work organisations, but the term 'organisation' helps to set their concerns within a wider context illuminat-
ed by both sociology and psychology. Studies indicate that care
should be exercised in using organisations primarily in terms of
single, articulated goals and in accepting any classification of
organisations, for example one based on the idea of the primary
beneficiary. Social work may have an unavoidable organisational form and context, but 'organisations' are not lying around in
the real world waiting to be collected and studied; they are more
elusive than their common name may suggest.

Smith, G. (1979) *Social Work and the Sociology of Organisations*,
  Routledge & Kegan Paul.
Warham, J. (1977) *An Open Case: The Organisational Context of
  Social Work*, Routledge & Kegan Paul.

Parole The term refers to release on licence of selected prisoners before their expected date of release; it is a procedure for modifying a sentence of the court through administrative action. A parole scheme was established in Britain in 1967, following a White Paper (*The Adult Offender*, Cmnd 2852, HMSO, 1965). Prisoners who have served one-third or twelve months, whichever is the longer, of their term may be released on condition that they accept the supervision of a probation officer; the sentence is not revoked, so a person on parole who breaks a condition of the licence may be recalled to prison. The system of decision involves newly created bodies, the local review committee, the Home Office Parole Unit, and the Parole Board, which finally makes a recommendation to the Home Secretary.

West, D. (ed.) (1972) *The Future of Parole*, Duckworth.

Participation This term refers to acting as an agent in co-operative work with others rather than being a passive recipient of service or ministration. It has been considered a desirable objective in social casework since the *Charity Organisation Society* and has more recently come to be similarly regarded in residential work. *Contract* work can be seen as taking steps to ensure active participation on the part of clients. Participation is also used to refer to a desirable form of involvement over a range of services and processes, such as planning. It can be viewed as an end in itself, as a way of discovering how decisions and plans are likely to affect those most concerned, or as a way of establishing a new power base. Schemes to encourage

135

participation may take a number of forms – neighbourhood councils, adding consumers to decision-making bodies, devolving responsibilities to groups or committees of consumers, recognising particular groups for consultation purposes, or improving the flow of information through surveys and meetings. One major problem, of course, concerns the relationship between participation in these forms and the 'participative' form of government called representative democracy.

Hatch, S. (ed.) (1973) *Towards Participation in Local Services*, Fabian Tract 419.

Rose, H. (1976) 'Participation: the Icing on the Welfare Cake', in *Year Book of Social Policy in Britain, 1975*, ed. K. Jones *et al.*, Routledge & Kegan Paul.

Patch system This term refers to a way of organising local authority social work: a designated geographical area is assigned to one or more social workers, and referrals arising in that locality are taken by them. To work according to a patch system does not necessarily entail that each social worker is responsible for a separate part of the locality. It can be that a team is given responsibility for providing the full range of social work services in a defined area and for planning for its area as a whole. Workers operate with a high degree of autonomy and aim to form working links with formal and informal helping networks in 'their' locality. In some ways the 'patch' way of working recognises an early dictum of C. S. Loch, Secretary of the Charity Organisation Society – 'Know your district' – which could also be taken as implying, then as now, that the social worker was concerned both with the particular clients presented in the locality and also with the locality as such. Most of the patch teams contacted by Hadley and McGrath claimed to have 'a distinctive community-orientated philosophy and a system of organisation and management designed to implement it'.

Cooper, M. (1981) 'The Normanton Patch System', in *Deprivation, Participation and Community Action*, ed. L. Smith and D. Jones, Routledge & Kegan Paul.

Hadley, R. and McGrath, M. (eds) (1980) *Going Local*, NCVO Occasional Papers, no. 1, Bedford Square Press.

Hadley, R. and McGrath, M. (1981) 'Patch Systems in Social Services Departments: More than a Passing Fashion?', *Social Work Service*, 26, 13-19.

Paternalism Paternalism refers to a situation, usually negatively evaluated, whether particular legislation (e.g. the compulsory wearing of car seat-belts) or kinds of relationship (e.g. social workers instructing clients on how they ought to behave for their own good) are being considered. The term refers to an abuse or exaggeration of behaviour which is quite proper and possibly praiseworthy in its original form (i.e. paternal behaviour in a parental relationship). Weale argues that paternalistic intervention exists when a person's freedom is inhibited in an attempt to secure for him welfare improvements against his own judgment. He indicates three criteria against which paternalistic intervention should be evaluated: the interference with a person's own *freely* chosen life-plan must not be severe; the intervention should be justified by reference to some element in the subject's own life-plan; there is some evident failure of reason on the subject's part which results in their inability to determine their own ends. Dworkin is concerned with suggesting and justifying principles governing the acceptable use of paternalistic power in imposing restrictions on what J. S. Mill called 'self-regarding' conduct.

Dworkin, G. (1979) 'Paternalism', in *Philosophy, Politics and Society*, 5th series, ed. P. Laslett and J. Fishkin, Yale University Press.
Weale, A. (1978) 'Paternalism and Social Policy', *Journal of Social Policy*, 7, 157-72.

Person/Personal What is to count as 'a person' is a subject of strong argument. Quinton has identified five 'personifying characteristics': consciousness, capacity for abstract reasoning, will or agency, capacity for moral praise and moral blame, and capacity for personal relations. Each of these can be found in a stronger or weaker form (e.g. 'rationality may be abstract and linguistic or concrete and practical') and 'Where the characteristics are present in their strongest form there is a complete personality, where in their weaker form a restricted one' (A. Quinton, *The Nature of Things*, Routledge & Kegan Paul, 1973, pp. 104-5). Explicitly 'person/personal' is important in welfare because of the emphasis on *respect for persons* in social work and social policy. It is also significant in discussions of the justification and methods of welfare activity. So, it is argued that social

P

137

welfare intervention is essentially political or that it is primarily intensely personal.

Halmos, P. (1978) *The Personal and the Political*, Hutchinson.

Personal Constructs/Personal Construct theory The notion of Personal Constructs and the theory of Personal Constructs originated in the psychological work of George Kelly. Constructs are interpretations of events or the terms by which we choose systematically to pick out from the flux of events certain continuities or stable features. Kelly's theory takes the form of a fundamental postulate and eleven corollaries. It is postulated that 'A person's processes are psychologically channelized by ways in which he anticipates events' (Kelly, quoted in Sechrest). An example of one of Kelly's corollaries would be that a person's construction system is made up of a infinite number of dichotomous constructs. The theory has been used in the exploration of aspects of social work practice.

Philip, A. and McCulloch, J. (1968) 'Personal Construct Theory and Social Work Practice', *British Journal of Social and Clinical Psychology*, 7, 115-21.
Sechrest, L. (1964) 'The Psychology of Personal Constructs: George Kelly', in *Concepts of Personality*, ed. J. Wepman and R. Heine, Methuen.

Personal social services It could have been expected that talk of the *personal social services* might have led to the exploration of 'personal' as the major criterion for categorising certain services as personal, but the term, first coined by the Seebohm Committee, refers usually to a list of particular services (e.g. the former children's departments, local authority welfare departments, etc.). Sainsbury, however, sees the personal social services as 'those concerned with needs and difficulties which inhibit the individual's maximum social functioning, his freedom to develop his personality and to achieve his aspirations through relations with others ...' (p. 3).

Goldberg, E. and Hatch, S. (1981) *A New Look at the Personal Social Services*, Policy Studies Institute, Discussion Paper no. 4.
Sainsbury, E. (1977) *The Personal Social Services*, Pitman.

Personality   It is difficult to define personality except in terms of particular psychological theories. Thus, from a behaviourist view, personality might be seen as the end product of someone's habit system. From other viewpoints, personality is seen as the characteristics of an individual that transcend the different roles he plays or as the dynamic and relatively integrated organisation 'within' the individual of the psychophysical systems that determine the behaviour and thought that characterise him. For a Marxist, personality might be seen as a variable that is related to material conditions. Within welfare not much systematic curiosity has been expressed at the interaction between the systems of society and of personality, though Spinley's early work was suggestive of relevant concerns. Theories of personality have assumed importance for social workers in their attempts to understand the development of growth of personality and also as presenting distinct models of man.

Ruddock, R. (ed.) (1972) *Six Approaches to the Person*, Routledge & Kegan Paul.
Spinley, B. (1953) *The Deprived and the Privileged*, Routledge & Kegan Paul.
Strean, H. (1985) *Personality Theory and Social Work Practice*, Scarecrow Press.

Philanthropy   The term philanthropia is of ancient Greek origin and rich in meaning. It seems originally to have included a citizen's love toward his equals, a king's benevolence to his subjects, reverence towards particular groups such as the elderly, as well as concern for orphans, the sick, and strangers. In more recent times the term has been narrowed to refer to altruistic activity (or charity) towards particular groups. The study of philanthropic giving is of interest for those concerned with the development of ideas about welfare and to those interested in social structure and change. Philanthropists have increasingly become subjects of adverse criticism, at least since Mrs Jellyby's 'telescopic philanthropy' in Charles Dickens's novel *Bleak House* – or the observation that the comfortably-off ladies of the *Charity Organisation Society* 'scrimped and iced in the name of a cautious, statistical Christ'.

Constantelos, D. (1968) *Byzantine Philanthropy and Social Welfare*, Rutgers University Press.

PHILOSOPHY

Jordan, W. (1959) *Philanthropy in England, 1480–1660*, Allen & Unwin.
Rosenthal, J.T. (1972) *The Purchase of Paradise: the Social Function of Aristocratic Benevolence, 1307–1485*, Routledge & Kegan Paul.

Philosophy 'Philosophy' in a welfare context refers to a process of logical analysis or to the substantive objective or point of an activity or programme. In the first sense, it is being increasingly realised that welfare relies heavily on certain key concepts which call for philosophical analysis – community, need, equality, person, and so on. These and other concepts are not decorations on the surface of the real world. 'Activities and human actions generally are only identified and specified through a system of concepts. A pattern of determined activity is only what it is in so far as it is described, identified and conceived in a particular way, according to social and linguistic rules, standards and conventions' (Plant, p. 4). Philosophy in the second sense refers not to an activity (that of philosophising) but to justification, usually in high-flown language. When visitors on 'inspection' panels in social work education enquire earnestly of a particular educational programme's 'philosophy' or 'underlying philosophy' they seem to expect not an analysis of its major concepts but some brief solemnisation of its objectives.

Plant, R. (1974) *Community and Ideology: an Essay in Applied Social Philosophy*, Routledge & Kegan Paul, pp. 1–7.
Timms, N. and Watson, D. (1976) *Talking About Welfare*, Routledge & Kegan Paul, pp. 1–38.

Planning Planning, particularly in welfare, has overtones of *social engineering* according to some blueprint of Utopia, but most people plan at least to a degree. To plan is to decide on a specific objective, to calculate the action required to achieve it, and to commit scarce resources to reach it. In a welfare context problems of a conceptual nature abound: 'Social-welfare planning is complicated by fuzzy definitions and vagueness about what welfare can contribute to development. Disagreement still exists as to whether planning for social security is different from planning generally ...' (Madison, p. 295). Recently a number of relatively sophisticated techniques have been introduced into welfare as aids to more effective planning, such as Forward

Planning (e.g. in 1962 the Ministry of Health for the first time asked local authorities to submit ten-year plans for the development of their health and welfare services) or Programme Budgeting, the attempt to relate expenditure to objectives in a routine manner. Particular problems arise when planning involves more than one department and/or discipline, as, for example, in the Joint Care Planning between local authorities and health authorities. This approach, introduced in the 1970s, involves Joint Consultative Committees, multi-disciplinary groups of officers, and Joint Finance, an arrangement whereby Health Service resources may be used to support local authority spending if this is likely to produce a better overall return.

Booth, T. (ed.) (1979) *Planning for Welfare*, Blackwell and Martin Robertson.
Madison, B. (1980) *The Meaning of Social Policy: the Comparative Dimension in Social Policy*, Croom Helm, pp. 275-99.

Poor Law The Poor Law, which had dominated social policy in thought and in action since Tudor times was statutorily abolished in 1948, but it continues to be of significance in social welfare. It is often claimed that the Poor Law attitudes, even the stigmatised (*stigma*) status of 'pauper', survive in present arrangements, and that to understand the present 'regulations' of the poor we need to understand the formation of the modern state and its concern with the classification, settlement, and control of paupers, rogues, vagabonds, and sturdy beggars, and with relief outside and within the workhouse. Poor Law history is subject to considerable present attention and some reinterpretation: of particular importance to students of welfare history are the careful attempts to re-interpret received versions of the major points in that history, e.g. the Amendment Act of 1834 and the work of the Poor Law Commission, 1905-9.

Corrigan, P. and Corrigan, V. (1979) 'State Formation and Social Policy until 1871', in *Social Work, Welfare and the State*, ed. N. Parry *et al.*, Edward Arnold.
Fraser, D. (ed.) (1976) *The New Poor Law in the Nineteenth Century*, Macmillan.

Positive discrimination This term refers to a policy of favouring particularly needy groups or areas with an 'unfair' share of resources. The term is often used in relation to local areas. The Plowden Committee, 1967, argued for positive discrimination in relation to *Educational Priority Areas*; the Seebohm Report, 1968, referred to areas that should receive extra resources; and the *Community Development Projects* and *Urban Aid Programmes* also embodied ideas of positive discrimination. The selection of areas rather than individual people or families as objects of positive discrimination had the advantage of securing more resources without any test of individual need, but the notion of *compensation*, rather than positive re-utilisation, has been criticised, as have ideas concerning the causation and nature of 'locality' problems. Some argue that policies of positive discrimination have had success in transforming the views local inhabitants had of their problem, but Room has called attention to the frequently sorry fate of many of these policies: 'their loss of legitimacy in the eyes of the powerful and the intensified loss of legitimacy of those original sponsors in the eyes of the deprived. Not, however, that such loss of legitimacy necessarily evokes any overt threat to social order' (p. 245). Positive discrimination can also be seen more generally as a principle in welfare. Thus, Pinker has distinguished positive discrimination practised by the privileged on their own behalf, within a *selectivist* or *universalist* framework, from positive discrimination on behalf of or by the underprivileged within a framework of universalism. The latter, in his view, is 'the only form of selectivity compatible with the idea of a welfare society because its ultimate goal is the achievement of optimal rather than minimal standards' (p. 190).

Batley, R. (1978) 'From Poor Law to Positive Discrimination', *Journal of Social Policy*, 7, 305-28.
Pinker, R. (1971) *Social Theory and Social Policy*, Heinemann, pp. 182-200.
Room, G. (1979) *The Sociology of Welfare*, Blackwell and Martin Robertson.

Poverty   As idea and reality, poverty is of major significance in welfare. Three questions are of particular practical and theoretical significance: who counts as poor, how is poverty measured, and what forms should a welfare response take? Rein identifies three broad conceptions of poverty: subsistence (sufficient to keep body and soul in a working state, one might say); equality (so that those are poor who, compared with others, lack opportunity and means to participate fully in the life of society); and externality (or the social consequences of poverty for the rest of society). Problems of measurement have become much more complex since the early studies of Charles Booth (*Life and Labour of the People in London*), especially now that the international context is seen as essential. Recent systematic attempts in America and, to a less organised extent in Britain, to combat the effects of poverty through central government initiatives have raised important questions concerning the delivery and effectiveness of innovative services, and the extent to which the problem of poverty demands redesigned services, redistributed resources, or radical social change. One highly-placed administrator in the American War on Poverty believed firmly in the second of these, though not everyone would see them as complete alternatives: 'What we must have is more income redistribution. After long hours of sociological discourse, one fact remains clear: the poor do not have enough money.' The work of the Royal Commission on the Distribution of Income and Wealth in this country shows how difficult income redistribution is (O'Higgins).

Higgins, J. (1978) *The Poverty Business: Britain and America*, Blackwell and Martin Robertson.
O'Higgins, M. (1980) 'Income Distribution and Social Policy: an Assessment after the Royal Commission on the Distribution of Income and Wealth', in *Year Book of Social Policy in Britain, 1979*, ed. M. Brown and S. Baldwin, Routledge & Kegan Paul.
Rein, M. (1970) 'Definition and Measurement of Poverty', in *The Concept of Poverty*, ed. P. Townsend, Heinemann.
Townsend, P. (1979) *Poverty in the United Kingdom*, Penguin.

Poverty trap   This term was coined in the early 1970s to refer to factors which prevented families raising their net income through increasing their earnings: these factors were outside their control. A family is trapped in and by poverty through the interaction of increased earnings, increases in tax payments, and national insurance contributions and the conditions of eligibility for coincidental means-tested *benefits*. Eligibility for several benefits at the same time can be affected by any increase in earnings. So, in 1976, for example, it was estimated that 50,000 families could be worse off in terms of net income after a £1 rise in earnings. Different kinds of poverty trap affect those in work and those not in work: the problem 'is endemic to means-tested benefits and is virtually impossible to avoid' (National Consumer Council).

National Consumer Council (1976) *Means-Tested Benefits*, pp. 22-4.
Royal Commission on the Distribution of Income and Wealth (1978) *Lower Incomes*, report no. 6, Cmnd 7175, HMSO.

Power Like some other notions in welfare discourse, the concept of power is a contested one: much hangs on how power is defined and its exercise detected. A person's view of power and the way it is legitimised (*authority*) is closely connected to his view of society. Lucas has distinguished power from the related ideas of influence and authority (not always clearly differentiated in welfare discussions) as follows:

'A man, or body of men, *has authority* if it follows from his saying "Let X happen", that X ought to happen ... A man, or body of men, *has power* if it results from his saying, "Let X happen" that X does happen ... A man, or body of men, *has influence* if the result of his saying "Let X happen", is that other people will say (perhaps only to themselves), "Let X happen" '(p. 16). This discusses the notions in the explicit context of 'saying', 'instructing', 'forcing', but others have argued that power is more significantly exercised in preventing matters ever getting to the point of speech, instruction, and so on: it is not decisions that should be studied in order to show who is powerful, but 'non-decisions'. Lukes has gone further than this 'by saying that A exercises power over B when A affects B in a manner contrary to B's interests.'

Lucas, J. (1966) *The Principles of Politics*, Clarendon Press.
Lukes, S. (1974) *Power: a Radical View*, Macmillan.
McLachlan, H. (1981) 'Is "Power" an Evaluative Concept?', *British Journal of Sociology*, 32, 392-410.

Prejudice 'Prejudice' can be described as a well-organised enduring predisposition towards negative or hostile appraisals: one is predisposed to negative judgments that require no supporting evidence in the situation. Prejudice may or may not lead to behaviour that is discriminative (*discrimination*). Prejudice has been explained in two main ways: those psychological influences that make individual bigots or as a function of the social group to which one belongs (Davey). In the former perspective, prejudice is invariably seen as pathological, but in the latter it can be seen as a 'rational' response to the systematically inferior position of one's group. Prejudice is significant in welfare in race relations policies and with regard to any group that is labelled 'minority'. It is also important, but has been little studied, in connection with social work.

Davey, A. (1981) 'Prejudice and Group Conflict', *Patterns of Prejudice*, 15, 3-14.
Smith, N. and McCulloch, J. (1978) 'Measuring Attitudes towards the Disabled', *International Journal of Rehabilitation Research*, 1, 187-97.

Presenting problem This term is used in social casework to distinguish what is initially offered by client or referring agent as the problem to be resolved from the 'real' or 'basic' problem as this comes to be defined. The presenting problem can be seen as a *symptom*, a representation or a concealment of the 'real' or 'basic' problem, and so the term has an important place in the language of social casework. The term is also important in considering whether the organisation or style of welfare activity encourages users of particular services to present their problems in particular ways. Social workers also use the term 'presents' (as in 'Mrs X presents as a person who is no stranger to grief') to describe relatively firm impressions gained from initial contact, though the term seems also to refer to the impression intended by the client.

P

Prevention It is considered better to prevent than to cure in welfare, as in many other fields of activity, but what is being forestalled, stifled, or not allowed to come into being is not always clear. Within the study and practice of public health it is usual to distinguish three levels of prevention. Primary prevention concerns steps to obviate the development of the disease in susceptible populations; secondary prevention takes the form of early diagnosis and prompt treatment once the presence of the disease is suspected; tertiary prevention aims at the limitation of the disability caused by the illness. Prevention was a particular objective for Children's Departments (*child care service*), but it was not always clear whether what was to be prevented was the child coming into care, his or her permanent harm, or the family and material conditions leading to the likelihood of public care. In this as in other areas of welfare (such as mental health) it is now appreciated that prevention at any of the levels mentioned above requires a varied set of interacting measures. While discussions of prevention usually call for more research, it is important, as Barter observed in relation to preventive mental health services, 'to appreciate how much we actually do know about populations at risk, the processes by which people become subject to psychological problems or remain free of them, and effective early intervention.'

Barter, J. (1979) 'Prevention', in *Seebohm Across Three Decades*, ed. J. Cypher, BASW Publications.
Billis, D. (1981) 'At Risk of Prevention', *Journal of Social Policy*, 10, 367-79.
DHSS (1976) *Prevention and Health: Everybody's Business*, HMSO.

Primary health care The term 'primary health care' conveys a comparatively new conceptualisation of the role of the general medical practitioner and the group of health visitors, nurses, etc. increasingly associated with the GP. It refers to the tasks of the diagnosis, treatment, and management near home of undifferentiated illness in a defined population to whom the doctor is accessible and for whom he accepts a continuing responsibility; and also to the prevention of disease and the maintenance of health. In developing countries the primary health worker is a non-medical practitioner, the member of the health care team closest to the community.

Hicks, D. (1976) *Primary Health Care: a Review*, DHSS/HMSO.
Rushton, A. and Briscoe, M. (1981) 'Social Work as an Aspect of Primary Health Care: the Social Worker's View', *British Journal of Social Work*, 11, 61-76.

Principles   Principles may be moral (social workers uphold the principle of client self-determination) or technical (to assume people are self-directing is an indispensable means of making them behave in a self-directing manner). Another way of making this distinction is to say that principles of conduct can be adopted as rules or guidelines or as ideals. 'Principle' may figure in an account of or in an explanation of performance. These distinctions are not always observed in social welfare, nor is it recognised that principles of conduct may well conflict in particular situations, that we cannot realise all our ideals or approximate to them, that we cannot follow all the rules applicable to a situation. So, in discussions of the principle of client *self-determination*, it is sometimes assumed that because other principles may conflict or even in some situations be decisive, such an outcome somehow weakens the former principle. See also *Values*.

Biestek, F. (1961) *The Casework Relationship*, Allen & Unwin.

Priorities   A priority is a line of action given precedence over other possibilities that are judged to be feasible at the time: the precedence is shown in immediacy of attention and/or the amount of resources devoted. Priorities can be established at different levels: for example, the DHSS Consultative Document on *Priorities for Health and Personal Social Services in England* (HMSO, 1976) was the first attempt in those areas by central government to establish priorities; it is also possible to speak of priorities within a particular local authority or within an individual social worker's *caseload*. At any level a distinction can be made between strategic priorities, concerned with overall allocation of available resources, and operational priorities, specifying how the total amounts of money, manpower, buildings, etc., will be used in terms of *service delivery*. Priorities can be established between localities (as in the different area priority policies, such as Housing Action Areas, and General Improvement Areas in housing legislation), between types of programme (e.g. *community care* contrasted with direct treatment), or between services for different client groups (e.g. the elderly). Priorities can be explicitly chosen after a rank ordering of the possible and feasible or become apparent as a result of people

147

coming to devote more time, resources, etc., to certain areas of activity. It is unclear how many priorities can be entertained by a person or programme at any one time. When a particular group or activity is said to have low priority what is usually meant is that it has no priority.

Algie, J. (1980) 'Priorities in Personal Social Services', in *Year Book of Social Policy in Britain, 1978*, ed. M. Brown and S. Baldwin, Routledge & Kegan Paul.
Whitmore, R. and Fuller, R. (1980) 'Priority Planning in an Area Social Services Team', *British Journal of Social Work*, 10, 277-92.

Prison welfare   The term 'prison welfare officer' is no longer in use – probation officers work in the field or in HM prisons – but the function of 'through-care', which it is hoped begins immediately after sentence, is of pressing contemporary significance. Since 1967 *probation and after-care* officers have been appointed on secondment to prisons. This exercise is an interesting example of the problems of creating a specialised welfare function, differentiated from the work of other staff (e.g. prison officers), in an environment not designed with therapy or self-realisation in mind. Prison welfare work is the responsibility both of the prison governor and of the chief probation officer. Prison welfare work can be directed towards the prisoner, or his family, or the prison system itself, but it is generally held that Home Office reports paint an unrealistic picture of possible achievements.

Pratt, M. (1975) 'Stress and Opportunity in the Role of the Prison Welfare Officer', *British Journal of Social Work*, 5, 379-96.
Smith, D. (1979) 'Probation Officers in Prison', in *Creative Social Work*, ed. W. Jordan and D. Brandon, Blackwell.

Probation and After-Care Service   A long-established service, originating in the Police Court Mission of the late nineteenth century, re-named in 1967 the Probation and After-Care Service. The Probation of Offenders Act 1907 defined the role of the probation officer as 'to advise, assist and befriend', and this has for long seemed to summarise the core of the work. Probation officers undertake a wide range of social work. The major functions are to supervise persons on probation or supervision orders, preparation of *Social Enquiry Reports* and after-care supervision of offenders on *parole*, as well as providing a social work service in prisons. Probation officers are responsible for serving the domestic court and preparing welfare reports in divorce cases concerning children. Increasingly, new ways of working with pre-delinquents and offering help in the community are being explored. *Community service* orders are administered by the Probation and After-Care Service.

Jarvis, F. (1976) *Probation Officers' Manual*, 2nd ed., Butterworth.

Problem family A term first coined in the 1940s, though the idea of a special problem group responsible for a whole range of problems in society is somewhat older. The term refers to a heterogeneous collection of families characterised by multiple problems (it used to be said that a family with a problem was different from a problem family), consequent contact with a number of 'helping' agencies who, because of the intractability of the family's problems, were unable to effect beneficial change, particularly in the organisation of daily life and in child care. A specialised form of social work was derived in response to these characteristics (Family Service Units), and attempts were made to understand the continued plight of these families in terms of emotional immaturity (Irvine) or response to severe material deprivation. The term has returned to more common use since the attention given to the idea of the cycle of *deprivation*, but more weight is now given to processes whereby families are *labelled* and to social-class factors.

Irvine, E. E. (1979) *Social Work and Human Problems*, Pergamon, pp. 95-155.
Rutter, M. and Madge, N. (1976) *Cycles of Disadvantage*, Heinemann.

Process recording Social workers, in training and in practice, can keep records of their work of different kinds (for example, summary records compress the most important actions and features in a case; diagnostic records concentrate on the changing understanding of a situation). Process recording originated in social casework, but is applicable in work with groups in a community or a more formal setting; it is applicable

149

whenever a process of one kind or another is significant for the work in hand. The object of the recording is to show the flow of the process (whether process is seen as that of politics or *relationship*, or of *help*) in sufficient detail so that *understanding* is cumulatively increased and a judgment can be made of the progress of work at any point. Process recording, which is often lengthy (though processes can, of course, be summarised), is used on training courses and is sometimes recommended for cases felt to be especially difficult.

Timms, N. (1972) *Recording in Social Work*, Routledge & Kegan Paul.

Profession/Professional relationship Professions are often defined in a rather idealised fashion: occupations with a service orientation whose work is systematically and continuously informed by a growing body of knowledge peculiar to the practitioner and governed by an acknowledged code of ethics. In welfare the relationship that social workers establish or ought to establish with their *clients* is similarly treated, so that it is seen not so much as a relationship governed by certain rules (e.g. do not exploit) but as one with an unspecifiable, almost mystical, content (*the* professional relationship). Professions/professional relationships are significant in a welfare context for two further reasons. First, effective *service delivery* is often considered to depend on the joint or related efforts of a number of distinct occupations – medicine, education, social work, and so on. Within such a grouping occupations are at different stages of professionalisation; it is sometimes suggested that social work is a semi-profession. Second, the professional identity of social work has been a question (often in examination papers) from at least 1915 – is social work a profession? It matters, of course, what *kind* of profession one is talking about (Johnson). Within the context of profession the definition, job descriptions, and training of those described as para-professionals are of theoretical and practical importance. Also of importance are the procedures and processes (of professional socialisation) whereby a person becomes recognised as a professional.

Austin, M. (1978) *Professionals and Paraprofessionals*, Human Sciences Press.
Johnson, T. (1972) *Professions and Power*, Macmillan.

Timms, N. and Timms, R. (1977) *Perspectives in Social Work*, Routledge & Kegan Paul, pp.196-207.

Psychiatric deluge   A description by Woodroofe of the unchallenged dominance of psychoanalytic (rather than generally psychiatric) ideas in American social work in the years following World War I. Woodroofe believed that the deluge came to England a decade or so later, but Yelloly's historical study argues that the situation resembled a drought rather than a deluge. Detailed research in America suggests that the dominance is more discernible in social work writing than in social work practice. (Field's is the latest study.)

Field, M. (1980) 'Social Casework Practice during the Psychiatric Deluge', *Social Service Review*, 54, 482-507.
Woodroofe, K. (1962) *From Charity to Social Work*, Routledge & Kegan Paul, Ch. 6, 'The Psychiatric Deluge'.
Yelloly, M. (1980) *Social Work Theory and Psychoanalysis*, Van Nostrand Reinhold.

Psychiatric social work   Psychiatric social workers work in organisations dealing with people who are mentally ill or emotionally disturbed; they usually work closely with psychiatrists. Typical workplaces for the psychiatric social worker would be the mental hospital and the child guidance clinic. The term is not in common use since the development of general training which replaced specialist training. For a considerable period the specially trained psychiatric social worker played an important part in the general development of social work in this country.

Irvine, E.E. (1978) 'Psychiatric Social Work', in E. Younghusband, *Social Work in Britain 1950-1975*, Allen & Unwin, vol. 1, pp. 176-94.
Timms, N. (1964) *Psychiatric Social Work in Great Britain, 1939-1964*, Routledge & Kegan Paul.

Psychopath   A term with a long and troubled history in relation both to the constituent notions of abnormal personality, resulting in behaviour falling between normality and *psychosis*, of persistent anti-social conduct, lack of conscience and of response to remedial measures, and to attempts to distinguish between types of psychopath. For example, a distinction has been made between aggressive and inadequate psychopath or between such

151

categories as the irresolute, the fanatical, and so on. A legal definition of psychopathic disorder is given in the Mental Health Act 1959 Section 4(3): 'a persistent disorder or disability of mind (whether or not including subnormality of intelligence) which results in abnormally aggressive or seriously irresponsible conduct on the part of the patient, and requires or is susceptible to medical treatment.' This does not assume that psychopathic disorder is a single entity, and the Butler Committee observed that 'there is now a multiplicity of opinions as to the aetiology, symptoms and treatment of "psychopathy", which is only to be understood by reference to the particular sense in which the term is being employed by the psychiatrist in question.' In a social welfare context consideration of psychopathy raises significant questions of the delineation of the boundaries between illness and moral misconduct and of the justification and effectiveness of particular treatments.

Home Office, (Butler) Committee on Mentally Abnormal Offenders (1975) *Report*, Cmnd 6244, HMSO, Ch. 5, 'Psychopaths'.
Prins, H. (1980) *Offenders, Deviants or Patients?: an Introduction to the Study of Socio-forensic Problems*, Tavistock.

Psychoses   These are usually considered to be more serious kinds of mental illness, which have a pervasive effect on the personality. They can be divided into the affective disorders (e.g. *depression*) and *schizophrenia (irrationality)*.

Irvine, E. (1979) 'Psychosis in Parents: Mental Illness as a Problem for the Family', in Irvine, *Social Work and Human Problems*, Pergamon.

Psychosomatic   This term refers to certain disorders in which psychogenic factors play a crucial causative role. Tuke, an early figure in the reform of mental health provision, argued that 'mind or brain influences, excites, perverts or depresses the sensory functions, muscular contraction, nutrition and secretion.' The central notion expressed in the term is that 'body' and 'mind/ emotion' are to be seen as an interacting unity. None the less, particular disorders have been singled out as 'psychosomatic', for instance asthma and various ulcerative conditions.

Punishment The idea of punishment can be used rather loosely, as in reference to 'punitive' attitudes on the part of people in positions of power. More strictly the notion of punishment contains a number of elements: punishment is something unpleasant inflicted by an authority for an offence of which the offender is guilty. Punishment is not the result of natural occurrence (such as a road accident), neither is it something imposed for the common good regardless of the culpability of someone judged to be an offender. Important general questions arise in any consideration of the possible justification of the right to punishment: retributivists look to what is the fitting response to identified wrongdoing, whilst others look to the likely consequences of punishment in the reform of the offender or the deterrence of others from similar kinds of rule-breaking. Within welfare, important considerations revolve around the idea of human responsibility for actions.

Bean, P. (1981) *Punishment: a Philosophical Criminological Inquiry*, Martin Robertson.

Honderich, T. (1976) *Punishment: the Supposed Justification*. Routledge & Kegan Paul.

Walker, N. (1980) *Punishment, Danger and Stigma*, Blackwell.

Wootton, B. (1978) *Crime and Penal Policy*, Allen & Unwin.

P

Quota system   A quota indicates a maximum proportion of a particular group that should be included in an organisation's service population (e.g. black children in 'white' schools). One of the best-known quotas in welfare concerns those on the Disabled Persons Employment Register. Under the Disabled Persons (Employment) Act 1944, employers of twenty workers or more are required to take up to 3 per cent of their staff from those on the Register. The discussion document, *Review of the Quota Scheme for the Employers of Disabled People* (1980) which followed a review by the Manpower Services Commission, suggested that the quota system for disabled people should be abandoned. It has been argued that the quota system for the disabled has never been markedly successful in placing disabled people in open employment, but that the legislation has subsequently taken on symbolic significance, standing for such widely shared values as the right to work and the independence believed to be within the reach of the disabled. Despite this, it now (July 1981) appears that this quota will be abolished, though some statutory protection will be retained. See also *Disability*.

Bolderson, H. (1980) 'Origins of the Disabled Persons Employment Quota and its Symbolic Significance', *Journal of Social Policy*, 9, 169-86.

R

Race relations Central government has been involved with a developing immigration policy (*immigration*) since 1962, but before 1965 was little involved with the treatment of coloured people, apart from pursuing a policy of dispersal in relation to education. After 1965 two major policies were pursued in attempts to combat racial discrimination (*discrimination*) and to foster what were termed good *community relations*. The first policy centred on the Race Relations Board and the Community Relations Commission (united in 1976 in the Commission for Racial Equality); the second on local Community Relations Councils (which now exist in about a hundred areas) and, at least in its beginnings, on the Inner City Programmes. One of the most pressing problems to be faced in a wide range of social provision is the extent to which British society is seen and accepted as a multi-racial society. See also *Inner city, Community relations, Unemployment.*

Little, A. (1977) 'The Race Relations Act, 1976', in *Year Book of Social Policy in Britain, 1976*, ed. K. Jones, Routledge & Kegan Paul.

Radical social work A radical is someone who works, more or less actively and consistently, for a basic or 'root' change in the governance, including the governing ideas, of any general social system. The change could be either in a 'leftward' or 'right-wing' direction, but usually in 'radical social work' the former is intended. So Galper, after reviewing some attempted definitions, states that 'radical social work is social work that contributes to building a movement for the transformation to socialism by its efforts in and through the social services. Radical social work, in this understanding, is socialist social work' (p. 10). However, those who are called or call themselves 'radical social workers' share neither the same political philosophy nor the same vision of an altered social work practice: they are as likely to be anarchists as Marxists, Christian Socialists as followers of different kinds of mystical tradition. Nor is radicalism necessarily associated with any particular mode: a radical casework, aiming, for instance, at raising the consciousness of poor people about their true class situation, is as conceivable as radical community work. Particular problems arise from grasping the connections between radical theorising and a radically changed practice, and appreciating the degree to which so-called traditional social work possesses radical tendencies. See also *Marxist theory*.

Galper, J. (1980) *Social Work Practice: a Radical Perspective*, Prentice-Hall.

Webb, D. (1981) 'Themes and Continuities in Radical and Traditional Social Work', *British Journal of Social Work*, 11, 143-58.

Rationality   In ordinary, everyday language we refer both to means to achieve objectives and to the objectives themselves as rational: the means were sensible and appropriate, as was the goal. Within the specialised languages of philosophy and sociology, 'rational' has a special place, and we sometimes speak of rationality as the single characteristic differentiating human from animal nature. It is sensible to take a clue from this, and not seek for an exclusive definition of rationality. Rational behaviour, then, may be taken to refer to the adoption of what the actor believes to be the most efficient means to his ends and to what is actually the most efficient means; his ends can be related to long-term goals or to the goals the actor ought to seek. In a welfare context, particularly one in which a comparative approach is made between social provision in different social cultures, one of the crucial questions concerns the extent to which criteria of rationality are universal. Lukes argues that some criteria are applicable in any context. The distinction between rational belief and rational action, and the use of the idea of rationality to assess social choices, are also significant for welfare discourse. See also *Irrationality*.

Lukes, S. (1970) 'Some Problems about Rationality', in *Rationality*, ed. B. Wilson, Blackwell.
Mortimore, G. (1976) 'Rational Social Choice', in *Rationality and the Social Sciences*, ed. S. Benn and G. Mortimore, Routledge & Kegan Paul.

Rationing Rationing is a way of systematically apportioning shares of scarce resources: rationing may be publicly acknowledged according to authorised criteria or may be accomplished through various informal procedures, such as deterrence, delay or misunderstanding. Judge has distinguished two levels of rationing: financial rationing is concerned with the high-level allocation of resources between competing claims, while service rationing refers to implicit or explicit procedures by which clients obtain access to social policy goods and services (or presumably do not). The debate about *universalism* and *selectivity*, and various schemes of *area* priority is concerned with explicit procedures whereby some areas/programmes/people receive more resources than others. Pricing is one method of rationing that has been seriously considered in welfare. 'All social services', it has been suggested, 'are rationed. Yet the effects of such rationing on the client are rarely fully explored' (Foster).

Foster, P. (1979) 'The Informal Rationing of Primary Medical Care', *Journal of Social Policy*, 8, 489-508.
Judge, K. (1978) *Rationing Social Services*, Heinemann.
Scrivens, E. (1979) 'Towards a Theory of Rationing', *Social Policy and Administration*, 13, 53-64.

Reality In a general sense reality is that which is the case. In a welfare context reality is what has to be changed or adjusted to. So Marshall argues that the distinctive function of a welfare service is 'to help those afflicted with disabilities or overwhelmed by circumstances to come to terms with life as it is, or as it can be made to be' (T. Marshall, *The Right to Welfare*, Heinemann, 1981, p. 18). Marxists argue that in order to understand any situation its material reality has to be grasped. Social workers often refer to reality-testing as one of the main functions of the personality, and to reality *confrontation* or to recognition of the reality of a situation as an objective in social work. More recently a distinct variety of therapy called 'reality therapy' has been developed. This focuses on immediate behaviour rather than feelings, on clients evaluating their actions, being committed to a plan of change, and 'no excuses'.

Glasser, W. and Zunin, L. (1973) 'Reality Therapy', in *Current Psychotherapies*, ed. R. Corsini, Peacock.

Reassurance   To reassure someone is to restore their confidence in their personal qualities, or in some aspect of present reality or in the future. It is a term used fairly frequently in social work, in two main ways. It can be used to explain behaviour (for example, sexual promiscuity could be seen as the result of a search for reassurance about one's sexual identity). It can also be used to describe the social worker's direct or indirect response to a client: the social worker could express confidence in the client's ability to solve a particular problem or could implicitly convey such confidence in assumptions of success. Reassurance is treated with some caution in certain social work texts, but this arises from failure to distinguish it from false reassurance, when there are insufficient grounds for the stated confidence, and from over-reassurance, when the social worker goes beyond what the grounds justify.

Rebate   To rebate is to make or allow a deduction in a sum otherwise fixed, as in deductions from full rents or full rates. The Housing Finance Act 1972 required local authorities to establish schemes of rent rebate for council-house tenants (and rent allowances for those in privately-owned accommodation). The present scheme of rate rebate operates under the Local Government Act 1974. Rebates under each Act are calculated on the basis of rent/rate, income, and needs allowance. The government is exploring (1981) the possibility of creating a single scheme of housing benefit, covering all low-income households, which would replace rate and rent rebates and allowances and the rent element in supplementary benefit.

Reciprocity   To reciprocate is to make a return, more or less acknowledged by the actors, for a benefit or favour received; relationships are often characterised by a high degree of reciprocity over a period of time. The notion of reciprocity is significant in social welfare for at least three reasons. First, mutual relationships between governments affecting the welfare of their citizens in certain respects often take the form of reciprocal arrangements. Second, reciprocity has for long figured in social welfare history as a basis for social welfare, and indeed citizenship itself. As Urwick argued: 'In the infinitely complex relationship of neighbour to neighbour, our actions are so numerous and sometimes so trivial that we do not think it worth while to look for any exact balance of act and reaction. But obviously the reciprocity must be there, or the social good – let us rather say, the social condition of any good – would not be maintained.' More recently, however, the idea of the unilateral *gift* as the basis of welfare has been explored. Third, the ability to engage in relationships marked by reciprocity may well be one of the important conditions for the development of patterns of effective informal care among neighbours, friends, and relatives.

Gouldner, A. (1973) *For Sociology*, Basic Books. Ch. 8, 'The Norm of Reciprocity', Ch. 9, 'The Importance of Something for Nothing'.
Urwick, E. (1930) 'The Principle of Reciprocity in Social Life and Action', London.
Uttley, S. (1980) 'The Welfare Exchange Reconsidered', *Journal of Social Policy*, 9, 187-205.

Recording   From the beginning of modern social work there has been emphasis on the importance of social work recording (as in the case record or case papers of the *Charity Organisation Society*). Thinking and practice is more advanced in relation to casework recording, and the recording of the ramifications of multi-scale interventions in group work and community work poses particular problems. Recording has a number of objectives: to render an account of service, to improve service and professional performance, as an aid to *supervision* of staff or students, as a possible contribution to research. It is doubtful, however, that much actual use is made of social work records. Problems of accuracy and objectivity are crucial, as are ethical questions concerning a person's right to consult 'their own record' and the uses to which information contained in the

159

records can be put. See also *Process recording, Confidentiality*.
Timms, N. (1972) *Recording in Social Work*, Routledge & Kegan Paul.

Referral If a person goes to a social agency on his own initiative he may be described for statistical purposes as a self-referral or as self-referred, provided he is taken on as 'a case'. All other cases come through some intermediary, direct or indirect (so, a person could be referred to a social agency in a telephone call, or by conversation or letter). What occurs during the process of referral (do those referred from one social agency to another feel 'rejected' by the former or put in touch with a more appropriate source?) is not well understood, and the distinction between self-referral and other kinds of referral is too crude to catch the complex, interweaving pathways by which people approach sources of help. 'Although "referral" is used to describe the process of people being sent by someone to someone, it is an ambiguous term which often fails to convey what was involved in reaching an agency and meeting an appropriate staff member' (S. Rees, *Social Work Face to Face*, Edward Arnold, 1978, p. 15).

Regional Planning Committee/Children's Regional Planning Committee These committees were established for each of the twelve regions in England and Wales under the 1969 Children and Young Persons Act to enable planning and use of provision over a wider area than a single local authority and to secure integrated provision (first, of residential accommodation) between local authorities and voluntary children's societies that had agreed to accept assisted or controlled status. Members of the Regional Planning Committees are nominated by local authorities; guidelines issued by the Department of Health and Social Security in 1972 suggested that juvenile court magistrates and probation officers were particularly suitable for co-option.

Register A register is an official list maintained for certain purposes (such as to ensure special attention or service). It is not always the case that these purposes are accomplished. It is questionable, for instance, how far the Disabled Persons

Employment Register actually helps the disabled to find work. Local authorities maintain registers of the blind, the partially sighted, the deaf, hard of hearing, and of other handicapped people, but full registration has not yet been achieved. In 1974 a DHSS circular initiated a system of management of suspected and actual cases of non-accidental injury to children which included the establishment of registers. These are usually maintained by the social services department, the Area Health Authority or by a Special Unit of the NSPCC. A circular of 1980 outlines criteria for registration which now include physical injury and neglect, failure to thrive and emotional abuse, and children in the same household as a person previously involved in child abuse. These criteria have been criticised as too broad and as failing to identify children at *risk* of abuse. Structural arrangements in relation to child abuse, including area review committees, *case conferences*, and 'at risk' registers are discussed in Hallett and Stevenson (1980).

Hallett, C. and Stevenson, O. (1980) *Aspects of Inter-professional Co-operation*, Allen & Unwin.

Rehabilitation   Rehabilitation is used more frequently in relation to restorative work with the physically or mentally disabled. Restoration of working capacity was one of the objects of the Disabled Persons (Employment) Act 1944 and of Employment Rehabilitation Centres. The term in the context of disability has been seen as referring 'to a combination of processes and techniques designed to improve or restore an individual's total functioning, i.e. not just restoring occupational functional ability but also improving social functioning and satisfaction. In some cases it may simply refer to the containment of disablement' (Wing). The term has also been used to describe a course of work with an offender (rehabilitation into society) or with a child separated from his home (resettlement or rehabilitation in his own family). In whatever context, it is clear that rehabilitation refers to a function or status that has been lost and to processes aimed at restoring the function or status: these processes may well involve others than the rehabilitatee and function/status cannot always be restored completely to its former condition.

RELATIONSHIP

Bolton, B. and Jacques, M. (eds) (1978) *Rehabilitation Counselling: Theory and Practice*, Baltimore, University Park Press.
Wing, J. (1974) *People with Handicaps Need Better Trained Workers*, CCETSW Paper no. 5, pp. 61-7.

Relationship As a general term, 'relationship' refers to a systematic connection between two factors, people, etc. Within welfare the term usually refers to the contact or affective bond between social worker and client which is described as *professional* and has often been seen (at least since Virginia Robinson's *A Changing Psychology in Social Casework*, Oxford University Press, 1931) as the main medium whereby significant change in the client and/or his situation is effected. Thus, the Morison Committee on the Probation Service, 1962, defined casework as '*the creation and utilization*, for the benefit of an individual who needs help with personal problems, of a relationship between himself and a trained social worker' (italics not original).

(Morison) Departmental Committee on the Probation Service (1962) *Report*, Cmnd 1650, HMSO.
Perlman, H. (1979) *Relationship: the Heart of Helping People*, University of Chicago Press.

Reporter See *Children's Hearings*.

Representative This can be a technical term in statistics (samples may or may not be representative of a wider grouping of instances) or a term referring to particular roles. Griffiths has usefully identified different senses in which the term in this second sense may be used. A person may be fairly typical of the group s/he represents; s/he may symbolically stand for some belief or sentiment; s/he may legally represent someone or represent their interests. Griffiths calls these kinds of representing another, respectively descriptive, symbolic, ascriptive and the representation of interests. In welfare the term 'representative' is used of social workers (in a symbolic and an ascriptive sense), while various policies or Acts of Parliament can be said to represent the success or failure with which the interests of distinct groups have been pressed.

Griffiths, A. (1960) 'How Can One Person Represent Another?',
Proceedings of the Aristotelian Society, Supplementary Volume
XXXIV, 187-208.

Resettlement units   This provision for 'homeless people who
require preparation for, and help with, independent living, as a
result of social disadvantage, ill-health, or prolonged institutional care or custody' (Supplementary Benefits Commission, *Annual Report 1976*, p.61) has developed from the casual ward of
the Poor Law and the reception centres created under the
National Assistance Act 1948. Almost all the resettlement units
are administered through central government and many also
provide re-establishment workshops on a day or residential
basis. Major problems with re-settlement units are the feasibility
of the aim of influencing people to lead a 'more settled way of
life'; the difficulty of seeing how the different kinds of user can
most appropriately be helped; and the issue of central or local
government responsibility. At the end of 1981 it was announced
that one of the best-known London units (Camberwell) was to
be closed, and 1,000 hostel places were to be provided through
the Housing Corporation. See also *Vagrancy*.

Supplementary Benefits Commission, *Annual Report 1976*, Ch.5,
    'People "Without a Settled Way of Living"'.
Wood, B. (1978) 'Homeless but not without Hope: Reception Centres
    and those who Use them', *Social Work Service*, 17, 1-6.

Residential care   Residential care is provision on a twenty-
four-hour basis for those who are judged to be unable to live in
their own homes. Such care has been of significance in welfare
since the days of the general workhouse, but has been provided
on an increasingly differentiated basis (e.g. for children, for
children with particular disabilities). Residential care raises a
number of important questions, as idea and as reality. Should it
be used as a last resort or as 'treatment' of choice in certain
circumstances? What models of residential care are most
appropriate in which circumstances (e.g. hotel, *therapeutic
community*)? Is residential care a form of social work or a setting
in which some social work can be practised? What are the best
forms of training for staff of different kinds? It is now less

common to hear opinions voiced that 'all residential accommodation should be abolished'. Careful research of a comparative kind, and such new approaches to problems of the quality of residential life and the interdependence of residential with other factors as are promised in the application of ideas of the production of welfare, indicate how exaggerated such a response has been. Tizard and his colleagues, for instance, argued that four factors are crucial for the pattern and the quality of life in residential centres: ideological variation (the centre is seen as school, hospital, domestic arrangement); organisational variation; staffing; and variation in response of residents.

Davies, B. and Knapp, M. (1981) *Old People's Homes and the Production of Welfare*, Routledge & Kegan Paul.
Jones, H. (1979) *The Residential Community: a Setting for Social Work*, Routledge & Kegan Paul.
Tizard, J. *et al.* (eds) (1975) *Varieties of Residential Experience*, Routledge & Kegan Paul.

Residual conception of welfare   See *Welfare.*

Respect for persons   Respect for persons is often claimed as a social work principle or the most important principle in social work, but Plant argues against such a domestic perspective and sees respect for persons as definitive of morality. It is not, however, easy to discern what is implied by respect for persons as ends. Downie and Telfer suggest that it is to value or cherish a person for what he is; his abilities to be self-determining and rule-following. 'To *respect* such a person is to make his ends one's own (show sympathy with him) and to take into account in all one's dealings with him that he too is self-determining and rule-following' (p. 37). Darwall has argued that there are two distinct ways in which persons may be the object of respect, and he calls these recognition respect and appraisal respect. What is of obvious importance is clarity about what kinds of behaviour or disposition count as respecting or being respectful, and also about that towards which respecting behaviour is directed – people seen under the description of persons.

Darwall, S. (1977–8) 'Two Kinds of Respect', *Ethics*, 88, 36–49.
Downie, R. and Telfer, E. (1969) *Respect for Persons*, Allen & Unwin.

Plant, R. (1970) *Social and Moral Theory in Casework*, Routledge & Kegan Paul, pp. 11-23.

Rights A right is a claim of special force. 'To say a person has a right to X, is to say more than that it would be desirable or good or justifiable that he receive X. It is to say that he is entitled to receive X, that X is properly his without further argument' (Jones). Rights can be based on legal or moral foundations, and can refer to some service a man may request or need or to an absence of obligation: in this last sense a man is said to have a right whenever others ought not to prevent him doing what he wants to do. 'Rights' play an important part in welfare. Over the years, benefit 'as a right' or 'as of right', contrasted with benefit that has to be earned through successful application or humiliating supplication, has been a touchstone by which much income maintenance provision has been judged. More recently 'welfare rights' has come to characterise an approach to work with several different client groups (the old, for example, or the emphasis on children as bearing certain rights). Within social work, 'rights' have always had a place, as in discussions of the client's rights of *self-determination*. See also *Welfare rights*.

Dworkin, R. (1977) *Taking Rights Seriously*, Duckworth.
Jones, P. (1980) 'Rights, Welfare and Stigma', in *Social Welfare: Why and How?*, ed. N. Timms, Routledge & Kegan Paul.

Risks A risk is the chance of encountering harm or loss. The concept is used in welfare in three, related, contexts. Within a large group certain individuals or sub-groups can be identified as 'at risk' of some more or less specifiable danger: a certain number of old people are at risk each winter, given certain economic circumstances, of hypothermia (fall of inner body temperature to an unacceptable level); or certain children can be registered as 'at risk' of abuse. Second, questions are raised concerning the extent to which people (in homes of various kinds, for example) should be protected from harm and not allowed to take risks or to enter risky situations. Third, behaviour in social workers and clients is sometimes understood as risk-taking of a calculated or implicit kind.

ROLE

Brearley, P. (1980) 'A Preliminary Framework for Risk Analysis', and 'Managing Risk and Taking Action', in *Admission to Residential Care*, Tavistock.

Role The concept of role has been used to understand aspects of welfare practice (changing the role of applicant to that of client), and of personality development: welfare provision is often role-specific – people are helped as deprived children, as unemployed, as members of a broken or breaking marriage. 'Role' refers to activity normatively expected of any particular social position (such as friend, politician), whilst role performance consists of the actual behaviour of someone occupying a particular social position. 'Role' is commonly found in company with a large number of related concepts, such as role-distance, role-set, role-conflict, role-taking. Sometimes these are collectively described as role-theory, but they are more appropriately viewed as conceptual elaborations used in a number of different theories, e.g. of *socialisation*. At least one sociologist (quoted by Morris) has complained that much writing on 'role' 'consists of pompous, nebulous and incredibly lengthy re-statements of what has been common knowledge for a very long time'.

Morris, B. (1971) 'Reflections on Role Analysis', *British Journal of Sociology*, 22, 395-409.
Ruddock, R. (1969) *Roles and Relationships*, Routledge & Kegan Paul.

Rural This term often forms part of a well-established wide-ranging dichotomy, that of country or city, of urban or rural ways of life. As Williams has argued: 'The "country way of life" has included the very different practices of hunters, pastoralists, farmers and factory farmers, and its organisation has varied from the tribe and the manor to the feudal estate, from the small peasantry and tenant farmers to the rural commune, from the *latifundia* and the plantation to the large capitalist enterprise and the state farm. The city, no less, has been of many kinds ...' (p. 9, italics original). A belief in the remedial influences of rural life has played some part in the development of welfare ideas and provision (e.g. the idea of the Garden City, country holidays for slum children, the rescue of children from the evils of city life and their establishment in children's villages). The specific

166

investigation of the extent and quality of social problems in country areas or of the provision required has not proceeded systematically. See also *Urban*.

Broady, M. *et al.* (1982) *Politics and Planning in Rural Development*, Bedford Square Press.
Seed, P. (1980) *Mental Handicap: Who Helps in Rural and Remote Communities?*, Costello Educational/Scottish Society for the Mentally Handicapped.
Williams, R. (1975) *The Country and the City*, Paladin.

R

S

Schizophrenia   This is preferably seen as a grouping of mental disorders of a severe kind, showing the following signs: disorder of thought (e.g. thought is experienced as inserted into the mind by outside agencies); psychosomatic disorders (e.g. stupor); emotional disorders (e.g. a flattening of tone, incongruity of mood); and so on. Questions of diagnosis are crucial, and Wing has noted: 'there is little doubt that some psychiatrists do use the term "schizophrenia" very widely, not to say vaguely, and that diagnosed on the shakiest evidence ... can be treated using powerful pharmacological and essential methods' (p. 21). This group of disorders is important in welfare for a number of reasons. Patients diagnosed as schizophrenic use considerable health and social services resources. Great interest has been shown in various theories of causation, and one important grouping of theories (that stressing the role of the family in the causation and continuation of the 'illness') could have important consequences for early welfare intervention of a correctional nature (*double bind*), and for the kind of social milieu to which schizophrenic patients might be returned after hospital treatment. In addition, studies of those diagnosed as schizophrenic have shed light on more general questions concerning the social factors in the causation of mental illness and the distribution of health service resources. See also *social class*.

Goldberg, E. and Morrison, S. (1963) 'Schizophrenia and Social Class', *British Journal of Psychiatry*, 109, 785-802.
Wing, J. (ed.) (1978) *Schizophrenia: Towards a New Synthesis*, Academic Press.

Scrounger   A scrounger is someone who begs or wheedles gifts.

The term 'welfare scrounger' or the description of someone as 'scrounging off the welfare' expresses moral disapproval of a considerable range of behaviour, encompassing those who claim benefits through frauds, those who do not comply with their national insurance contribution liabilities, and those who are more generally seen as not making efforts of which they are deemed capable towards independence from outside help or who manipulate welfare systems. In welfare, the 'scrounger' is important as part of the image of certain recipients of benefit which is emphasised at particular times in the media – Deacon (1978) argues that in 1976 public concern over possible abuse was expressed more widely than at any time since the 1920s – and because of the resources devoted to the detection and prosecution of fraud. Cases of social security frauds approved for prosecution increased from nearly 9,000 in 1970 to about 27,800 in 1977.

Deacon, A. (1976) *In Search of the Scrounger: the Administration of Unemployment Insurance in Britain, 1921-1931*, Bell.

Deacon, A. (1978) 'The Scrounging Controversy: Public Attitudes towards the Unemployed in Contemporary Britain', *Social and Economic Administration*, 12, 120-32.

Segregation To segregate is to set someone under a particular description apart from similar others for particular purposes. Segregation is usually negatively valued in welfare discussion. Segregation units exist in prisons to separate prisoners who are dangerous or in danger, disturbed or disruptive. See also *integration*.

Selectivity The ideas of selection and selectivity have been used in welfare in a number of ways: to refer to the processes whereby clients are selected by organisations (Greenley); to describe the choice of priorities or of some people for greater opportunities (as in selective education). Most frequently, however, the term 'selectivity' refers to a general principle of allocation 'to certain applicants on externally imposed conditions' (Jones *et al.*, p. 44); this principle is usually contrasted with '*universalism*', though it is now argued that both principles are applicable in the real social welfare world of 'selectively financed universal services selectively used' (Reddin). The selectivist principle is constituted by a number of assumptions: services should go to those who need them and not to those who do not (this need can largely be measured in terms of means to pay); pricing and consumer choice should be much more widely used as a means of resource allocation; selective use of resources should be encouraged to restrain public expenditure. Selective measures are usually directed towards individuals but it is possible to select certain needy groups as *priorities* or to allocate resources selectively on an area basis. See also *Positive discrimination, Stigma*.

Greenley, J. (1980) 'Organisational Processes and Client Selectivity in Social Welfare Services', in *Welfare or Bureaucracy?*, ed. D. Grunow and F. Hegner, Oelgeschlager, Gunn & Hain, Cambridge, Mass.

Jones, K. *et al.* (1978) *Issues in Social Policy*, Routledge & Kegan Paul, pp. 44-58.

Reddin, M. (1969) 'Universality *versus* Selectivity', *Political Quarterly*, 40, 12-22.

Self-determination A much used and much discussed notion in social work: reference is frequently made to the client's right to self-determination, and this means not a right to a particular 'thing' (as in a right over one's own body) but a right in relation to one's action (to do what one wishes as long as this does not interfere with similar rights of others) and a claim that someone should help one in the way one wants. Self-determination is a complex notion, referring both to an objective and to the most favoured means of social work (client self-direction), to the avoidance of coercive imposition, and to freedoms of various kinds (e.g. not to be a client against one's wishes). Discussion in welfare has centred on the coherence of the principle of self-determination (is it a single principle or, as some have suggested, two principles – those of client participation and non-interference on the part of the social worker except in essentials?); on its desirability (some see it as an elaborate sham); on the limitation of the right; and on the relationship between being self-determining and being determined by others or by outside, causative factors. See also *Determinism*.

McDermott, F. (ed.) (1975) *Self-Determination in Social Work*, Routledge & Kegan Paul.

Self-help 'Self-help' is used in two ways: as a description of an objective of social work (to help people to a state in which they can help themselves and are not 'relying' on social service) or as referring to a comparatively recent development in welfare, that of the self-help movement. In the latter sense 'self-help' refers to independent 'self-cure' and/or reforming groups which rely on the recruitment of sufferers from a common condition who help each other. Groups arise because of criticism of the 'helping' professional's lack of understanding of a particular condition, growing faith in the 'healing' and support capacities of small groups, a decision to combat *stigma* and decline of support from institutions. Katz and Bender suggest a classification – groups concerned with personal growth, social advocacy, alternative living, 'outcasts', and groups with more than one main objective.

Katz, A. and Bender, E. (1976) *The Strength in Us: Self-help Groups in the Modern World*, New York, Franklin Watts.
Robinson, D. and Henry, S. (1977) *Self-help and Health: Mutual Aid for Modern Problems*, Martin Robertson.

Self-knowledge Seen as an objective of social work in some instances: to increase a person's self-awareness. Generally accepted as an objective for students in social work education, but opinion differs on the best means of increasing self-knowledge (directly, as through interpretation, or indirectly); on the boundaries of self-knowledge (awareness that primarily derives from knowledge of the influence of family relationships or that also includes awareness of one's political and moral beliefs and their impact on one's behaviour); on the 'individualistic' form of 'self-knowledge', so that some would argue that self-knowledge must include or even be constituted by realisation of one's social-class membership and the 'real' interests of that class. It has also been argued that awareness of one's own values is important for planners and decision-makers. 'This will help them guard against injecting their own values into policy, rather than shape it in the image of the choices that make up the general consensus' (B. Madison, *The Meaning of Social Policy*, Croom Helm, 1980, p. 42).

Service delivery This relatively new phrase relates to a number of recent concerns in welfare – social provision should be broken

171

down into a number of discrete services (e.g. *day care*), but these should be viewed as parts of a connected set of services; services should be delivered to or on behalf of those requiring them in acceptable ways; services should be seen as the product of a network of service personnel and capable of delivery to the client or his network in an efficient manner. See also *Systems theory, Social services.*

Kahn, A. (1976) 'Service Delivery at the Neighbourhood Level: Experience, Theory and Facts', *Social Service Review*, 23-53.

Settlements University settlements were established towards the end of the last century, following the creation of the first, Toynbee Hall, by Canon Barnett in 1884. The settlement was an attempt to bridge the chasm between the social classes through a residence of 'university people' in poor areas and the establishment of educational, friendly, and local resident contacts. Women's settlements played an important part in the starting of social work training. The notion of a university group 'settling' a locality was no longer dominant by the early twentieth century, but settlements were centres for a range of services, particularly clubs for different ages. By the 1960s the relevant organising body changed its title from British Association of Residential Settlements to the British Association of Settlements and Social Action; the idea of the involvement of local communities as agents of change had replaced the earlier notion of local people as individual recipients of the offerings of what C.R. Ashbee caricatured in his novel, *The Building of Thelema* (Dent, 1910) as 'a refined colony of academic thinkers, who had come ... to study and improve the poor under the guidance of the ubiquitous rector ...'

Abel, E. (1979) 'Toynbee Hall, 1884-1914', *Social Service Review*, 53, 606-32.

Sex Sex refers either to gender (male or female) or to a range of behaviour, which might appear to present few problems of a definitional nature. However, reflection on the idea of infantile sexuality (*Freudian theory*) or discussion of the relative contribution of the enforcement of shame and of sexuality in rape suggests that sexual behaviour is a more complex notion: it is not simply a case of certain behaviour but behaviours seen by those interacting as 'sexual'. Sexual behaviour has recently become of more serious and apparent interest in welfare. The sexual needs of disabled people, for example, have come to be recognised and some sex counselling is being made available; the social definition or *labelling* of certain kinds of sexual conduct as 'abnormal' has received attention, as has the role of sex orientation in social work; new services have been established to deal in innovative ways with victims of sex attacks (e.g. rape crisis centres). See also *Women*.

Armytage, W., Chester, R. and Peel, J. (eds) (1980) *Changing Patterns of Sexual Behaviour*, Academic Press.
Hart, J. (1979) *Social Work and Sexual Conduct*, Routledge & Kegan Paul.
Plummer, K. (1975) *Sexual Stigma*, Routledge & Kegan Paul.

Sick, chronically Covered by the Chronically Sick and Disabled Act 1970. One of the aims of the 1974 Health Service reorganisation was to divert resources to the chronically sick. See also *Disability*.

Sick role A role played by someone who has gained access to the status 'sick'. The term originates from the sociology of Talcott Parsons, who believed that the sick role had the following elements: exemption from the responsibilities of normal day-to-day roles; the sick person cannot be expected to recover simply by his own unaided efforts; but the sick role has its own responsibilities, since the role-player is expected to get well as soon as possible and to co-operate with the professionals. The idea of the sick role as exemplified by Parsons should not be divorced from the conception of illness as *deviance* that must be controlled so that the social equilibrium is maintained. Emphasis on the sick role as such highlights the controlling function of health care, but may also lead to an underestimate of the social factors in the genesis of disease (see, e.g. Brown).

Brown, G. (1976) 'Social Causes of Disease', in *An Introduction to Medical Sociology*, ed. D. Tuckett, Tavistock.
Parsons, T. (1951) *The Social System*, Routledge & Kegan Paul, Ch. 10.

SOCIAL ACTION

Social action See *Community action*.

Social administration The term could be thought to refer to the business of running social agencies as well as to those who teach about the working of such agencies (occasionally attempts are made to distinguish the latter by name – social administrationists, for example). Usually the term refers to an area of academic interest (not so much a discipline) that developed from the Social Studies Departments established in certain universities earlier this century and mainly concerned with the preparation of future social workers. In its beginning, social administration was concerned with the history and functioning of the social services, and distinguished from the study of other governmental organisations which were the concern of public administration. The main study of social administration still centres on social services, but it has an existence separate from social work training and is viewed in a more complex and extended context:

— social administration is frequently linked with *social policy* and seen as a composite;
— traditional social services are studied in a wide perspective of *welfare*;
— a comparative basis is seen as increasingly important;
— social services are linked to social needs and their satisfaction.

'Social administration is thus concerned, for instance, with different types of moral transaction, embodying notions of gift exchange, of reciprocal obligations, which have developed in modern industrial societies in institutional forms to bring about and maintain social and community relations' (Titmuss).

Rodgers, B. (1968) *Comparative Social Administration*, Atherton Press.
Titmuss, R. (1968) *Commitment to Welfare*, Allen & Unwin.

Social care See *Care*.

Social class This refers to one form of social stratification about which there continues to be considerable debate. For Marxists, classes are determined by relation to the means of production, and 'class' cannot be understood except in terms of class conflict between those who own those means and the exploited class, and in terms of class consciousness. For Weber, social classes are, rather, aggregates of people who possess the same life-chances. Others see social class in terms of a clustering of characteristics such as educational level, lifestyle, and so on. Elucidating and elaborating these and many other theoretical distinctions is work for sociologists, though some of the complexity of the idea of social class could profitably find its way into practical and theoretical work on relationships between social policy, social work, and social class. However, social class is of crucial importance in welfare. Social-class factors influence access to and use of a whole range of social and other services, whether this is seen in terms of different housing classes with differential access to property in a market situation (Rex and Moore), or differential socialisation into distinct ways of defining and solving problems. Social class also figures centrally in accounts of the development of the *Welfare State*, whether in terms of the distribution of civic, political, and social rights to larger social classes (*citizenship*) or of working-class success in wresting concessions from the ruling class.

Reid, I. (1977) *Social Class Differences in Britain: a Sourcebook*, Open Books.
Rein, M. and Rainwater, L. (1978) 'Patterns of Welfare Use', *Social Service Review*, 52, 511-34.
Rex, J. and Moore, P. (1967) *Race, Community and Conflict*, Oxford University Press.

Social conscience   The term, as used in welfare, has two main uses; to refer to what some people may have made moral judgments and resolved to act *about* (i.e. social problems, faults in society) and to the promptings and dictates of a developing body of judgments seen as residing somehow *in* society. In the first sense it is sometimes said that people enter social work or go in for *social reform* because of their social consciences: they believe they ought to act in the attempt to remedy a social fault. In the second sense (which has some connection with Durkheim's *conscience collective*, though this idea has not been developed) it has been suggested that social workers should

175

maintain an unswerving identification with 'the social conscience', and that one set of explanations of historical changes in
social policy can usefully be described as 'the social conscience
thesis'. Baker argues that the latter contains a number of
assumptions: social policy represents benevolent state activity;
changes in social policy result from a deepening sense of social
obligation and an increase in knowledge of unmet need;
improvements are cumulative and irreversible.

Baker, J. (1979) 'Social Conscience and Social Policy', *Journal of Social
Policy*, 8, 177-206.

Social control 'Control' is a very wide-ranging term. Thus,
Room says: 'Means-testing is itself a form of rationing and
hence control – for it involves the application of formal criteria
to determine entitlement' (p. 201). 'Social' refers to the interest in
which 'control' is exercised (e.g. towards social solidarity) or that
over which control is exercised (e.g. social relations). To control
is to govern or to exercise a governing influence over someone,
and both senses are present in 'social control', since it refers to
all the means by which a society is maintained in its present
social order, remains the kind of society it is, and also to those
means that are acknowledged specifically as agencies of control, such as the law. Social policies and social workers can
act as 'agents' of control in both senses, though Marxists
would make little distinction. A recent line of argument seeks
to explore the sense in which 'social control' creates rather
than is created by social *deviance*. In this context, welfare
measures are seen as intensifying and hence amplifying
deviance.

Day, P. (1981) *Social Work and Social Control*, Tavistock.
Room, G. (1979) *The Sociology of Welfare*, Blackwell and Martin
Robertson, Ch. 6.
Watkin, C. (1975) *Social Control*, Longman.

Social engineering The term is not used very precisely, but
refers generally to those who seek social change through
planned contrivance. Usage of the term often conveys a negative
evaluation, but Popper has distinguished piecemeal from Uto-
pian social engineering in any work of social reconstruction. He

favours the former because our knowledge of society is unequal to the task of reconstruction according to a fully detailed blueprint; because agreement is more likely on the removal of a specific abuse; and because of the injustice of imposing the total burden of change on those contemporary with the revolution. Rees takes seriously the idea of changing society as an engineer would go about change, and challenges the coherence of the notion of engineering society: 'we do not make the language we speak. Nor does its persistence depend on our decisions. Neither do the activities for which policies are put forward – industry, education, and the rest. Policies are put forward in the day's work.' The term 'social engineering' has also been used in relation to the law. Roscoe Pound described lawyers as social engineers concerned with three types of legal interests: public, social, and private.

Popper, K. (1945) *The Open Society and its Enemies*, vol. 2, Routledge & Kegan Paul.
Pound, R. (1954) *An Introduction to the Philosophy of Law*, Oxford University Press.
Rees, R. (1947) 'Social Engineering', *Mind*, 56, 317-31.

Social Inquiry Reports (SIRs, SERs)   The Criminal Justice Act 1948 gave probation officers the duty to inquire, in accordance with any directions of the court, into the circumstances or home surroundings of a person with a view to helping the court to determine the most suitable disposal of the case. Curnock and Hardiker suggest that in carrying out the inquiries and reporting to the court probation officers may take different roles: advising sentences by offering diagnosis and prognosis; playing 'a more classical justice role by acknowledging the inevitability of a tariff sentence, given the seriousness of an offence' (p. 12); attempting to persuade the court that a particular person be kept out of prison. Other controversial aspects of the social inquiry system concern whether pre-trial inquiry may be considered an infringement of individual liberty, and the extent to which the objective of the inquiry can be and should be to help the subject of the inquiry or to help the court to reach an appropriate decision.

Curnock, K. and Hardiker, P. (1979) *Towards Practice Theory: Skills and Methods in Social Assessments*, Routledge & Kegan Paul.

SOCIAL JUSTICE

Social justice 'Justice', says St Thomas Aquinas, 'makes the will prompt to deal fairly', but fair dealing can be to deal equally with individuals in a group or to give someone their due, and what is due to a person can be expressed in terms of rights, or deserts, or needs. Stevenson has used a distinction between creative justice (concerned with response to the uniqueness of individuals) and proportional justice (fairness as between individuals) in a study of supplementary benefits. Our basic intuition of justice as fairness has been considerably developed by Rawls, who has explored two basic principles: that everyone has the right to as much liberty as is consistent with a like liberty for all; and that 'social and economic inequalities are to be arranged so that they are both (a) to the greatest benefit of the least advantaged, and (b) attached to offices and positions open to all under conditions of fair equality of opportunity' (Gorovitz). The view that justice is the first virtue of all social institutions has obvious implications for the institutions of social welfare. The attempt by Runciman to apply Rawls to the study of the public view of justice has been described by Robert Pinker as of 'great relevance to the debate between universalism and selectivity' (*Social Theory and Social Policy*, Heinemann, 1971, p. 110). Interest has also been focused on the unequal provision local authorities make in relation to 'identical' problems, and the consequent need for *territorial justice*. In addition, arguments have developed in connection with a distinction between natural plight and evil situations created through human agency. Thus it has been argued that poverty is an evil but not an injustice that arises from any person's fault and against whom a claim for restitution can intelligibly be pressed.

Gorovitz, S. (1976) 'John Rawls: a Theory of Justice', in *Contemporary Political Philosophers*, ed. A. de Crespigny and K. Minogue, Methuen.
Runciman, W. (1966) *Relative Deprivation and Social Justice: a Study of Attitudes to Social Inequality in Twentieth-Century England.* Routledge & Kegan Paul.
Stevenson, O. (1973) *Claimant or Client?*, Allen & Unwin.

Social movements This term refers to a form of collective behaviour concerned with furthering an acknowledged cause or establishing a particular programme. So in a welfare context reference is made to the mental health movement, the social imperialist movement towards the end of the nineteenth century, and so on. The objectives of a movement are not always clearly articulated and allegiance may be of different degrees, but Traugott argues that movements are not ephemeral instances of collective behaviour; they are identified rather by criteria of positive solidarity and an anti-institutional orientation. Wilkinson presents a tenfold typology in terms of religion, rural and urban discontent, nationalist and race, imperialism, class interest, moral protest, revolution and counter-revolution, youth, women, and intellect. Movements under each of the descriptions have played an influential role in the history of social welfare.

Traugott, M. (1978) 'Reconceiving Social Movements', *Social Problems*, 26, 38-49.
Wilkinson, P. (1971) *Social Movements*, Pall Mall.

Social planning   See *Planning*.

Social policy   The name of an area of study (*social administration and social policy*) and of that which is studied; policies that in some way or another count as 'social'. Neither meaning is entirely free of problems. As an academic subject 'social policy' seems to have either fairly tight or hardly visible boundaries: it may be concerned with services traditionally recognised as 'social', or with services identified as means to the same end (e.g. social integration) whatever their common-sense label, or with 'the means whereby societies prevent, postpone, introduce and manage changes in structure' (Townsend, p. 2). In the interests of academic boundary maintenance, attempts have been made to distinguish sharply (rather sinful) economic policy from (saintly tending) social policy, but it is now recognised that the study of social policy is impoverished if divorced from economic (and political) contexts. Students of social policy now call attention to the lack of theoretical underpinning of their subject, and recent developments include attempts to connect social policy with political theories of substance. Thus, Room sets social policy study within the traditions of liberalism, Marxism,

179

and social democracy. Others refer to liberal, conservative, and socialist theories of welfare. The major problem with 'social policy' as the name of what is studied lies partly in the ambiguity of 'social' (already mentioned) but also in defining and studying 'policies' or even 'policy change'. Is policy what an *organisation* (and who counts as a member is problematic) is seen to have done over a period of time, or the announcement of official (and good) intentions? Is social policy the 'policy' of 'society' or of government?

Room, G. (1979) *The Sociology of Welfare*, Blackwell and Martin Robertson.
Townsend, P. (1975) *Sociology and Social Policy*, Allen Lane.

Social problem   This term is used in at least two different ways in welfare: individuals or families are said to have 'social' as distinct, say, from 'medical' problems (they have problems amenable to the efforts of social workers or to those who can change the client's environment); we also refer to general contingencies (*family violence*, crime, child abuse) as social problems (problems of some dimension and significance that 'society ought to respond to on a societal scale'). It is now recognised that contingencies come to be defined as social problems through social processes of some complexity, and that it is always appropriate to ask in relation to any such contingency for which interests it *is* a problem, and what sort of threat is posed. In posing these questions, issues of *social control*, including the operation of the law, and the potentially problematic features of many accepted social institutions, such as the family, are increasingly considered. Social problems call for research and action from a psychological (e.g. Frieze *et al.*), sociological (e.g. Schrager and Short), and an economic (Claassen) perspective. See also *Deviance*.

Claassen, A. (1980) 'The Policy Perspective: Social Problems as Investment Opportunities', *Social Problems*, 27, 526-39.
Frieze, I. *et al.* (1979) *New Approaches to Social Problems*, Jossey-Bass.
Schrager, L. and Short, J. (1978) 'Towards a Sociology of Organisational Crime', *Social Problems*, 25, 407-19.

Social reform   This carries with it perhaps an air of continuous progress, especially when connected to ideas of the evolving *social conscience.* Such a connotation is excluded in a recent attempt to distinguish innovatory and developmental social policy changes from reforms which constitute 'a new way of doing something with which the State is already involved. Legislation or administrative structures are literally, re-formed. We would also include in this category instances where the objectives of an existing policy are altered radically; for instance in the matter of housing subsidies (Hall *et al.*, p. 19). Motives for advocating changes in law and social provision can be described in liberal or conservative terms, but exposed only within a cynical or a Marxist vocabulary. The precise influence of political theory on particular reforms is, however, a matter of controversy (as in discussions of the place of Benthamism in the reforms of the 1830s). In welfare history certain periods of 'reform' have been given special attention (e.g. those leading to what has been called the mid-Victorian Administrative State or the Liberal Reforms of 1906-14). Students of *social administration* often claim to be in the business of social reform as part of their 'discipline', and the Webbs and their colleagues in the Fabian Society offer both a lesson of gradualism (implicit in the idea of careful scholarship though innocent of any explicit theorising) and the active pursuit of change. Reform is a catholic notion embracing those convinced about one particular legislative change and those attempting gradually to re-model society as *social engineers.*

Hall, P. *et al.* (1975) *Change, Choice and Conflict in Social Policy*, Heinemann.

Hart, J. (1965) 'Nineteenth-Century Social Reform: a Tory Interpretation of History', *Past and Present*, no. 31, 39-61.

Hay, J. (1975) *The Origins of the Liberal Welfare Reforms 1906-1914*, Macmillan.

Roberts, D. (1960) *Victorian Origins of the British Welfare State*, Yale University Press.

Social security   The social security system consists of governmental income maintenance services including those of national insurance and supplementary benefit. Important questions concern the relationship of these two measures of social protection, the relationship between social security and other social welfare services, and the role of social security in income redistribution.

SOCIAL SERVICE/SOCIAL SERVICES

The beginnings of the present British system are to be found in the Old Age Pensions Act 1908 and the National Insurance Act 1911, but the structure of present provision owes most to the Beveridge Report. The system has been criticised on a number of grounds (e.g. adequacy for particular groups, such as the retired) but George has called for a radical social security service aiming at the reduction of income inequality and of stratified social relationships, through mechanisms which encourage free access and respectful treatment, and are not inferior to market provision. Lynes has suggested the correct context within which a system of social security should be judged: it 'is much more than a source of income geared to particular events or circumstances ... It is a social institution which both reflects and modifies the ideologies and aspirations of society; which can perceptibly change the pattern of distribution of income and wealth; and which, above all, can symbolise the cohesion of a society or of classes within a society' (quoted in Madison).

George, V. (1973) *Social Security and Society*, Routledge & Kegan Paul.

Kaim-Caudle, P.R. (1973) *Comparative Social Policy and Social Security*, Martin Robertson.

Madison, B. (1980) *The Meaning of Social Policy*, Croom Helm, Chs 5, 6 and 7.

Social service/Social services   Both elements in these terms – 'social' and 'service' – pose problems: the idea of service is considered by some to perpetuate divisions between (self-designated) servants and those (possibly) served, and to militate against ideas of communal response; 'social' here – as elsewhere – is ambiguous as between object (services oriented to social relations) and auspice (services that are in some way socially authorised). Social services may be widely defined as all programmes concerned directly or indirectly with state mediation of access to life-chances or, more narrowly, to refer to the range of more or less discrete services that are the province of local authority social services departments. Significantly, the Seebohm Report (1968) which led to the present departments referred to social service rather than social services in the attempt to conceive of a new community-oriented service which abandoned over-concern for separate eligibility requirements for discrete services and embraced the possibility of new forms of user participation in self-service. Developments since 1968 have resulted in some clarification of *social work* as a service in itself and as a mode of service delivery, but questions concerning the extent to which centralised social services have failed and should be replaced by more participatory forms are now being actively pursued. See also *Welfare*.

Hadley, R. and Hatch, S. (1981) *Social Welfare and the Failure of the State: Centralised Social Services and Participatory Alternatives*, Allen & Unwin.

Pinker, R. (1971) *Social Theory and Social Policy*, Heinemann, pp. 146-53.

Social skills   Social skills are successful ways of negotiating social pathways and achieving objectives in a manner that is not socially disruptive. Some would reduce such successful habits to very small units, as the management of eye contact, while others would see as a social skill such overall tasks as the management of an interview. Recently, within welfare, training in ordinary life-skills (maintaining social space, handling encounters, equipment, and so on) has been emphasised as a concrete problem-solving method, either in the form of systematic search for and establishment of particular skills or of a more generalised training in sensitivity, such as through T-groups.

Cooper, C. (1974) 'Psychological Disturbances Following T-Groups', *British Journal of Social Work*, 4, 39-49.

Priestly, P. *et al.* (1978) *Social Skills and Personal Problem Solving*, Tavistock.

Social work   For some, spending time on defining social work is simply ensuring more attention is paid to the claim of social workers to professional status (*profession*) than to the realities of their simple but necessary tasks of acting as the poor man's secretary/adviser and delivering various practical services in a reasonably friendly manner. Others emphasise professional social work and wish to distinguish *the* social work task from work that might be undertaken by para-professionals or those not trained. Such differentiation is not easy. For instance, sight of a recent definition by the professional association is enough to frighten even hardened readers of the literature: 'Social work is the purposeful and ethical application of personal skills in interpersonal relationships directed towards enhancing the personal and social functioning of an individual, family, group, or neighbourhood, which necessarily involves using evidence obtained from practice to help create a social environment conducive to the well-being of all.' This manfully attempts to encompass within the one fold the three 'methods' of social work – *casework, groupwork* and *community work* – but the descending cloud of professionalism obscures any distinction between what social work is and what it ought to be. In describing social work it is a necessary first step to question its assumed unitary nature and also to bear in mind the historical changes in 'social work' which as a description of work other than traditional 'charitable' work made its first appearance towards the end of the nineteenth century. What started as, in part, a reservation away from the statutory *Poor Law* has now become, through historical change – in the eyes of some commentators – a bureau-profession acting as guardian of the new negatively privileged status group of benefit claimants (*benefit*). It is important to ask, of any definition of social work, what is social work being distinguished *from* and *why*.

Dolan, P. (1980) 'The Social Work Task: a Rulebook for Social Work', in *Social Welfare: Why and How?*, ed. N. Timms, Routledge & Kegan Paul.

Parry, N. and Parry, J. (1979) 'Social Work, Professionalism and the State', in *Social Work, Welfare and the State*, ed. N. Parry *et al.*, Edward Arnold.

Social work assistants As the name suggests, these workers were originally seen as taking on particular tasks within a case (e.g. helping the professionally trained social worker by undertaking escorting, transporting, supplementary visits). In this perspective the assistant worked as an ancillary, but social work assistants also have cases assigned to them (typically old people or others thought to have relatively 'straightforward' needs, having problems not complex enough to require the skills of a professionally trained social worker). Development of this second kind has been encouraged by the dominance of the case as the unit of work, but it raises interesting questions – is social work of an 'assistant' quality, not simply social work, whoever does it; would service not be more effectively delivered through a system of case-sharing?

Hallett, C. (1978) 'Ancillaries', in DHSS, *Social Service Teams: the Practitioner's View*, Olive Stevenson and Phyllida Parsloe, Introducers, HMSO.

Socialisation   On a societal scale, 'socialisation' refers to those processes whereby full membership of a society or social group is learned, social values are absorbed, and appropriate role behaviour governed by recognised norms is inculcated. Within welfare the concept is significant because certain groups of people (service-users or non-users) are sometimes collectively described as in a predicament because of inadequate socialisation through one or more faults in the main institution in which the lessons of social life are learned, such as the family or other kinds of primary group. In this context some have conceptualised a major task of social work as the resumption or correction of early socialisation or as concerned specifically with adult socialisation (i.e. that learning which occurs after the main 'stages' of child development). It is also possible to use 'socialisation' in relation to the 'correct' behaviour of a particular social position, so that no one can refer to adequately or inadequately socialised clients. On either scale there are dangers of assuming that in any person 'socialisation' fully takes, as it were, and of failure to differentiate between the one assumed homogeneous society with agreed values and norms and the various sub-cultures which have different relations with 'society'. It is also important to note more recent developments in research into early childhood socialisation which suggest that the task of parents is not to mould some neutral human stuff but rather to synchronise with the infant's already partially organised behaviour.

McBroom, E. (1970) 'Socialization and Social Casework', in *Theories of Social Casework*, ed. R. Roberts and R. Nee, University of Chicago Press.
Schaffer, R. (1977) *Mothering*, Open Books.

Special schools   Schools, approved by the Secretary of State, which offer special educational treatment, on a day or residential basis, for handicapped children. Under the 1944 Education Act the following categories of handicap were recognised: the blind, the partially sighted, the deaf, the partially hearing, the educationally sub-normal, the epileptic, the maladjusted, the physically handicapped, the speech defective, and the delicate. In 1971 education authorities were given responsibility for the education of mentally handicapped children. A White Paper, DHSS, *Special Needs in Education* (Cmnd 7996, HMSO, 1980) followed the Warnock Report which it described as 'a landmark in the development of policy and practice in the important area' of special education. The White Paper proposes to abolish the system of ascertainment of children as belonging to a category of handicapped and to base provision on the concept that certain children have special educational needs. A minority of these children will be the subject of a formal record and regular review. The local education authority will decide whether a child should be recorded, but children will be recorded only on the basis of a *multi-disciplinary* professional assessment. Children with special needs will, whether recorded or not, be educated, as far as is reasonable and practical, with those without such needs, but maintained and non-maintained special schools will be retained and a new category created of independent schools for the admission of 'recorded' children.

DHSS *et al.*, (Warnock) Committee of Enquiry into the Education of Handicapped Children and Young People (1978) *Special Educational Needs*, Cmnd 7212, HMSO.

Specialisation 'The issue of specialisation in the provision of social services generally, and of social work in particular, is one of the most important raised in this report' (DHSS *Social Service Teams: the Practitioner's View*, Olive Stevenson and Phyllida Parsloe, Introducers, HMSO, 1978, Ch. VII, 'Specialisation'). It has reappeared after a period in which specialisation in social work could not apparently be discussed without the addition of 'narrow': narrowness was built into the idea of training experience in a particular branch of work and into the idea of developed expertise. Specialisation in a social work context is now envisaged in different ways: by client groups (the aged, children); by particular condition (e.g. mental handicap); by method of intervention (e.g. community work) or by mode of work (e.g. family therapy); or by particular aspects of service (e.g. *intermediate treatment*). See also *Generic*.

Hey, A. (1979) 'Specialisation in Social Work', in *Seebohm Across Three Decades*, ed. J. Cypher, BASW Publications.
Stevenson, O. (1981) *Specialization in Social Service Teams*, Allen & Unwin.

Status passage   An individual may occupy many social positions throughout a life-span. Each social position involves a status, and the sum of all the individual's statuses defines the structure of his social identity. As one status changes into another during the life-time, it is accompanied by rites of passage. Marriage is an example of a status passage accompanied by rites. It is at these periods of transition or status passage that problems and stress can occur which often present themselves for social work intervention. See also *Youth*.

Glaser, B. and Strauss, A. (1971) *Status Passage*, Routledge & Kegan Paul.
Hart, N. (1976) *When Marriage Ends: a Study in Status Passage*, Tavistock.

S

Stigma   To carry a stigma is to have been stigmatised or publicly marked so that other invidious treatment follows. Stigma has become an important concept in welfare for understanding the effects of the structure and operation of social services and in describing one of the main tasks of social policy – providing appropriately differential welfare response without stigmatising the recipients. The term is widely used in social welfare, but it is important to note the distinction between what has been called 'felt stigma' (feelings of relatively permanent devaluation) and 'stigmatisation' (the social processes by and through which people are devalued). Pinker's treatment does not pursue this distinction, but presents a number of complex variations: particular stigmas (e.g. of dependency and obligation); stigma equivalents; degrees of stigma, and so on.

Pinker, R. (1971) *Social Theory and Social Policy*, Heinemann.
Plant, R. *et al.* (1980) *Political Philosophy and Social Welfare*, Routledge & Kegan Paul, pp. 133-5.

SUBNORMAL

Subnormal   See *Mental handicap*.

Super-ego   Super-ego is one of the dynamic elements in Freudian personality structure – along with *id* and *ego*. It is an unconscious structure arising, according to Freud, from the resolution of the *oedipal* conflict. *Kleinian theory* would place the origins of super-ego development much earlier in the life of the child. The super-ego is best seen as a censoring activity based on introjection of parental commands of some kind, though sometimes what is said to be introjected is a phantasy parental figure or a parental super-ego. Super-ego is important in psychoanalytic explanations of *depression*, but it is misleading to treat the term as synonymous with 'conscience'. See also *Guilt*.

Supervision   This term is used in two main ways: in relation to court orders (e.g. a suspended sentence supervision order; or a supervision order of a child aged between 12 and 14 made to a local authority); or in relation to the educational or professional oversight of social work students and trained practitioners respectively. Student supervision by fieldwork teachers (the now preferred description of those formerly known as supervisors) is usually considered to consist of three main roles – administration, supporter, teacher. Critically supervision has been seen as a major means of *social control* or alternatively as a specific social work contribution to the development of professional excellence. In relation to the supervision of practitioners a distinction can be made between management or the fullest degree of accountability for the work of others and responsibility for professional development. In addition, questions have been raised concerning the present availability, use and perception of supervision.

Deacon, R. and Bartley, M. (1975) 'Becoming a Social Worker', in *Towards a New Social Work*, ed. H. Jones, Routledge & Kegan Paul.
Martel, S. (ed.) (1981) *Supervision and Team Support*, Bedford Square Press for the FSU.
Pettes, D. (1979) *Staff and Student Supervision: a Task-Centred Approach*, Allen & Unwin.

Supplementary Benefits Commission (1966–80)   The first central government agency to administer assistance benefits was created in 1934, the Unemployment Assistance Board; in 1940 it became the Public Assistance, and in 1948 the National Assistance Board. In 1966 the last-named was replaced by the Supplementary Benefits Commission within the new Ministry of Social Security. The Commission was responsible for the award of supplementary benefit, subject to decisions of Appeal Tribunals, for the award of Family Income Supplement, and for most of the means-testing required for legal aid. The Supplementary Benefits Commission was abolished in the 1980 Social Security Act: executive functions were devolved to supplementary benefit offices, policy matters to the minister, and the advisory function to the Social Security Advisory Committee which also incorporates the former National Insurance Committee.

Donnison, D. (1976) 'Supplementary Benefits: Dilemmas and Priorities', *Journal of Social Policy*, 5, 337-58.
Donnison, D. (1981) *The Politics of Poverty*, Martin Robertson.
Leach, S. (1981) 'Relationships between Supplementary Benefits Offices and Social Services Departments', *Policy and Politics*, 9, 349-71.
Stevenson, O. (1973) *Claimant of Client?: a Social Worker's View of the Supplementary Benefits Commission*, Allen & Unwin.
Webb, A. (1975) 'The Abolition of National Assistance: Policy Changes in the Administration of Assistance Benefits', in *Change, Choice and Conflict in Social Policy*, ed. P.D. Hall *et al.*, Heinemann.

Support/Supportive work   In Freud's terms this kind of social work activity is nearer to cure by love than cure by analysis, though there is some doubt as to whether social work that is supportive aims at marginal improvements in social functioning rather than anything that might count as cure. 'Support' or sustaining/encouraging activity is sometimes a euphemism for routine check-up with little purpose; at other times, it describes a necessary phase of work with any client (support seems particularly appropriate when the social worker is encouraging the client to tell his story, allaying any fears of the agency); finally, support or supportive work is a special 'treatment', with a specific cluster of techniques (such as logical discussion, advice and guidance, reassurance, setting realistic limits) considered appropriate for clients in particular diagnostic categories. In any usage it is important to be clear not simply about how the support is offered and whether it is actually received, but also what aspects of the person and/or situation are being supported.

Stuart, R. (1976) 'Supportive Casework with Borderline Patients', in *Differential Diagnoses and Treatment in Social Work*, ed. F. Turner, Free Press.

Symptom   Symptoms manifest a particular illness; more generally the term is used to refer to specific signs of something seriously amiss. Thus, in welfare, we may speak of certain forms of treatment as doing little more than alleviating symptoms or we may refer to poor housing conditions as a symptom of fundamental urban decay. In social work the *presenting problem* has sometimes been dismissed as merely symptomatic. At least two general problems are raised by symptom-talk: the identity of that which is manifested through what are called 'symptoms' and the relation of 'symptom' to other signs and to the more fundamental, treatment-attracting entity. As Austin has argued (*Philosophical Papers*, ed. J. Urmson and G. Warnock, Clarendon Press, 1970, pp. 105-6): 'We never talk of "symptoms" or "signs" except by way of implied contrast with inspection of the item itself. No doubt it would often be awkward to say exactly where the signs or symptoms end and the item itself begins to appear: but such a division is always implied to exist.' Welfare talk of prevention sometimes includes reference to the desirability of action on the appearance of the first symptoms, say, of delinquency, but this usually means action following swiftly on detected delinquent acts.

Systems theory   Strictly not a theory but a set of concepts for making and understanding working connections between 'parts' within a permeable or closed boundary. Systems are of very many different kinds, but they are viewed as 'open' or 'closed', and open systems in some kind of exchange relationship with their environment have a number of characteristics including the importation of energy, through-put, and output, equifinality (a system's ability to reach the same final state from differing initial conditions and by a variety of paths), and the steady state (or dynamic homeostasis). (See Davies, pp. 104-16, for social work illustrations.) A systems approach has recently become attractive as a possible means of linking the different methods of social work into a *unitary approach*, and of providing a basis for a new coherence for social work and for a knowledge base. It also recognised that the target system (towards which efforts should be directed) was not always the same as the client system (on whose behalf efforts were to be made); and that *service delivery* also constituted a system.

Davies, M. (1977) *Support Systems in Social Work*, Routledge & Kegan Paul.
Pincus, A. and Minahan, A. (1973) *Social Work Practice: Model and Method*, Peacock.

T

Take-up 'Take-up' refers to the actual receipt of some benefit for which one is entitled to make a claim. The take-up rate is the percentage of those receiving related to the total number estimated to be eligible. Estimates are liable to error both in relation to the total eligible and to those taking up the benefit (as some benefits run for up to twelve months, those counted as receiving may in fact no longer be below income limits). Reasons for the comparatively low take-up rates include ignorance (despite publicity), complexity of the schemes, *stigma*, and invasion of privacy.

National Consumer Council (1976) *Means-Tested Benefits.*

Task (the social work task) Davies has recently argued against any singular notion of the task: 'for there is no such thing as *the* social work task; it is not even certain that there is any such activity as social work, in the sense that nursing, teaching and hairdressing, for example, are self-explanatory terms' (p. 3). See also *Social work*.

M. Davies (1981) *The Essential Social Worker*, Heinemann.

Task-centred casework At first sight it may appear strange that in such a practical business as social work a method or approach is singled out as focused specially on defining and achieving tasks. This has to be understood historically as a reaction against a period in the development of social casework when social workers were encouraged to go for a walk with a relationship and to undertake a kind of therapy by stealth. The task-centred approach emphasises in contrast the value of agreed objectives, of time-limited contact, and the client's own views. It was pioneered in the United States by Reid and Epstein in 1972, and the most recent extension is Reid. The approach concentrates on helping clients to carry out agreed tasks (often outside the interview) aimed at leading to changes in specified conditions. Reid argues that a shift has to occur from 'what is wrong' to what is needed, and this cannot take place if the client remains trapped in *existential* issues, such as who am I?

Goldberg, E. and Stanley, S. (1979) 'A Task-centred Approach to Probation', in *Pressures and Change in the Probation Service*, ed. J. King, Institute of Criminology.
Reid, W. (1978) *The Task-Centred System*, Columbia University Press.

Tax credit Schemes of tax credit are suggestions for a kind of negative income tax. A tax-credit system is 'a reform which embodies the socially valuable device of paying tax credits, to the extent that they are not used up against tax due, positively as benefit' (Cmnd 5116, 1972), and which reduces or eliminates the overlap between the systems of income tax and social security. Negative or reverse income tax schemes are of various kinds (e.g. the social dividend or state payment of a prescribed minimum to all regardless of other income, or the Friedman-type reverse tax, which would guarantee an income to half the poverty-line minimum for families with no other income). 'The choice of Reverse Income Tax Scheme depends on which consideration is judged primary – fully adequate help to the poorest, preserving incentives, or minimum cost in tax levied and (implied in this last aspect) maximum "selectivity" in concentrating help on the poor' (Christopher). Townsend, among others, has heavily criticised the whole idea of negative income tax.

Christopher, A. *et al.* (1970) *Policy for Poverty*, Institute of Economic Affairs.
Treasury Department (1972) *Proposals for a Tax Credit System*. Cmnd 5116, HMSO.
Townsend, P. (1975) *Sociology and Social Policy*, Allen Lane, pp. 128-34.

Team A team is an inter-disciplinary or *multi-disciplinary* work group. Social services departments are usually organised on the basis of area teams, but social workers in hospitals could be said to be part of a Health Services team together with doctors, nurses, and so on. Team work has been extolled in social work (see *child guidance*), but the 'team' in question is usually an inter-disciplinary group rather than any case-sharing social work. In any reference to teams (and these abound in social welfare) it is important to be clear that teams can be of significantly different kinds. Webb and Hobdall have recently suggested a simple taxonomy in terms of homogeneity and heterogeneity of both task and skill. This produces the collegial term, the specialised team (in which specialisation by task does not necessarily imply the existence of a hierarchy), the apprenticeship team, and the complex team.

Parsloe, P. (1981) *Social Services Area Teams*, Allen & Unwin.
Webb, A. and Hobdall, M. (1980) 'Co-ordination and Teamwork in the Health and Personal Social Services', in *Teamwork in the Personal Social Services and Health Care*, ed. S. Lonsdale *et al.*, Croom Helm.

Technique   A technique is a systematic, routineised means of achieving a known objective. So there are techniques of *planning* such as Forward Planning, Programme Budgeting, and so on. Reference is also frequently made to the various techniques used by social workers, and attempts have been made to identify them (e.g. environmental *manipulation, support, advice*, etc.), but no agreement has been reached on an exhaustive list. Other problems concern the psychological and moral issues that are raised by questions concerning the efficiency of techniques and their application to problems of a personal nature. Can one have a technical attitude towards persons? In discussion, technique is sometimes treated as synonymous with style ('She has a good interviewing technique or style'), with skill ('His interviewing technique is highly accomplished') or with what is better seen as a collection of techniques, a method ('They used a groupwork technique').

Terminal care   See *Death*.

Territorial justice   Territorial justice obtains when resources

194

are distributed to an area directly in proportion to the needs of that area. The statistical definition is a high correlation between indices of resources use and an index measuring the relative needs of the population of an area for the service. Davies argues that needs indices have to be designed specifically for each service and its chain of substitutes. A different scale of analysis is, of course, required if what is in question is not justice between areas but a just provision between individuals within the areas (Pinch). Since the pioneering studies of Davies, the idea of territorial justice has been mentioned frequently in discussion of social policy, though other writers have not always acknowledged his acceptance of the difficulties involved in measuring the degree of territorial justice.

Davies, B. (1968) *Social Needs and Resources in Local Services*, Michael Joseph.

Pinch, S. (1979) 'Territorial Justice in the City: a Case Study of the Social Services for the Elderly in Greater London', in *Social Problems and the City: Geographical Perspectives*, ed. D. Herbert and D. Smith, Oxford University Press.

Theory The term has many uses, but it can perhaps best be generally approached through teasing at such questions as what does it mean to have, or to build, a theory? Having a theory, for instance, enables us to use certain descriptions, perform certain operations (such as make predictions), and explain particular phenomena. In welfare discussion 'theory' figures in two specific ways. *Social administration* is often criticised as a mass of facts and figures cohering around insights and/or rhetoric but devoid of its own theory. In relation to social work a similar criticism is made of undue reliance on unrepaid loans from sociology and psychology. In addition, levels or kinds of theory often remain unspecified, so that espoused theories of a very general nature are not distinguished from the more mundane practice theories (as contrasted with theories that explain social work and those purporting to describe and explain social work clients). Finally, social work education has long stressed that particular relationship between 'theory' and 'practice' (the terms are significantly singular) that rejoices in the name '*integration*'.

Curnock, K. and Hardiker, P. (1979) *Towards Practice Theory*, Routledge & Kegan Paul.

Therapeutic community The 'therapeutic community' is an influential innovation in the treatment of mental hospital patients, arising from small group research and clinical experience in and after World War II, and associated originally with Maxwell Jones. The two words 'community' and 'therapeutic' convey the main contentions of what came to be something of a *social movement*: that the social structure of the hospital be radically altered so that the previously unrealised therapeutic potential of social relations might be used through social analysis for maximum treatment effect. As the idea developed, particular emphasis came to be given to notions of democracy, permissiveness, and communalism, and consideration of the world 'outside' the hospital led some to make a distinction between the therapeutic community and what could be termed a therapeutic community approach towards larger social groupings. Clark's review uses a distinction between milieu therapy (in which milieux are the dominant treatment form), therapeutic milieux (environments consciously designed to facilitate milieu or social therapy), and the therapeutic community (or small, face-to-face residential group relying on the analysis of social relations as a major treatment tool).

Clark, D. (1977) 'The Therapeutic Community', *British Journal of Psychiatry*, 131, 553-64.
Manning, N. (1976) 'Innovation in Social Policy: the Case of the Therapeutic Community', *Journal of Social Policy*, 5, 265-79.

Therapeutic paradox See *Double bind.*

Transactional analysis A transaction is a unit of social intercourse, and categorising and attending to such units marks a particular kind of psychotherapy associated originally with Berne. This has been adopted as a model by some social workers. Berne characterises linked transactions or conversations as rituals, procedures, games, etc., and assumes 'within' each 'transaction' three possible positions from which interaction can be organised: that of adult, child, or parent. A person may transact from any of these ego positions addressed to any of alter's three positions. Transactions can also be classified as complementary or crossed, simple or ulterior, and so on.

Berne, E. (1966) *Games People Play*, Deutsch.

Transference This term refers to an important systematic phenomenon which it is the aim of the mode of Freudian analysis 'free association' to produce and of the interpretation to resolve into *insight*. Transference can be positive or negative; in either sense it refers to what comes to be experienced first by the analyst and then, through interpretation, by the analysand and as the patient behaving and feeling towards the analyst as if he were a significant, usually parental, figure in the patient's early life: the analyst becomes the object of a set of feelings/thoughts/responses which 'belong' to the past and not the present (see also *counter-transference*). In developing ideas of casework as a kind of therapy, the notions of 'transference' and 'transference interpretation' came to be used and criticised. Irvine's central discussion (of 1956) of the issues concluded that the basic element in social casework consisted in enabling the client to experience a new, helpful kind of *relationship* with the caseworker: 'If the transference is interpreted, I think the aim will usually be not so much to explore the inner world which is projected in the transference as to remove the veil of distortion and enable the client once more to experience the reality of the relationship'.

Irvine, E. (1979) 'Transference and Reality in the Casework Relationship', in *Social Work and Human Problems*, Pergamon.

Treatment Treatment is used frequently in discussions of social work activity in a strong sense and a weak sense. Strongly, 'treatment' refers to a course of measures designed to cure or alleviate what is seen under the explicit or implicit description of 'illness'. In a weak sense treatment refers to systematic behaviour towards another according to some *principle*. 'Treatment' in the former sense was developed in social casework in the years following what has come to be known as 'the *psychiatric deluge*', and it has become fashionable to accuse those responsible for *typologies* of 'social illnesses' and of their cures of following 'the' medical model. (The use of the singular prevents

197

us from seeing that there is more than one, and that a public health model (*prevention*) has much to offer social work.)

Tribunals   Administrative tribunals exercise judicial or quasi-judicial functions outside the regular judicial system subject to the rules of natural justice and the instrument of government conferring jurisdiction. The growth of administrative tribunals and the elaboration and reform of their procedures have been a marked feature of social welfare since the establishment of courts of referees under the National Insurance Act of 1911 which heard and decided appeals from the decisions of insurance officers. Tribunals, taking or reviewing decisions independently, have since been established in relation to taxation, employment rights, supplementary benefits, rent, immigration, and mental health. Advantages of the tribunal system have been seen in terms of speed, cheapness, openness, and impartiality, but more recently concern has been expressed concerning the rights of applicants, their lack of knowledge, and their possible need for assistance in making an appeal. Since the Tribunals and Inquiries Act 1971, a Council on Tribunals exercises general supervision over the work of tribunals.

Bell, K. *et al.* (1974, 1975) 'National Insurance Local Tribunals', *Journal of Social Policy*, 3, 289-315; 4, 1-24.
Bell, K. (chairman) (1980) *The Functions of the Council on Tribunals: Special Report*, Cmnd 7805, HMSO.
Fennell, P. (1977) 'The Mental Health Review Tribunal', *British Journal of Law and Society*, 4, 186-219.
Fullbrook, J. (1978) *Administrative Justice and the Unemployed*, Mansell.

Typologies   From time to time interest is expressed in research circles in the development of connected typologies of clients and of *treatment*. Such typologies would consist of a limited number of descriptions of problems systematically connected to a limited set of prescriptions. The elements in either the problem or the treatment categorisations should possess sufficient commonality and be based on some explicit theoretical position; elements should also be mutually exclusive. One of the best known typologies of treatment in social casework is that developed by Hollis, who identifies sustaining procedures, procedures of direct influence, ventilation, different kinds of reflective consideration, and environmental treatment.

Hollis, F. (1972) *Casework: a Psychosocial Therapy*, Random House.
Ogren, E. *et al.* (1979) 'Typologies in Social Work Practice', *Social Work in Health Care*, 4, 319-29.

U

Unconscious Freud spoke on occasions of the unconscious as a special realm or part of the mind inaccessible to ordinary investigation or introspection. Such a pictorial representation is misleading only if it detracts from the central idea that what is significant is not the attempt to demonstrate that *the* unconscious somehow exists but rather the possibility that wishes, symbols, purposes can be systematically kept from our awareness. *Freudian theory* contains a complex theory of unconscious processes, including the structural notions of conscious, pre-conscious, and unconscious and of primary processes which operate without relation to reality or any sense of contradiction. The idea of unconscious wishes and unconscious forces has been influential in social casework, and the attempt was made to distinguish social casework from psychotherapy by arguing that the former was directly concerned only with the conscious and pre-conscious. However, insufficient attention has been given in social welfare discussion to the logical analysis of Freud's ideas (MacIntyre) or to the possibility of their re-formulation in behavioural terms (Miles). See also *Jung*.

MacIntyre, A. (1958) *The Unconscious: a Conceptual Study*, Routledge & Kegan Paul.
Miles, T. (1966) *Eliminating the Unconscious*, Pergamon.

Understanding 'Understanding' is a term much used but little analysed in social work. Generally speaking, 'understanding' refers to the results of an exertion to use an idea or set of ideas to grasp a situation so that appropriate action (including contemplation, successfully conveying the sense of the situation to others) can be taken. The idea may be something relatively simple, such as 'I understand that now I see that is what X intended', or something more complex such as a theory ('I understand that in terms of Freud's instinct theory'). It is sometimes suggested that clients value a social worker's attempt to understand as much as his achievement in so doing. Social workers distinguish kinds of understanding: for example, between understanding derived from 'heart' knowledge or 'head' knowledge. Such a distinction is perhaps better seen as understanding from distinctive points of view, that of the participant and that of the experienced observer. These perspectives produce different understandings, but it is not the case that one is a deeper or superior version of the other. 'Understanding' is also an activity at the centre of much social legislation and of the work of those who devise, execute, or study social policy. The study of understanding (or hermeneutics) has much to offer our attempts to unravel this activity.

Bauman, Z. (1978) *Hermeneutics and Social Science*, Hutchinson.
Timms, N. and Timms, R. (1977) *Perspectives in Social Work*, Routledge & Kegan Paul, pp. 135-9.

Unemployment   To be unemployed is not to be in a remunerated occupation though able to work, expecting and expected to be in regular work and under official retirement age. It is difficult to measure unemployment rates with fine accuracy, but it is clear that over the last ten years high levels of unemployment have become a marked feature of most industrialised economies. Unemployment is significant for a number of reasons in welfare terms. What are the social implications of any change in the dominant objectives of full employment? What of human suffering and the waste of human potential on a large scale? Unemployment is not a condition spread evenly across a society, and those most at risk are the relatively unskilled, the long-term unemployed who are likely to be older and to present problems of ill-health, the young and those in minority *ethnic groups*. To alleviate problems, special programmes for the unemployed have been developed (C. Short, 'Ameliorative Programmes', in Burghes and Lister), but the re-adoption of full employment as an explicit objective of public policy is being increasingly urged (Field and Lister).

UNITARY APPROACH/UNITARY MODEL

Burghes, L. and Lister, R. (eds) (1981) *Unemployment: Who Pays the Price?*, CPAG.
Field, F. and Lister, R. (1978) *Wasted Labour: a Call for Action on Unemployment*, CPAG.
Showler, B. and Sinfield, A. (1981) *The Workless State*, Martin Robertson.
Sinfield, A. (1981) *What Unemployment Means*, Martin Robertson.

Unitary approach/Unitary model   This is a term of recent origin in social work, describing a movement away from the conceptualisation of social work as a grouping of distinct, separable methods (for instance, *casework, groupwork,* and *community work*) aimed at correcting problems in either the client, or his immediate environment, or 'society' in general. The unitary approach, usually based on a version of *systems theory*, assumes that social work is one thing, differentially manifested, and that its targets and those for whom social work is undertaken can all be encompassed in one over-arching framework. Goldstein argues, for example, that the overall objective of social work is the management of social learning; this learning is guided by the influence of the professional social worker. The unitary approach is not without its critics: some see it as an excessively wordy product of consensus thinking, confining rather than liberating the client; others see it as flawed in other respects – 'All talk of a unitary approach to social work is nonsense as long as there is no common concept of human nature. The unity is false because it is generated by the exclusion of the moral' (Wilkes, quoted in Olsen).

Goldstein, H. (1973) *Social Work Practice: a Unitary Approach*, University of South Carolina Press.
Olsen, R. (ed.) (1978) *The Unitary Model*, BASW Publications.

Universalism   This refers to a principle for organising the basis of social services (compared to *selectivity*) so that all contribute equally and all are equally entitled to draw equal benefit. There are no social services in Britain organised on such a principle, but 'universalism' covers an important range of arguments concerning attitudes towards welfare, and its objectives. These arguments include the extent of *stigma* in relation to the reception of public services – and the importance of combating this by structural means; the use of social services to encourage the high objectives of social *integration*; the inappropriateness of the operation of market forces in situations in which the rationality of the consumer is reduced. It is now accepted that neither selectivity nor universalism provides an exclusive principle, but the relationship between them is not easily stated, as can be seen from the description of the challenge as residing 'in the question: what particular infrastructure of universalist services is needed in order to provide a framework of values and opportunity bases within and around which can be developed socially acceptable selective services aiming to discriminate positively, with the minimum risk of stigma, in favour of those whose needs are greatest' (Titmuss, p. 135).

Jones, K. *et al.* (1978) *Issues in Social Policy*, Routledge & Kegan Paul, pp. 44-58.
Titmuss, R. (1968) *Commitment to Welfare*, Allen & Unwin.

Urban 'Urban' is that which pertains to the city or town, but, as Williams argues, 'Between the cities of ancient and medieval times and the modern metropolis or conurbation there is a connection of name and in past of function, but nothing like identity. Moreover, in our own world, there is a wide range of settlements between the traditional poles of country and city: suburb, dormitory town, shanty town, industrial estate' (p. 10). The central areas of large cities resemble urban villages, and the urbanised areas surrounding cities have been described by Pahl as a dispersed city. The description 'urban' is important in welfare because it draws attention to differential spatial patterning of social problems and centres of resource. An urban way of life, consequent on increase in size and density of population and characterised by severe anonymity and greater heterogeneity than that found in a folk society, has sometimes been seen as the source of many social problems. It is now argued that the local–national distinction is of greater significance than the rural–urban. In this perspective the so-called urban manager (*gatekeeper*) assumes importance as a power-holder at an intermediary position in the system of resource allocation. See also *Rural.*

203

URBAN PROGRAMME

Donnison, D. with Soto, P. (1980) *The Good City: a Study of Urban Development and Policy in Britain*, Heinemann.

Pahl, R. (1968) 'The Rural–Urban Continuum', in *Readings in Urban Sociology*, ed. Pahl, Pergamon.

Pahl, R. (1979) 'Socio-political Factors in Resource Allocation', in *Social Problems and the City*, ed. D. Herbert and D. Smith, Oxford University Press.

Williams, R. (1975) *The Country and the City*, Paladin.

Urban Programme   This was established under the 1969 Local Government Grants (Social Need) Act which authorised central government to give grants to local authorities which in its view are required in the exercise of their functions to incur expenditure by reason of the existence in any urban area of special social need. By 1976-7 nearly £30,000,000 had been spent on the Urban Programme in England and Wales and the *Community Development Project* was financed from urban programme funds. On the basis of the DoE White Paper, *Policy for the Inner Cities* (Cmnd 6845, July 1977), a Partnership Scheme was announced and the Comprehensive Community Programmes and Inner Area Programmes. The main thrust was to go beyond social projects of the earlier phase and to include industrial, environmental, and recreational provision; resources were to be increased but used more selectively, with priority going to specially selected partnerships between central government and certain local authorities. In each Partnership area an Inner Area Programme will be devised covering the totality of local authority policies and such other public sector activities as industry and employment. The Urban Programme is the responsibility of the Department of the Environment. See also *Inner city*.

Community Development Project (1979) *The State and the Local Economy*, London, CDP.

V

Vagrancy Controlling the wanderer with no settled abode or regular work has been a feature of social policy since Tudor times. 'The great object of our early pauper legislation seems to have been the restraint of vagrancy' (Poor Law Report, 1834). More recently, vagrant men and women were seen in terms of destitution, and the definition of destitution has changed from that stressing personal inadequacy of one kind or another to the more operational notion of sleeping rough or regularly using night shelters or *resettlement units*. The Housing (Homeless Persons) Act 1977 has led to a demand that 'vagrants' should not have to rely on special accommodation such as night shelters, but should be entitled to a permanent home in local authority housing.

Cook, T. (ed.) (1979) *Vagrancy: Some New Perspectives*, Academic Press.
Leach, J. and Wing, J. (1980) *Helping Destitute Men*, Tavistock.

Values 'Values' are used in descriptions of the principles and guiding rules of social work; e.g. *self-determination, acceptance, the non-judgmental attitude* are all described as values of casework or of social work in general. 'Values' refers to the objectives of social work processes (as in individualisation of service), to the objectives of social work (as in 'improved social functioning'), and to rules for meeting both sorts of objective. 'Value' is also used in discussions of social policy: 'Social policy is the battlefront in which clashes between socialist and capitalist social values occur. The major values involved in these ideological clashes have been freedom, individualism and equality' (Wilding and George); or welfare policy is seen as actively

205

VANDALISM

helping to create standards of value (Marshall), or increased governmental activity in welfare is seen as a result of a change in values, such as a move towards self-realisation (Robertson). Whatever their use, 'values' are seldom analysed in social work or social policy with care. This is partly because 'a man's values are like his kidneys; he rarely knows he has any until they are upset' (Jones).

Jones, R.H. (1970) 'Social Values and Social Work Education', in *Social Work Values in an Age of Discontent*, ed. K. Kendall, New York, Council on Social Work Education.
Marshall, T. (1972) 'Value Problems in Welfare Capitalism', *Journal of Social Policy*, 1, 15-32.
Robertson, A. (1980) 'The Welfare State and "Post-Industrial" Values', in *Social Welfare: Why and How?*, ed. N. Timms, Routledge & Kegan Paul.
Wilding, P. and George, V. (1975) 'Social Values and Social Policy', *Journal of Social Policy*, 4, 373-90.

Vandalism   The term is used to describe a considerable range of behaviour – the so-called ideologically motivated industrial violence of the nineteenth-century Luddites, the destruction of medieval buildings to make way for Victorian railways, the apparently random smashing of communal facilities on certain council estates, the illegal but socially protected damage of student rags, and so on. The main element concerns the destruction or spoiling of any part of the material environment that is not one's own property. Questions of definition are crucial. Some would define the damage as of its essence mindless, others stress spontaneity, while others see at least some kinds of vandalism as the attempt to reassert a control over the environment that is experienced as lost.

Murray, R. and Boal, F. (1979) 'The Social Ecology of Urban Violence', in *Social Problems and the City: Geographical Perspectives*, ed. D. Herbert and D. Smith, Oxford University Press.
Pearson, G. (1976) 'In Defence of Hooliganism', in DHSS, *Violence*, ed. N. Tutt, HMSO.
Ward, C. (ed.) (1973) *Vandalism*, Architectural Press.

Ventilation   Ventilation was identified as a social work procedure by Hollis, mid-way, as it were, between sustaining and directing and reflection on past or present situations. Ventilation has to do with the expression of strong feeling that the person concerned (in Hollis this is not always the main client) usually keeps from expressing. The purpose of such expression is taken to be catharsis or, in more mundane terms, 'getting it off one's chest' without, as it were, simply voiding it. Catharsis, with its overtones of moral improvement, is a rather crude approximation, but the important point is that 'feeling' is expressed with a view to achieving a purpose over and above display. Ventilation is to be distinguished from abreaction, a psychiatric technique for re-establishing the association of abnormal emotional excitement with the memory of the event that first caused it and facilitating complete expression of feelings in relation to it. In discussion of ventilation, a vulgarised view of *emotion* is often assumed.

Hollis, F. (1972) *Casework: a Psychosocial Therapy*, 2nd ed., Random House.

Victim This term is generally considered to refer to an innocent person who suffers serious harm, usually at another's hands. (One could perhaps be described as a victim of one's own depression, etc.) In welfare, services can be provided as specific *compensation* (in 1964 the Criminal Injuries Compensation Board was established to compensate those who had sustained injuries directly attributable to a crime of violence) or on the general grounds that 'victims' of social change should be 'compensated'. Recently, the operation of income maintenance and of social control services have been criticised as 'blaming the victim'. There is increasing interest in support schemes for victims, such as Rape Crisis Centres, and a growing realisation of the significance of the reactions of other people to victims.

Coates, D. *et al.* (1979) 'Reactions to Victims', in *New Approaches to Social Problems*, ed. I. Frieze *et al.*, Jossey-Bass.

Violence 'Even a cup of tea may be stirred violently' (Harris), so questions of definition are of some consequence. Generally speaking, we can consider violence in terms of the unjustified use of force, often vehement force, in order to inflict physical injury on people or damage to property. It can be public or domestic, though Tutt argues that normally violence is 'part of a repertoire of behaviour within a pre-existing relationship and is usually taking place between people who know each other, not in consequence of attacks by unknown thugs or assassins' (*family violence*). The subject of violence is important in welfare for a number of reasons. First, social services and social workers often operate in particular or local situations generally accepted as 'violent' (e.g. Northern Ireland). Second, social administrators and social workers are expected to understand and respond to both actual *vandalism* and those 'moral panics' (Cohen) which often distort reality in the public mind. Finally, it is claimed that 'violence' is systematically misunderstood unless the violence of society is brought into the picture. As Engels wrote: 'Murder has also been committed if society places hundreds of workers in such a position that they inevitably come to premature and unnatural ends' (quoted in Harris).

Cohen, S. (1973) *Folk Devils and Moral Panics*, Paladin.
DHSS (1976) *Violence*, ed. N. Tutt, HMSO.
Darby, J. and Williamson, A. (eds) (1978) *Violence and the Social Services in Northern Ireland*, Heinemann.
Harris, J. (1974) 'The Marxist Conception of Violence', *Philosophy and Public Affairs*, 3, 192-220.
Nielson, K. (1981) 'On Justifying Violence', *Inquiry*, 24, 21-58.

Voluntary society In a welfare context a voluntary society is a welfare organisation that is non-statutory. It should not be confused with an organisation of, or using exclusively, *volunteers*. Voluntary societies have been a feature of welfare provision at least since the nineteenth century – for instance Barnardo's in the field of child care. As state services developed it seemed that voluntary societies had the primary task of pioneering provision that might eventually be taken over by the state. The most recent systematic consideration of the role of voluntary societies is to be found in the report of the Wolfenden Committee (*The Future of Voluntary Organisations*, Croom Helm 1977), which proposed 'the development of a new long-term strategy' involving central government, 'local intermediary bodies' (centres for development work and liaison and support services for other organisations), and central intermediary bodies. An important series of questions concerns the relationship between the statutory and voluntary sectors: should the aim of voluntary societies be to complement statutory provision, to act as agents by providing services that are the equivalent of or a substitute for those of the local authority, to provide an alternative service based perhaps on a set of distinctive values, to represent the citizen and act as a pressure group? The interest of central government in the voluntary sector is illustrated by the formation of the Voluntary Services Unit in 1972.

Hatch, S. (1980) *Outside the State: Voluntary Organisations in Three English Towns*, Croom Helm.
Rowe, A. (1975) 'The Voluntary Services Unit', in *Year Book of Social Policy in Britain, 1974*, ed. K. Jones, Routledge & Kegan Paul.

Volunteers   In social welfare, 'volunteer' is not readily defined. Clearly, a volunteer undertakes unpaid work, but in present society may be said to earn moral credit. The volunteer engages in a non-reciprocal relationship with the organisation that uses his or her resources, but various satisfactions may be considered to accrue from work that is not in any sense compelled. Moving to a more concrete level, any of the following (and others) could be described as volunteers: a person in the Women's Royal Voluntary Service, a lay magistrate, a selected ex-offender in a new careers scheme, a disabled person in a self-help group, and so on. In this wide sense the volunteer has a long history in welfare (as a committee member, for example), but current interest in the volunteer as providing a direct and arguably a special service stems from the Aves Report (*The Voluntary Worker in the Social Services*, Allen & Unwin, 1969). Volunteers were at one time regarded ambivalently by professional social workers, but systematic provision for the use and training of volunteers is a significant feature of contemporary welfare. New organisations and roles have been created. In 1973 the Volunteer Centre was established to encourage the substantial extension of the direct involvement of volunteers, to improve the effectiveness of volunteer participation, and so on. It runs a unit

VOLUNTEERS

to offer service to Volunteer Bureaux (of which there were 215 by April 1980), originally started by what are now called *Councils of Voluntary Service*. At a local level statutory authorities may employ Volunteer Service Organisers.

Thomas, M. (1974) 'The Volunteer Centre', in *Year Book of Social Policy in Britain, 1973*, ed. K. Jones, Routledge & Kegan Paul.

W

Wants The idea of 'wants' appears simple, but appearance deceives. Kenny, for example, has argued that wanting X is always wanting to get X, and that getting X describes a state of affairs and not a particular thing. He lists three conditions for saying 'A wants something': A must be able to say what counts as getting what he wants and what he wants to do with it; and what is wanted must not already be in his power. It is important to grasp that a want is not a stirring in a private breast; a want is intelligible in so far as it relates to public standards. 'Want' has assumed some importance in recent welfare discussion partly because of emphasis on giving consumers what they want (and the accompanying assumption that this can be directly observed); and partly because in the discussion of *need* attempts have been made to give primacy to market-satisfiable wants, leaving needs as wants for which no one is prepared to pay. See also *Interests*.

Kenny, A. (1973) *Action, Emotion and Will*, Routledge & Kegan Paul.
Plant, R. *et al.* (1980) *Political Philosophy and Social Welfare: Essays on the Normative Basis of Welfare Provision*, Routledge & Kegan Paul, pp. 25-36.

Welfare 'Welfare' is used to describe certain services or institutions and also the ideas of individual and social well-being by which those services or institutions are informed. In this context it is also important to consider the complementing notion of diswelfare: for many, social service provision represents not an increment in welfare but a partial *compensation* for diswelfares incurred as a result of social change. While ideas of welfare and compensation for diswelfare may be said to inform the social services, it should be appreciated that 'welfare is only to a very limited extent the product of social services or of social policy. Its roots lie deep in the social and economic system as a whole. Its realisation and enjoyment depend, therefore, on a number of other rights ... including those to property and personal freedom, to work and to justice' (Marshall, p. 93). It has become increasingly common to identify different models of welfare; Pinker, for example, discusses the models derived from classical political economy, from Marxism, and from the effort to make 'a welfare society in which the terms of exchange and the understandings of obligation and entitlement were decently conditional, neither vulgarly egoistical nor impossibly altruistic' (p. 245).

Honderich, T. (1981) 'The Question of Well-being and the Principle of Equality', *Mind*, 90, 481-504.
Marshall, T. (1981) *The Right to Welfare and other Essays*, Heinemann.
Pinker, R. (1979) *The Idea of Welfare*, Heinemann, Ch. 12, 'Three Models of Social Welfare'.

Welfare rights   The history of social policy is, at least in part, the extension of welfare provision as a *right*, but what is called the Welfare Rights Movement is a more recent development. 'Movement' suggests perhaps greater unity of purpose than is the case, since concern for welfare rights can have a *reformist* (see *social reform*), a *radical* (see *radical social work*) or an anarchist basis. So those advocating a welfare rights approach may be seeking solutions to problems created by lack of awareness to entitlement or by difficulties in access to *gate-keepers*. Or they may pursue the general policy of reducing the elements of *discretion* in favour of stipulated, public rules to particular entitlements; or they seek to push and test the law to its limits in defence of the poor who are defined as those whose rights are diminished, obscured or simply not recognised. These alternatives are to be found in varying combinations, of course. Some local authorities have appointed social service staff as welfare rights officers, and the *Community Development Project* became interested in a welfare rights approach. It has been argued that *advocacy* on behalf of another to help to secure their rights is demeaning, and also that 'every "welfare right" implies a claim on someone else's productive obligation, and the increase in the number of academic courses in "welfare rights" for students of social policy and social work indicates a perilous insulation of these subjects from economic realities and popular notions of justice' (R. Pinker, *The Idea of Welfare*, Heinemann, 1979, p.249). Another problem concerns the framework within which rights within the social services should be considered. Watson has argued that the United Nations Universal Declaration of Human Rights is to be preferred to the European Convention because it includes social and economic rights.

Watson, D. (1977) 'Welfare Rights and Human Rights', *Journal of Social Policy*, 6, 31-46.

Welfare society 'Welfare society' is more difficult to define than 'Welfare State' to which it is related. This relationship has been seen in the form of stages of development, with 'welfare society' as the inevitable sequence to a situation of enforced minima. Others see the relationship in potentially negative terms. Thus, Sinfield talks of 'the Welfare State in an anti-Welfare Society'. Again, 'welfare society' can be used to point a contrast between ways of looking at provision and service: 'welfare society' emphasises alternative ways, through informal care and the *voluntary societies*, of achieving similar *or* more ambitious objectives. For some, 'welfare society', 'caring society', 'compassionate society' are ways of speaking about social relations: sometimes status distinctions between those caring and those being cared for are acknowledged, sometimes an attempt is made to transcend them. Perhaps the most clear version (in very general terms indeed) of a welfare society is to be found in Marx, whose version of the final resolution of class warfare is a society arranged, somehow or other, so that all human needs are met, all human *wants* satisfied.

Sinfield, A. (1978) 'Analyses in the Social Division of Welfare', *Journal of Social Policy*, 7, 129-56.

Welfare State Titmuss called the 'Welfare State' an 'indefinable abstraction', and it is certainly difficult to put into any reasonably sized nutshell. Indeed, some would distinguish as a *social security* state what others would see as a Welfare State in so far as it guaranteed minimum standards of income, nutrition, and health for all as of right. Others would define as a Welfare State what yet others see, somewhat dimly, as an objective for the future, an egalitarian and democratic *welfare society*. The term 'Welfare State' was coined in the early 1940s to refer to developments in state provision which formed some kind of coherence, perhaps as a commitment by the state to modify market forces in such a way that what in Britain Beveridge described as four common enemies were defeated – Want, Disease, Ignorance and Squalor. Later, Titmuss and others argued for a compensation effect, so that the Welfare State was seen also as offsetting the costs and insecurities of 'the diswelfare state'. Questions concerning the meaning of the term are significant in both academic and public discourse ('cradle to grave provision'). Also important are questions about the origins and growth of welfare in the modern state – as the result of developments of *social conscience*, as the price to be paid for industrial progress, as the result of working-class success in the class struggle. More recently, arguments have been mounted concerning the counter-productivity of welfare law and provision.

Campbell, T. (1981) 'Counter productive Welfare Law', *British Journal of Political Science*, 11, 331-50.
Titmuss, R. (1968) *Commitment to Welfare*, Allen & Unwin.

Women A woman is an adult female human, but in welfare it is the social roles clustered around 'woman' that are significant. First, social welfare policies are seen as defining what women should do ('social welfare policies amount to no less than the *State organisation of domestic life*', Wilson, p. 9). Second, women number significantly amongst the 'providers' of welfare (both formal and informal) and amongst those for whom various services are provided (*family violence*) or to whom they are directed. For instance, it has been a continual complaint that social workers attend much less to foster fathers, fathers of children at child guidance clinics, etc., than to the mothers involved. Third, attention has recently been given to systematic prejudice against women, and this has led some to establish alternative services for women by women.

Gottlieb, N. (ed.) (1980) *Alternative Social Services for Women*, Columbia University Press.

Wilson, E. (1977) *Women and the Welfare State*, Tavistock.

Work through Originally this was a psychoanalytic term referring to the rather lengthy process whereby a new insight is slowly absorbed and digested into the analysand's 'real' life: the insight is worked at from different angles so that the *ego* learns increasing toleration of less distorted derivatives from the past. It can also be used to describe a process of spontaneous recuperation (as in working through one's grief). In social work the term is used in a very general way to describe almost any more or less systematic discussion of a fraught subject. ('I raised the problem of poor school attendance, and the mother and I worked through this.')

Y

Youth This term refers to young people as a social category. Musgrove argued that young people constituted a class of their own in so far as they were a grouping based on the differential possession of power and authority; he also stated that from the middle of the nineteenth century 'social legislation and changing social conventions *made* the adolescent' (p. 34). Other writers are less confident that the creation of the social category can be dated, but draw attention to the fact that talk about youth often assumes that young people are somehow classless, participate in a single relatively homogeneous youth culture, and are inevitably at odds with the dominant, adult culture. The extent to which generational identity and its consciousness are a reality in any society has implications for the extent to which resources are distributed between age groups in a population. See also *Adolescence, Youth Service*.

Murray, C. (ed.) (1978) *Youth in Contemporary Society: Theoretical and Research Perspectives*, NFER Publishing Co.
Musgrove, F. (1964) *Youth and the Social Order*, Routledge & Kegan Paul.
Musgrove, F. and Middleton, R. (1981) 'Rites of Passage as the Meaning of Age in Three Contrasted Social Groups', *British Journal of Sociology*, 32, 39-55.

Youth Service 'For one reason or another it [the Youth Service] has always been in a state of emergency since its inception in 1939 and by the 1970s there was little sign of a total strategy that would give it the solid underpinning of a universal and professional service' (E. Younghusband, *Social Work in Britain: 1950-1975*, Allen & Unwin, 1978, vol. 2, p. 275). The service of youth originated in the nineteenth century and took various forms, of which youth clubs organised by local or national voluntary bodies was one. Statutory intervention dates from the Second World War and particularly after the Albemarle Report, which found the service neglected and held in poor regard. The Service is still extremely unevenly spread and hampered by difficulties concerning the identity of youth work (an extension of teaching or a form of social work or of community work), the relationship between club and 'unattached' work, and the place of such new ventures as *intermediate treatment*. Marsland has identified four current objectives that are presently canvassed for the Youth Service: to be transformed into a generalised community service (following the Milson–Fairbairn Report many localities are served by what they call a Youth and Community Service); to be submerged in a de-specialised, generic organisation for youth affairs; to become an instrument of explicit social change; to be re-directed towards immediate crises and problems.

DES (1969) *Youth and Community Work in the Seventies* (Milson-Fairbairn Report), HMSO.
DES (1960) *The Youth Service in England and Wales* (Albemarle Report), Cmnd 929, HMSO.
Marsland, D. (1980) 'Novelty, Ideology and Reorganisation: Threats to the Value of Youth Work', in *The Ignorance of Social Intervention*, ed. D. Anderson, Croom Helm.